Escape to the City

VIOLA FRANZISKA MÜLLER

Escape to the City

Fugitive Slaves in the
Antebellum Urban South

The University of North Carolina Press *Chapel Hill*

This book was published with the assistance of the Authors Fund of the University of North Carolina Press

Set in Arno Pro by Westchester Publishing Services
Manufactured in the United States of America

Library of Congress Cataloging-in-Publication Data
Names: Müller, Viola Franziska, 1987- author.
Title: Escape to the city : fugitive slaves in the antebellum urban South / Viola Franziska Müller.
Other titles: Fugitive slaves in the antebellum urban South
Description: Chapel Hill : The University of North Carolina Press, [2022] | Includes bibliographical references and index.
Identifiers: LCCN 2022020615 | ISBN 9781469671055 (cloth ; alk. paper) | ISBN 9781469671062 (pbk. ; alk. paper) | ISBN 9781469671079 (ebook)
Subjects: LCSH: Fugitive slaves—Southern States—History—19th century. | Free Black people—Southern States—History—19th century. | Slavery—Southern States—History.
Classification: LCC E450 .M854 2022 | DDC 973.7/115—dc23/eng/20220518
LC record available at https://lccn.loc.gov/2022020615

Cover illustration: Mathew Benjamin Brady, *View of Richmond, Virginia* (ca. 1860–65), Record Group 111: Records of the Office of the Chief Signal Officer, 1860–1985, National Archives (NAID 524454). Courtesy of Wikimedia Commons and U.S. National Archives and Records Administration.

To my parents, Doris and Hugo

Contents

Figures, Graph, Maps, and Tables

Acknowledgments

This book is the result of years of academic training, reading, teaching, traveling, extensive archival research, discovering, hard work, personal growth, and—perhaps most importantly—shared experiences. As this enumeration already suggests, writing *Escape to the City* was by no means a one-woman show, and many people were directly and indirectly involved in its making. I would like to take this opportunity to thank them.

Since this book grew out of my PhD dissertation, I would first like to extend my gratitude to my supervisor Damian Pargas. Thank you for continuously supporting me! Your enthusiasm and positivity made work so much easier. A huge thanks also goes to Marlou Schrover, my second supervisor, who played a very important role during the final stages of the writing process. Also, I was fortunate for having close colleagues with whom I could engage in inspiring discussions and share sources. Thank you, Oran Kennedy and Thomas Mareite. My research was generously funded by the Dutch Research Council (NWO); the Bonn Center for Dependency and Slavery Studies contributed to the maps in this book.

At UNC Press, my thanks go to Debbie Gershenowitz for believing in this book and for her invaluable editing work, and to Andrew Winters, Elizabeth Orange, Dino Battista, Carol Seigler, Michelle Wallen, Iris Levesque, Kristen Bettcher, and Brett Keener for their great work. David Durà and Madge Duffs took care of the maps and images. I am also immensely thankful to the two reviewers without whose generous commitment this book would not be the same.

Besides my supervisors and editorial team, I am indebted to people who had no visible reason to support me, but did so nevertheless. Be it reading earlier versions of chapters, sharing sources with me or providing me with invaluable advice, I am grateful to Jeffrey Kerr-Ritchie, Sven Beckert, Gregg Kimball, Edward Papenfuse, and numerous librarians who caringly engaged with me and helped me navigate the archives. A particular thank-you is in line for Seth Rockman, who has played an important role in my turning a dissertation into a full-fledged book.

On a similar note, I would like to thank people who read parts of my research that were published as articles elsewhere but nevertheless implicitly feature in this book. Mariana Dantas, Nico Pizzolato, Irene Fattacciu, and Christian De Vito supported me in this way, as did the participants of the Nineteenth-Century US History Workshop and the 2018/2019 fellows of the Center for the Study of Slavery and Justice, both at Brown University. I am grateful to everybody who bothered to read and/or comment on my work. I received valuable feedback from Catia Antunes, Michael Zeuske, Ariadne Schmidt, Jan-Bart Gewald, Jessica Roitman, Aviva Ben-Ur, David Doddington, Jared Hardesty, Bram Hoonhout, and Anna Derksen. At Leiden, the Small Gathering of the Economic and Social History section provided me with various opportunities to benefit from my colleagues' knowledge and to test my ideas. Likewise very important was the feedback I received from colleagues affiliated with the N.W. Posthumus training school for Economic and Social History. These include Laura Nys, Laurence van Goethem, Thomas Verbruggen, Regina Grafe, Pepijn Brandon, and Ben Wubs.

During my time at the European University Institute, I could count on Ian Hathaway, Jorge Díaz Ceballos, Gašper Jakovac, Nikos Mavropoulos, Nicoletta Asciuto, Andreas Greiner, and Giacomo Tagiuri. Thanks, also, to Laurie Anderson for her help with the book proposal. The altruistic commitment to somebody else's work is one of the reasons why this profession has such a strong social side to it and shows that history writing is a joint effort.

Furthermore, during my research trips, I was extraordinarily lucky to meet wonderful people who prevented long periods in unknown lands from turning into lonely and monotonous loops of days. Thank you for hanging out with me and showing me around, Thomas Ginn, Dominic Nell, Marco Delsante, Elizabeth Belcher, Kit Gillespie, Krystal Halverson, Meg Ryan, Jake Gambino, Grace Garcia Varano, Katherine Bertrand, Jana Blakes, Mark Martin, Sarah Shapiro, Simeon Simeonov, Mimi Cabell, Kai Franz, Ian Stirton, John Wheeler, Bridgette Sloan, Candelaria Martínez, Jane and William Bertrand, and my sister Saskia.

Almost last but not least, I am grateful to all my friends, regardless of whether they were with me or supported me over a distance. This particularly applies to those who are not in academia and who kept me sane and balanced; I am more than happy to have them in my life. The same goes for my family and especially for my parents, Hugo and Doris. The one person who was *always* with me during the last years and who had to read more versions of this book than anyone else is David de Boer. It is hard to imagine having done all this without you, David!

Escape to the City

Rethinking Slave Flight

You establish a spot within the slaveholding States
which would be a city of refuge for runaway slaves.

—James Buchanan

In 1836, James Buchanan, then senator from Pennsylvania, delivered a speech in which he outlined his views on the question of whether slavery and the slave trade should be abolished in the District of Columbia. As a Democrat, Buchanan sided with the political interests of southern slaveholders, and he predictably favored rejecting the proposal outright. Interestingly, one of his main concerns was that the abolition of slavery in Washington would turn the District into a "city of refuge for runaway slaves."[1] Was Buchanan not aware that D.C. and other southern cities already provided shelter and camouflage for thousands of fugitives from slavery—despite their lying within slaveholding territory? What *would* have changed, in the case of abolition, was the legal status of the federal district. Abolishing slavery would have turned D.C. into "free soil" territory, where no person could be legally enslaved. It would have undoubtedly exacerbated the local runaway issue, but it would certainly not have created it.

Buchanan's opposition to transforming a city within the slaveholding South into free soil for fear that it would unleash a runaway slave crisis was connected to the most heated political debates of the antebellum period (c. 1800–60)—debates that placed slave flight at the center of national and international discussions and conflicts, but that also failed to appreciate the diverse and complicated geography of refuge for enslaved people living in the U.S. South. Southerners themselves tended to obsess more over the dangers of sharing their borders with free soil territories than the dangers of internal runaways within the South itself. Throughout the nineteenth century, the southern states, and their representatives in Washington, continuously exercised pressure on places like Spanish Florida, Mexico, and especially the northern United States because of their relatively open acceptance of fugitive slaves from the South. This resulted in severe tension, sometimes leading to drastic political events, including the annexations of Florida in 1821 and of Texas in 1845; the Mexican-American War of 1843–45; the Fugitive Slave Act of 1850; and the American Civil War of 1861–65. Far-reaching and well-documented political measures, wars, and diplomatic crises that came out of (or were related to) disagreements over escaped slaves produced reams of written evidence and entire archives for historians to pore through. Partly because of their visibility, people who fled enslavement to free soil regions not only dominated contemporary discussions of the "fugitive slave issue," but also subsequent historical scholarship.

This focus is striking considering that vast numbers of runaway slaves remained within the slaveholding South—not just as "absentees" or scattered "maroons," but as permanent refugees in urban areas, where runaways illegally lived camouflaged within the African American populations. There, they could not expect to ever be legally free. Fugitives who went to Canada, Mexico, or even the northern states might have hoped to one day become citizens or—in an ever distant future—reach equality with Whites. These hopes stood beyond the reach of those who decided to remain in the South: after all, their entire strategy to shake off slavery was to attract as little attention as possible. Consequently, these men, women, and children moved clandestinely toward and within the cities. Set in Baltimore, Richmond (Virginia), Charleston, and New Orleans, and putting to the forefront issues of mobility, illegality, networks, and labor in the urban space, this book tells their stories.

Runaways as Migrants

Freedom is the overarching theme of American history. Not all accounts are optimistic and recognize freedom as a linear or expeditious process, yet, they often do see freedom as the ultimate goal that, even if unachievable, guided Americans' lived experiences.[2] Does this claim hold true for southern fugitivity? Certainly, successful runaway slaves left unrequited toil behind, but did these men and women also gain freedom by fleeing slavery? The answer to this question depends on what we understand as "freedom." We can think of freedom largely as not being forced to work against one's will for the benefit of others.[3] We can also think of it as civil and legal rights or social inclusion in American society as "legitimate persons," something that Frederick Douglass called "full freedom."[4]

This book proposes that freedom—regardless of the discussions about its definition and meanings—cannot fully capture the struggles of antebellum southerners of African descent. As historian Joseph Miller also emphasized in his plea for a thorough historization of slaveries, we need to view enslaved people "more fully than [...] as mechanically resisting the lack of Freedom that the modern historian imagines as the primary privation that they endured."[5] The very fact that so many absconders from slavery stayed in the slaveholding states means that the way we typically understand notions of freedom in the context of American slavery was not on these people's minds as an ever-present, all-encompassing goal. Yes, significant numbers of enslaved Americans were aiming to raise their voices, to be heard, and to disclose their intellectual potential. They were spearheaded by Frederick Douglass, the most prominent figure we choose to remember most vividly. Yet, most people's highest priority was to be self-asserted, meaning to live socially and economically independently from a master or mistress who held a claim to their labor, families, and places of residence. This was also possible in the South.

Notably, in a society where enslavement was justified on basis of law, thousands of enslaved people could only escape slavery *against the law*.[6] Those who stayed in the South remained within the jurisdiction of the very slaveholding society that stipulated they were slaves; their legal status did not change. The subsequent lives that these men and women built for themselves in southern cities therefore had, likewise, no basis in law; their sheer presence in the cities was illegal. This brings them close to present-day undocumented migrants, a consideration that implies that they were living somewhere without the authorization to do so.[7]

Migration research, however, is rarely occupied by questions of freedom and unfreedom to evaluate the experiences of refugees and their receiving communities. So, what if we leave the question of freedom aside temporarily and, instead, think about fugitive slaves as living in conditions of statelessness, predisposed to being undocumented, vulnerable to discretionary policing, and susceptible to coercive labor? This book attempts to focus on new perspectives put forward by the methods of migration studies. This approach demonstrates that the experiences of southern-internal fugitive slaves can indeed best be understood by applying concepts more commonly associated with contemporary debates on migration, such as "illegality" and "undocumentedness."

Enslaved southerners exited slavery without authorization, used false papers and identities, overstayed their officially sanctioned passes or used expired slave passes, or did not return to their masters and mistresses after a set period of time. These criteria rendered them undocumented as a consequence.[8] This drawing on twentieth- and twenty-first-century analogues offers an innovative way to rethink the conditions of fugitive slaves as workers and residents and allows us to concentrate on fugitive slaves' legal and economic precariousness. By doing so, *Escape to the City* departs from the predominant African American historiography that emphasizes the slavery-to-freedom narrative and brings to the fore a new perspective to understand the social history of Black Americans before the Civil War.

By putting aside the presumption that freedom was the omnipresent animating energy of enslaved people's lives, a new set of questions immediately come into focus when studying fugitivity. Who were the fugitives, from where did they come, why did they decide to go to southern cities, how did they get there, and who supported them? Which preconditions had to be fulfilled so that these men and women were in a position to make such an endeavor work? Once in the city, how did they navigate the physical and social spaces of the urban environment? How did they avoid recapture? Where did they live? Equally important are questions about their economic lives. When enslaved people planned to stay in a city for a long period of time, what were their prospects for employment? How and where did they find work? Lastly, these methods require us to ask how the cities reacted to the newcomers. Fugitive slaves gravitated to cities inhabited by free Black people, other enslaved people, White Americans, and White immigrants, who were citizens, noncitizens, workers, employers, poor, or wealthy. What were the attitudes of these other social groups to the presence of fugitives?[9]

Thinking of runaway slaves as refugees also underscores the urgency of their escape from oppressive conditions and shifts the focus to their agency. After all, fleeing slavery was a decision. Not everybody was able to take this decision and not everybody who took this decision succeeded or acted the same way. Still, individuals weighed the costs, including the risks and consequences, and benefits of migration.[10] Migration historians argue that, usually, people prefer to stay at home but are, for a variety of reasons, compelled to leave in order to, for instance, escape political persecution, improve their material conditions, or create a better future for their children.[11] Although all of these can also be additional factors for slave migrants, the fact that these people were legally property, and "home" referred to the place where they were forced to labor for someone else, does change the picture. American slavery, one of the most absolute, oppressive, and restricting labor regimes in history, adds a context in which migration decisions (and in fact all decisions enslaved people took) cannot be analyzed without taking the specific environment into consideration. Nevertheless, it also holds true for fugitives from slavery that migrating in the sense of fleeing implied a rupture and necessitated a total reorganization of one's familiar life.[12] Pretending to be free and living in a city among Black people embodied this rupture and reinvention.

What follows is an exploration of why spaces of refuge arose in southern cities, and how fugitive slaves navigated those spaces. The account begins with the growth of the free African American population around 1810 and stops in 1860, shortly before the American Civil War.[13] During this period, the slave system became stronger rather than weaker, as chapter 1 explores. Slavery's increasing integration into global markets and its intensification in the nineteenth century led Dale Tomich to conceptualize it as the "second slavery."[14] In this era, manumission schemes were curtailed and people were increasingly sold away from their families, giving enslaved men and women little hope to be released and the realization that if they wanted out, they had to free themselves.

But who were these fugitives? The vast majority of enslaved Americans were not in a position to make an escape attempt. We recognize this clearly with accounts like that of Solomon Northup, who tried innumerable times to get out of slavery. "There was not a single day [...] that I did not consult with myself upon the prospect of escape," Northup remembered later. But there were a "thousand obstacles" that prevented him from succeeding for twelve long years.[15] It was not the lack of power of volition or physical fitness that impeded people like Northup from breaking free. Some, however, did succeed.

In the nineteenth century, increasingly globalized labor and manufacturing processes restructured the American economy and introduced new arguments regarding how and where to employ enslaved workers. These developments laid the cornerstone for the "new fugitive slaves," a small part of the enslaved population able to escape bondage. In chapter 2, we see that features typically attributed to fugitive slaves—foremost, being male and being skilled—did not determine who ran away. Instead, this book puts forward a new model that foregrounds horizons created by physical mobility, autonomy, and exposure to other people who were not slaves or slaveholders. For these people, the mechanisms of control were weaker than is often assumed and they were aptly suited to finding their way in the burgeoning cities.

Collective Resistance

When looking at fugitive slaves as migrants, probably the most important condition was that, contrary to most migrants in modern history, they broke the law by fleeing. In the logic of the antebellum United States, they stole a body that belonged to another person—they legally stole themselves. Furthermore, they forfeited loss of money and future labor for their owners. In this aspect, the understanding of slaveholders clashed dramatically with that of fleeing slaves, who very obviously resumed ownership of their *own* bodies. What is more, people who broke free from bondage had an idea that what they did was *right*.[16] And although their actions were illegal in the eyes of those enacting the laws, for those oppressed they were licit and fully justified. With this conviction, every person who escaped slavery dealt a blow to that institution and exposed its weaknesses.

Running away was a challenge to slavery, an act that Shauna Sweeney has called a "covert but public rebellion."[17] Yet, fugitives from slavery rarely acted alone: other Black southerners were crucial to their survival. The free part of this population grew substantially in the postrevolutionary era and tended to congregate in cities and towns. To understand how and why it became possible for fugitives to find shelter there, it is paramount to study closely both the cities and the relationship between the newcomers and their receiving communities. Analyzing fugitive slaves together with their host societies in southern cities unearths distinct social realities. Why would Black city dwellers not expose fugitive slaves? Why would they, even more actively, shelter them or help them find work? These actions carried considerable risks. In this context, tracing fugitives in southern cities also has the potential to reveal their and their helpers' attitudes vis-à-vis the system they were fleeing from and the society they were fleeing to.

Baltimore, Richmond, Charleston, and New Orleans are ideal places to throw light on the urban dimension of fugitivity across the South; they were among the largest cities in the antebellum era and contained the largest numbers of African American residents, both free and enslaved.[18] To turn places like these into hospitable places for fugitives, a number of solidarities and institutional resources had to be mobilized. Throughout the South, free Black Americans had varying social experiences that extended to fugitives as newcomers in their communities. Yet, generally, shared exposure to slavery, discrimination, and general support for abolition were factors that substantiated cooperation. Expanding family networks, Black churches, and increasingly segregated neighborhoods facilitated escape and refuge.

While historian Martha Jones, in her study of Baltimore's free Black community, acknowledges the threat of deportation, insecure property, restrictions of commonly held rights, and increasing regulation as negatively impacting Black Baltimoreans' lives, she argues that they were at times able to make use of legal tools to successfully claim rights they felt entitled to.[19] *Escape to the City* emphasizes a different, more ominous picture. As a collective, as chapter 3 shows, Black southerners experienced dramatic discrimination and criminalization over the course of the antebellum era, culminating in the illegalization of tens of thousands. By putting them into the spotlight this book explores how, analogous to fugitive slaves, parts of the receiving society likewise had an illegal or undocumented status. This means that they either had no permission to live where they were living, had no documentation, or had false documentation.[20] These people, unlike some of the figures in Jones's study, could not publicly claim political rights and had often no connections to the more esteemed Black urban classes, who had access to the legal system. In short, the most vulnerable remained silent.

Instead of viewing fugitive slaves as solitary actors who fought to leave enslavement behind, this perspective makes us consider the involvement of broader parts of the Black population. Becoming aware of the indispensable role that the free Black communities played leads to de-emphasizing individual strategies of fleeing people and pushes us to reconceptualize this kind of fugitivity as collective action. In this regard, southern-internal flight converges more with studies of maroons, rebellions, and large-scale insurrections.[21] Likewise, students of northbound flight have long stressed the collaborative element of informal escape networks like the Underground Railroad or local associations of protection and resistance.[22] In the South, it was the strong link between fugitive slaves and their urban host communities, who were all exposed to arbitrary policing, extralegal violence, and civil disability before the law, which laid the cornerstone for their survival. Yet, real freedom remained elusive: all African Americans were illegal in one way or another, always in violation of some law, always presumed criminal. As a result, the urban fugitive fit right in.

Cities of Refuge

Once in the cities, fugitives had met their first milestone. Now, being clandestine, they camouflaged themselves amid the urban Black populations and had to navigate the physical and social spaces in the urban South. The people in this book lived in or moved to cities whose names already reveal the historical dominance of their oppressors. Charleston, New Orleans, Baltimore, and Richmond carry explicit names that lay bare the rule of people who built up their cultural, social, economic, and political hegemony on European legacies of colonialism and imperialism.

Despite still being understudied, cities and towns in the context of American slavery are of special interest because they deviated from the far more common plantation slavery. The very nature of labor, the construction of the social environment, and the mechanisms of control were fundamentally different for urban than for rural-agricultural slaves.[23] Studying cities provides promising insights due to the intense interplay between different groups, the relative density of court and police records, and the specific nature of the urban labor markets. Fundamental issues in urban history include governance, planning, segregation, injustice, and criminality.[24] These dynamics, which also run through this book, created contested and shifting spaces.

As port cities and centers of commerce, Baltimore and Richmond in the Upper South, and Charleston and New Orleans in the Lower South provide dynamic settings for long-term research. Baltimore and New Orleans were the largest, demographically most diverse cities in the South. In Charleston, residents of African descent formed the majority until the 1850s and the city had the highest percentage of slaves of all American cities. In general, large-scale slaveholding decreased in the urban South between 1810 and 1860. Richmond was the exception. With its massive use of enslaved workers in tobacco manufacturing and iron production, Richmond ranked first in combining slavery with industrialization.[25]

Southern cities had many faces, and Black urban dwellers encountered people in cities who had traveled widely and those who had never set foot outside of city limits. In Southern cities, Black people saw blatant violence but also felt the effects of reform movements. They saw abject poverty next to neat squares and organized parks. Black men and women who could not read or write crossed paths with other Black people who went to the theaters and races for amusement. They could rent apartments and sign contracts but were not allowed to vote. Cultural values were adopted from the countryside, economic visions from the North. And slavery, last but not least, created deep lines of division among the heterogeneous urban populations.[26] In the middle of all these contradictions and complexities, runaways from slavery—men, women, and sometimes children—tried to avoid capture and a return to bondage.

How did they carve out spaces that allowed them to move under the radar of those who dominated the urban space? Nineteenth-century cities were messy places, renowned for the undesirable mixing of different kinds of people, and they were full of strangers and short-term visitors. In these chaotic spaces, people on the run could hide with a little luck and a lot of strong networks.

Historians, social scientists, and geographers have done valuable work conceptualizing alternative geographies in the context of slavery. They have shown that people of African descent constructed perceptions of their physical surroundings differently than White people, which affected the spatial organization of their actions.[27] In southern cities, alternative geographies constituted places of empowerment and resilience simply because Black people could do things there on their own.

In a way, these Black geographies were already sites of refuge in themselves. Following runaway slaves into the cities reveals how they organized themselves in the urban space and sheds light on the relation of their community to the world around them. In the antebellum American South, the urban space was contested and shifting, and structured along gender, race, work, and, increasingly in the nineteenth century, class. Access to the public space depended on these factors and varied over time—long stretches of it and even determined by the time of day. Fugitive slaves who wanted to stay in southern cities had to navigate the social worlds they found there. Chapter 4 explores these aspects. Putting them center stage directs the perspective of this study to perceptions of different urban groups, usage and appropriation of physical places, and relations of power.

Runaways needed information to contact allies, find places to hide after dark, and socialize. It was to their advantage that a large number of illegal and undocumented city dwellers already depended on these Black geographies. Although there were substantial risks and dangers involved, particular racial and ethnic demographics marked off certain spaces as more congenial for fugitives than others. Seen through this lens, antebellum southern cities emerge as sites of danger, oppression, and struggle, but also as sites of Black resistance, solidarities, and sanctuary. *Escape to the City* investigates how fugitive slaves navigated them, and where they could breach the geographies of domination to find spaces of refuge.

Knowledge about racial and legal codes in the cities also helped runaways to survive economically, as chapter 5 addresses. Those who were familiar with the place, or had networks that fed them essential information, usually succeeded in finding work because they were able to read the "landscape of labor." Attention to labor has fallen somewhat short in recent decades as historical studies of resistance and agency have partly redirected scholars' attention to culture and away from work.[28] Yet, the question of where fugitive slaves worked is fundamental because work occupied a central position in their lives and largely decided where they could go and stay.

This perspective also helps explain why White southerners did not try very hard to stem the tide of fugitive slaves heading to southern cities. Fugitives who stayed within the South may not have caused political crises like their counterparts in the North but their sheer numbers were at least equally potent. Historian Simon Newman has stressed that when running away turned into an act of resisting slavery with explicit consequences for the larger community, it took on a political dimension.[29] Because they broke the law by running away and because they deprived their owners of their legal property, which they "hid" in the cities, fugitive slaves had a considerable effect on state and municipal politics. As will be shown, their presence influenced, among other areas, the regulation of self-hiring of slaves, police surveillance, and prison infrastructure, and it impacted urban politics and the economy.

Slaveholders were traditionally responsible for legislation regarding racial control in the cities. Yet, as the final chapter discusses economic developments, the expansion of suffrage to lower-class White men, and foreign immigration gradually brought about a restructuring of civic power and visions of Black labor. In this light, it is telling that there were also segments of the White population—especially urban employers—who had very little incentive to try to keep runaway slaves completely out of the cities. Ultimately, it was a combination of social and economic developments that facilitated the fugitives' cause.

A Chaotic Choir

The U.S. South as a space of refuge for enslaved people has a thin historiography. Apart from a relatively small but important body of work on temporary runaways and maroons, the bulk of historical scholarship of the United States has focused on men and women who freed themselves by setting foot on free soil.[30] Permanent and long-term runaways from slavery, who by intent and by outcome never migrated out of the slaveholding South, have barely been the focal point of historical studies. This is surprising given that contemporaries did not conceal their awareness of them. Northern U.S. journalist Frederick Law Olmsted, for one, found that "throughout the South slaves are accustomed to 'run away.'"[31] Although Olmsted's main argument rested on temporary flight, it was well known that runaway slaves were often absent for months, for years, or for good. After all, the innumerable notices in newspapers furnished long-term slave flight with a high visibility.

Slave flight within the southern states was a phenomenon known to contemporaries, yet individual southern fugitives from slavery could only be successful in their endeavors when they managed to stay invisible to the authorities (and to people who might betray them). Writing a history about them is challenging because people fleeing and hiding have left few traces in the archives. Political and societal discussions that explicitly addressed fugitive slaves in southern cities were rare, which has led historians to hitherto largely ignore them. This seems at first sight contradictory to the claim that runaways put themselves on the political agenda. It is important, therefore, to keep in mind that southern political leaders had reasons not to frequently emphasize this issue. One example is the official liability to protect the property of slaveholders; property rights over slaves had, in theory, to be enforced like other property rights. Political disputes with the northern states that were based on accusations of facilitating slave flight are another example. And when it came to slaveholders themselves, there was a common understanding that it was their own responsibility to retrieve their runaway slaves if they were still in the same jurisdiction. Despite these complexities, there are a variety of sources that confirm fugitive slaves' presence in southern cities and shed light on their experiences.

Throughout the antebellum period, and even before, the vast majority of southern newspapers daily published advertisements in which slaveholders asked readers to look out for their escaped human property. A great many enslaved men, women, and children were assumed to be somewhere outside the slaveholding South, but even more were thought to be hiding *within* the South, particularly in cities. While a good amount of these announcements reflect the beliefs and suppositions of slaveholders, there are likewise plenty of runaway ads that confirm that an escaped person was in a given place. Formulations by subscribers that a fugitive "was seen in Baltimore"; "has been secreting himself about this city for three months"; "I am informed he has passed as a freeman"; or "she has been seen recently in the neighborhood of Franklin-street" are frequent.[32]

Historian Gerald Mullin has stressed that these newspaper notices are fairly objective when compared to other sources. The subscribers of the announcements neither defended slavery nor justified their involvement in it.[33] Yet historians should be mindful when using runaway ads as quantitative sources. The contextual background of these announcements, and the reasons for slaveholders not to use them or to place them at a much later point in time, means that those fugitives who were advertised for in newspapers were the least likely to be found—this is why they were publicly wanted in the first place. The until now strongest empirical evidence for this claim derives from a perusal of names of people listed as runaway slaves in the Police Jail of the

Third Municipality of New Orleans from February 1839 to March 1840. The inventory delivered no matches with electronically searched newspaper announcements during the same period.[34] Consequently, runaway slave advertisements represent only a fraction of men, and even fewer women, who escaped bondage.

Apart from these sources, there were countless announcements by jails, workhouses, and other detention centers for slaves and free Black people, which point to the presence of fugitive slaves in the cities.[35] This phenomenon did not escape contemporaries. In May 1838, for example, a Black man "calling himself Sam, who has for some time passed in the City, as a free Negro," was apprehended and "Lodged in the Work House" in Charleston. The workhouse clerk, who hoped to find Sam's legal owner through the "Committed to Jail" advertisement, also "believes there are several runaways in the same situation in this place" and recommended to "let the officers look to it!"[36] In most places for most of the antebellum period, runaway slave jails were local. Only Louisiana established a centralized state depot to improve the management of internal runaways, doing so in 1857.[37]

Slaveholders furthermore compiled plantation management books, diaries, and private correspondence, and composed legal petitions and court documents. In legal sources, we can sometimes also hear the voices of escaped slaves, albeit in a distorted manner, constructed and reflected on by White people and squeezed into standardized legal statements.[38] Less distorted are autobiographies and interviews. Unlike runaway slave narratives written by (mostly) men who fled to the North, there are no equivalents to cover southern-internal flight. Yet, some of the autobiographies by formerly enslaved people deal with experiences in the South that can be used to understand the activities and motivations of southern fugitive slaves.[39] Combining these sources with newspaper articles, legislative ordinances, political speeches, travel accounts, church registers, municipal records, and city directories, *Escape to the City* provides perspectives from as many angles as possible.

By consulting diverse evidence from Baltimore, Richmond, Charleston, and New Orleans, this book attempts to counterbalance the silence about southern urban fugitives in the historical archives. At the same time, the fact that they are hard to find in the archives testifies to their success as people whose strategy was to be invisible. Despite all the obstacles, it is possible to write their history, even with scarce sources.

Stressing the importance of studying slave resistance, the late historian Stephanie Camp addressed the question of *how*. "Assuming that few new sources will come to light," she reasoned, "we need innovative ways to read our existing ones."[40] Following her call, this book draws many "reverse conclusions," for example, from people who failed (and were imprisoned) to shed light on those who succeeded. Asking negative questions, such as why these people are not in the archives and why they did not cause large political discussions, provides a starting point for comprehension. About *how to write* the history of fugitive slaves, this study converges with other historians' view that it is not possible to reconstruct the entire life history of even one enslaved person based on archival material. A prosopographical approach, however, leads the fragmentary voices in the archives to form a choir. Aptly formulated by historian Michael Zeuske, this will be a "chaotic choir," with many contradictions, and solo parts will be rare. Yet, it will be a choir capable of carrying and transmitting a narrative.[41]

CHAPTER ONE

The Urgency to Escape

In the late eighteenth and early nineteenth centuries, the geography of slavery in the Americas was radically transformed. People born during the American Revolutionary War heard and perhaps read about the destruction of the institution in some parts of the hemisphere, and its expansion and entrenchment in others. Even before this generation could have remembered anything, they witnessed the ongoing abolition process in the U.S. northern states. As young adults, they heard word of the sensational slave rebellion in St. Domingue and the subsequent abolition of slavery and proclamation of the second republic in the Americas. In their mid-twenties, newspapers covered the illegalization of the transatlantic slave trade, and throughout their adult lives, they saw slavery being defeated in Central America, Mexico, British Canada, and several places in the Caribbean and South America. Yet during this same period, news coverage simultaneously informed them about the growth of the institution in the southern United States, Cuba, and Brazil.

During the antebellum period, the United States of America came to constitute the largest slaveholding republic in the world. By 1860, shortly before the legal abolition of the institution of slavery, nearly four million men, women, and children were held in bondage. These people were trapped in a system that commodified their bodies, reduced them to chattel, rendered them legal property, and put them to forced labor as a natural state of servitude. The same period also witnessed significant increases in escapes of enslaved people, which cannot be explained by the numerical growth alone. Why, then, did more people than ever before flee enslavement?

A number of major developments precipitated slave flight, including diminishing opportunities to legally exit bondage, the expansion of slavery, and the intensification of the domestic slave trade. These factors indicate that the slave system was getting stronger rather than weaker. Manumission schemes were curtailed, an end to slavery was out of sight, and people were increasingly sold away from their families. This led enslaved men and women to see that, if they wanted out of bondage, they had to take care of it themselves. Running away certainly was neither the only nor the best way out, yet for thousands of enslaved people it became a tangible option.

American Slavery

Enslaved people at all times and in all places wanted to be free. Many slave narratives, written by formerly enslaved people after they had fled slavery, give insight into how Black Americans felt when they first realized that they were enslaved, and all of them explicitly deal with the longing to break free. Louis Hughes recalled that within his enslaved family, "It had been talked of (this freedom) from generation to generation."[1] Lunsford Lane, who later bought himself and his family out of slavery, accounted that "when I began to work, I discovered the difference between myself and my master's white children." Early on, Lane also recognized the realistic fear of being sold south, which "seemed infinitely worse than the terrors of death. To know, also, that I was never to consult my own will, but was, while I lived, to be entirely under the control of another, was another state of mind hard for me to bear."[2]

The colonies, and later the country that became the United States of America, whose economy was built upon coerced labor, had introduced the first enslaved people from the western coast of Africa in 1619. Over the next nearly 250 years, until the institution was finally abolished in 1865, slavery continuously evolved.[3] In the Age of Revolutions, Enlightenment ideals, most visible in the American, French, and Haitian Revolutions, had major impacts on the institution of slavery. The shift of moral consciousness, partly paired with religious convictions, that took place at this time led many people in Europe and in the Americas to regard slavery as a symbol of "all the forces that threatened the true destiny of man."[4]

The reassessment of the legitimate treatment of the poor, the weak, and the different led, among other changes, to challenging the physical treatment of slaves, which came to constitute a step toward a critique of slavery itself.[5] A mix of ideological change brought about by the pushing against slavery by Black people and an economic loss not too painful for slaveholders ultimately led to the prohibition of the transatlantic slave trade in 1807 and the abolition of slavery as an institution in various states, nations, and countries throughout the Americas. These included the American northern states, all of which had either abolished slavery or introduced gradual abolition schemes by 1804.[6] American leaders such as Thomas Jefferson and James Madison supported the idea that, when slavery was expanding into the new territories in the West, it would cover less ground and eventually peter out. This "diffusion" theory would bring an end to slavery without the federal government interfering in states' rights, Jefferson thought.[7]

The Age of Revolutions also had a profound impact on slavery in the southern states, although with a different outcome. Instead of emancipating all enslaved people by formally ending slavery, manumission and self-purchase schemes were facilitated which liberated thousands, even as bondage remained intact. Enslaved people themselves played an active role in this process. The Revolutionary era was a turbulent time that furnished African Americans with new opportunities to contest their bondage. Many slaves took the chance to flee from slavery or to exchange military service for their free status. Others actively pressed their owners for manumission or purchased themselves or their family members out of slavery.[8]

In the South, moral concerns regarding slavery during this time coincided with weakening tobacco production, which had been the backbone of slavery in Virginia, the largest and oldest slave society of the new country. Although historian Manisha Sinha has underlined that it was mainly abolitionist mobilization, revolutionary ideology, and slave resistance that spurred individual manumissions, decreasingly fertile soils in the Upper South made tobacco-based slavery seem doomed after the Revolution. In 1782, Virginia enacted an ordinance to ease legal constraints on manumissions. Between that year and 1806, ten thousand bondspeople benefited from this legal relaxation.[9] Hopes were high in Virginia and other states that manumissions would bring liberty to a growing number of Black people.

Manumissions, whereby slaves were officially and legally set free, had always been a part of the system of slavery; the possibility to manumit was in many aspects in the interest of masters. It offered a motivation for their bondspeople "to behave well," provided the slaveowners with a reward mechanism, and, in the case of self-purchase, allowed owners to negotiate above-market prices with their slaves.[10] Consequently, the prospect of manumission for a few could be used to maintain the subjugation of the masses. The reasons why slaveowners set their bondspeople free or allowed them to "purchase" their own freedom varied from a cash payment to satisfaction of what was perceived good and loyal service to religion, ideology, or a self-understanding of a "benevolent" slaveholder.[11]

Thanks to this plethora of motivations, which for the first time had a palpable impact on larger demographic developments, manumissions skyrocketed. The free Black population became the demographic group with the fastest growth rates. By 1810, 10 percent of people of African descent in the Upper South were free. And although the number of manumissions was much smaller in the Lower South than in the Upper South, between

TABLE 1.1 Free people of African descent, 1790–1860. Numbers of free people of African descent between 1790 and 1860, divided between the entire country, northern states, southern states, Upper South, and Lower South.

	1790	1830	1860
United States	59,500	319,600	488,100
Northern states	27,100	137,500	226,200
Southern states	32,400	182,100	262,000
Upper South	30,200	151,900	225,000
Lower South	2,200	30,200	37,000

Source: Berlin, *Slaves Without Masters*, 46, 136.

1790 and 1810, the number of free Black people in South Carolina and Georgia almost tripled.[12] Slavery in the United States appeared to be retracting.

A Closing Door

Antislavery sentiments between the American Revolution and until about 1810 led to spikes in manumissions in the South, and formal abolition became so tangible that it was discussed at the state level in Virginia, Maryland, and Delaware. The latter two states even had abolitionist societies operating within them.[13] Before support for such plans ever reached a critical mass, however, endorsement of slavery suddenly rose again. One important factor was the question of what to do with Black people who were released out of slavery. Unsupervised and uncontrolled, the free Black population was perceived as troublesome.

At the opening of the new century, there existed already a modest, self-preserving free Black population. When manumissions were curtailed, the free African American population of the United States had increased sufficiently as to ensure and expand its future autonomous growth. In 1810, 108,300 free Black people lived in the southern states. In the decades to follow, this population grew substantially, although the Upper South always counted a considerably higher number than the Lower South. In 1820, 134,200 southern free African Americans were divided into 114,000 living in the Upper South and 20,200 living in the Lower South. Thirty years later, in 1850, numbers had increased to 238,200 across the entire South, with 203,700 populating the Upper South and 34,500 the Lower South (see table 1.1).

The best motivation for enslaved African Americans to push against slavery was to see other people who looked like them and were free. White Americans recognized this, too. In 1860, a Tennessee lawmaker warned: "Their mere presence [of free Black people], the simple act of walking our streets, and traveling our highways by the farms of the countryside is sufficient to incite insurrection in the slaves, for the desire for freedom is innate in the human breast."[14] With the growth of this free population, one of the most basic justifications of American slavery—the claim that free Blacks were not capable of living in freedom—weakened.

White southerners panicked. Having held Black people in captivity for generations, they were deeply frightened of retaliation, especially in places where African Americans constituted the majority. St. Domingue taught them that this was not sheer fantasy. Southerners evoked the horrors of the Haitian Revolution (1791–1804) for the next several decades as a way to strengthen their demands for more repression against free and enslaved African Americans.[15]

These depictions of free people of color as dangerous elements peaked with every real or perceived insurrection of the enslaved, such as with Gabriel Prosser's attempt to march enslaved coconspirators into Richmond in 1800, after the Denmark Vesey conspiracy of 1822 in South Carolina, and following Nat Turner's 1831 rebellion in Virginia.[16] After each event, slave repression and suspicion of free Black people intensified. In the wake of Vesey, the South Carolina Assembly adopted "An Act for the Better Regulation and Government of Free Negroes and Persons of Color" in the same year, which provided a number of hefty restrictions on Black movement. Among other forms of control, every free man of African descent was required to have a White guardian who would vouch for his good behavior.[17]

In territories newly incorporated into the American nation, these developments were visible in a more radical and accelerated manner. In Florida, which was part of the Spanish overseas empire until 1821, people of African descent enjoyed a higher status than in the regions that emerged out of the British Empire. When Florida became part of the United States, authorities hurried to adjust it to the social systems of the other slave states until it "looked less disturbingly Caribbean and more comfortably southern," as historian Jane Landers has put it. In short time, Black peoples' world was turned upside down as they saw their social, political, and economic rights curtailed, and manumissions almost entirely abolished.[18] For most White Americans, the free Black population posed a danger, and it was a priority to contain its growth.

This was devastating for bondspeople because manumission and self-purchase were legal ways out of slavery. The advantage of a legal procedure was that one's free status was certified and former slaves turned into legitimate residents of the societies in which they lived. Yet, manumissions in the U.S. South became increasingly complicated to enact. The exact practices varied in different places and tightening legislation affected people in different states at different times. The overall developments, however, were similar: the laws became stricter. Virginia was the first state to enact a law in 1806 that stipulated that manumitted bondspeople had to leave the state. Consequently, manumission rates in Virginia decreased dramatically.[19]

Legislatures had to balance the right of slaveholders to set their own slaves free against the demands of larger society, which called for public safety. Therefore, at least in the early decades of the nineteenth century, the practice was not abolished but rather so much complicated that it was drastically reduced. For example, manumissions in New Orleans were severely curtailed over time and some of the legislation went far beyond the strictness of other southern states. In 1830, slaveholders who wanted to emancipate their slaves were required to post a bond of $1,000 to make sure that the emancipated person left Louisiana. From 1852 onward, the law required manumitters to pay $150 shipping costs for the transportation of the manumittee to Africa, and five years later, the practice was prohibited altogether.[20] By the mid-1830s, emancipators officially needed judicial or legislative consent in most states. Over time, the doors to a legal path out of slavery closed almost entirely. In the last years before the Civil War, only Delaware, Missouri, and Arkansas granted the right of manumission to slaveholders.[21]

Significant for the Upper South were "delayed manumissions." T. Stephen Whitman has analyzed these patterns unique to Maryland and concluded that delayed manumissions were an important tool for slave control in the city of Baltimore. After 1815, future emancipation decreased but still constituted one-third of individual manumissions. People immediately manumitted were on average older than those who would be released at some point in the future. Whitman calculated that the average age for both men and women released without deferment was forty, an age at which slaveholders could no longer expect high profitability. Enslaved women typically had already given birth to children who were born the property of their mothers' owners.[22] Younger people were hardly targeted by this mechanism, and runaway slave advertisements and petitions testify to the escapes of term slaves.[23]

Further hampering legal avenues to exit slavery, self-purchase became more expensive, and it was not unusual that slaveholders in American Louisiana charged up to 20 percent above the market price.[24] Bondspeople who wanted to purchase a free status faced almost insurmountable obstacles unless they made their own money as hired slaves. Strategies to achieve this included for plantation slaves to work in their free time in their own gardens and sell the surplus produce in the markets, or for hired slaves to work additional hours or spend less on lodging and food. Even when they against all odds managed to save enough of their wages (which almost always implied living a very arduous life), they had no legal security and depended on the word of their owners.

Slave narratives contain accounts of (mostly) men who worked tirelessly to make and save enough money to buy themselves or loved ones out of slavery and were betrayed by people with more power. Moses Grandy, for example, was defrauded by two masters, who decided to take the sum agreed upon and additionally make the same sum by selling Grandy. The third attempt to buy his freedom was successful. Yet instead of the originally agreed-upon $600, Grandy paid $1,850.[25] Theoretically, the possibility of purchasing oneself (or a loved one) remained, but due to the rising slave prices and the curtailing of manumissions, bondspeople collectively understood that their chances of becoming free in a legal way were rapidly shrinking.

The Expansion of Slavery

Dubbed the "second slavery" by Dale Tomich, slavery after 1810 was not only marked by massive plantation complexes, it also became compatible with industrial production and was increasingly integrated into global capitalist markets.[26] The main factor was cotton. The invention of the cotton gin in the 1790s, a machine that allowed its user to separate the cotton fibers from the seeds with an efficiency unheard of until this time, increased the demand for raw cotton. Suddenly, investments in cotton caught the attention of people with money, and the future of slavery seemed profitable again. With the burgeoning Industrial Revolution in Great Britain, the demand rose seemingly boundlessly. Tons of raw cotton were shipped via southern rivers to the port cities and transported to Manchester in England. Slavery, opposed by the British public, was a by-product that was shrugged off by businessmen and the government in order to fuel the ever-hungry textile industry, and the southern states became the main suppliers of cotton to Europe.[27]

American planters saw moneymaking opportunities in the global economy, and old and new slaveholders began to curtail manumissions. To be able to respond to the massive demand for cotton, plantation slavery in the United

States intensified and expanded geographically. Rapid soil exhaustion and the growing demand from manufacture sites in Europe drove cotton and slavery westward and southward. The United States expelled Indian groups and tribal nations from their native lands, on which cotton and sugar were then cultivated. When the United States purchased the Territory of Louisiana from France in 1803, it doubled its size overnight. Enslaved workers produced monocultural crops on mass plantations in the new commodity frontiers. During the "first slavery," colonialism and slavery were interdependent and the latter only took place at the margins of the empire. Now it moved to the core of society.[28] This was when southerners recommitted to slavery. Before that, an eventual end to slavery had seemed plausible. But now, slave-based plantation work and investments in enslaved human beings became more profitable than ever before.[29] It became clear that slavery was not just going to die out; Jefferson's diffusion theory was an illusion.

Historian Sven Beckert has underlined that the uniqueness of American cotton-growing lay in the planters' control of and access to extensive supplies of land, labor, and capital, and that the expansion of this business sector rested on the physical and psychological violence of mass slavery.[30] Cotton had the power to generate fortunes for those who were able to command labor power. In contrast to the Chesapeake region (eastern Virginia and Maryland), where slavery had been self-maintaining since the 1720s and planters were not entirely dependent on the constant influx of new laborers, in the Deep South, slavery swallowed many more lives. The sizes of the production units grew. By 1860, 11 percent of people enslaved in the Upper South toiled on plantations with 50 to 199 slaves; in the Lower South, it was 30 percent. Massive cotton plantations in the Deep South propelled the economy, with Alabama, Mississippi, Louisiana, and Georgia producing almost 80 percent of the country's cotton in 1859.[31]

Those fleeing from Deep South plantations tried to escape the discipline of a labor system built around drill, violence, and fear. Slave labor on the sugar and cotton plantations was constructed around the gang system, with set working hours and a fixed quantity of cotton to be picked or cane to be cut each day.[32] In the early years of the nineteenth century, 11 percent of enslaved Americans lived on cotton plantations; on the eve of the Civil War it was 64 percent.[33] The amount of cotton these people picked increased yearly. In 1790, 1.2 million pounds were produced in the American South; this number had risen to 2.1 billion in 1859. The most astonishing detail about this is that cotton production grew not only because slavery as an institution expanded simultaneously. Rather, biological and technological inventions, paired with a faster picking rate of enslaved workers, increased cotton productivity.[34] It was a relentless labor regime that devastated the lives of hundreds of thousands.

This commitment to and expansion of bondage revealed the contradictions in the context of Atlantic revolutions and abolitions. Specifically, it forced southerners to defend racial slavery—long justified on the basis of a perceived mental and physical "inferiority" of Black people—in the wake of revolutionary ideals that underscored liberty and equality.[35] While the racial basis for chattel slavery had generally been accepted by its defenders since the late seventeenth century, it obtained a new quality in the nineteenth century. Black people came to be seen as not only suitable for slavery but indeed *un*suitable for freedom.[36] In order to justify the maintenance of their captivity at a time of humanitarian liberalism and to exclude people of African descent from the claims of the Declaration of Independence, southern slaveholders created the idea of dependent, childlike slaves who were grateful to their masters for guidance and care. Slavery, earlier seen as a "necessary evil," became an ideology in the southern states at the same time that it was extinguished in the majority of the surrounding areas.[37]

The consequences were a stronger politicizing of slavery and a defense of its benign intentions through an alleged paternalism. Until the end of the eighteenth century, a patriarchal master-slave relation was pervasive, which demanded absolute obedience from the subordinate and accented the authority of the master through quickly enforced violence. Slave control was based on physical immobility and coercion. Around the turn of the century, the nature of that slavery changed. In contrast to other places where humanitarian trends led to the abolition of slavery, southern slaveholders answered with what from their perspective was a "more humane" form of slavery. The shift from patriarchy to paternalism provided the master—in his view—with an aura of generosity, solicitude, and benevolence. The forbidding patriarchal slaveholder became a loving father who cared about his dependents and in return expected gratitude and affection.[38] These developments were strongly influenced by religion. A Christian man felt, as head of his household, responsible for all his dependents: wife, children, and slaves.[39]

When the South saw slavery vanish from almost all countries and regions around it, slaveholders needed the support of other White people to defend the institution against all the attacks it was exposed to during the second slavery.[40] The Democratic Party was the one institution slaveholders relied on for their endeavors to corroborate the system. To justify and defend it in the nineteenth century, they depended on a broader base of support, yet the majority of White people did not own slaves. And so, under the banner of White supremacy, Democrats advocated for racial privilege and aimed to construct solidarity and unity among slaveholding and non-slaveholding Whites and Whites in the South and in the North.[41] It was the most dominant political party in the South for most parts of the antebellum era.

Besides cultural superiority, White supremacy promised socioeconomic advancement and promoted slaveowning as an important milestone. The number of small slaveholders increased drastically after the Revolution as a result of the decline of primogeniture. Distributing property, including slave property, to a number of heirs instead of only the firstborn son enlarged this social class while reducing the absolute wealth of every one of them. The result was a new slaveholding middle class who shared the planters' efforts to keep the institution of slavery in place and to defend it against slave flight— and for small slaveholders, the loss of a slave constituted a much larger loss. Securing slavery for the future was best done by increasing the range of people benefiting from it.[42]

As Barbara Fields has reminded us, the goal for planters was always to produce cotton (and, by extension, sugar, tobacco, indigo, rice, and wheat) and get rich from it. White supremacy was a necessary by-product.[43] It was, however, not waterproof, and while more White people were joining the slaveholding classes during the antebellum period, non-slaveholding Whites never held a uniform view vis-à-vis African Americans. Nevertheless, as a group, they were characterized by resentment toward Black people and endorsement of slavery.

High profitability paired with the political power of the planters resulted in the elimination of most criticism of the institution. Revolutionary talk about abolition waned and nearly disappeared from the South. By the 1830s, formal abolition was farther away than ever before. The great demand for slaves swelled the ranks of those in bondage and the enslaved population skyrocketed from 700,000 in 1790 to 1.2 million 20 years later, and culminated in nearly 4 million on the eve of the Civil War (see table 1.2). Fueled by the rise of cotton and the fear of slave revolts, slavery increasingly removed any hope of emancipation via the actions of the owners, so many enslaved people decided to take matters into their own hands and seek relief by flight.

Broken Families

The expansion and intensification of slavery, paired with shrinking opportunities to exit the system in a legal way, stimulated enslaved people to con-

TABLE 1.2 Enslaved population, 1790–1860. Numbers of enslaved people between 1790 and 1860, with indications for the entire country, Maryland, Virginia, South Carolina, and Louisiana.

	1790	*1830*	*1860*
United States	698,000	2,009,000	3,954,000
Maryland	103,000	103,000	87,000
Virginia	294,000	470,000	491,000
South Carolina	107,000	315,000	402,000
Louisiana*	—	110,000	332,000

*Louisiana was not part of the United States until 1803.

Source: *Return of the Whole Number of Persons within the Several Districts of the United States, According to "An Act Providing for the Enumeration of the Inhabitants of the United States"* (Philadelphia: Childs and Swaine, 1791), 3; Department of Commerce and Labor Bureau of the Census, *Heads of Families at the First Census of the United States in the Year 1790: South Carolina* (Washington, D.C.: Government Printing Office, 1908), 8, https://www.census.gov/library /publications/1907/dec/heads-of-families.html, April 16, 2019; Joseph C. G. Kennedy (ed.), *Population of the United States in 1860; Compiled from the Original Returns of the Eighth Census under the Secretary of the Interior* (Washington, D.C.: Government Printing Office, 1864), 193, 214, 452, 513; Berlin, *Slaves Without Masters*, 396–97.

sider flight as a way out. Another factor was the breaking up of enslaved families caused by a significant increase in the volume of slave sales. Sale had always been inherent to slavery but during the second slavery it became much more common. As the United States expanded, it took its racialized system of slavery with it. The transformation of new lands into slave soil was accelerated by developments in the old Chesapeake region and the low country on the eastern Atlantic shore. The labor-intensive tobacco production was largely replaced by the cultivation of grains and other aliments, which allowed Upper South planters to dispose of surplus members of their enslaved labor force.[44]

Contrary to the numerous manumissions that had taken place during the Age of Revolutions, from the early nineteenth century on, slaveholders rarely considered manumitting their slaves but identified another opportunity to generate profit: they sold their slaves into the new regions, where arduous work; an unfamiliar, harsh climate; and the separation from family and friends would mark their future lives. The higher death rates and the growing number of plantations increased the demand for enslaved laborers in the new cotton and sugar regions of the Deep South. Slavery was everywhere. It infused the South's economy, politics, religion, and social relations.

Slaves ceased to be mere laborers and instead turned into human capital that could be bought, sold, and traded. James Steer from Louisiana, for example, recognized the promising economic prospect of investing in slaves in 1818: "For a young man, just commencing life, the best stock in which he can invest Capital, is, I think, negro Stock. [...] negroes will yield a much larger income than any Bank dividend."[45] In the antebellum period, 88 percent of bank loans secured by mortgages in Louisiana, and 82 percent in South Carolina, used enslaved people partly or fully as collateral.[46] On a macro level, the entire commercial and financial structure of cotton production was infused by the reliance on enslaved bodies, "both on the ability of enslavers to extract cotton from them and on the ability of enslavers (or bankruptcy courts) to sell them to someone else who wanted to extract cotton," according to historian Edward Baptist.[47] Being at the same time a body with a monetary value, a commodity, an investment, the ultimate financial security, and a political support instrument (foremost in the context of the Three-Fifths Compromise), enslaved men, women, and children in the antebellum period were much more to slaveholders than a source of cheap labor.[48]

Between 1790 and 1860, the internal slave trade displaced approximately one million enslaved people from Maryland, Virginia, and the Carolinas to Kentucky, Tennessee, Georgia, Alabama, Mississippi, Louisiana, and Texas.[49] An additional two million were forced to relocate within the same states. For the displaced this could mean that they were separated from their loved ones, although they often did not live far away.[50] Those in the cities were not necessarily spared. Places like Baltimore, Richmond, and Charleston fed bodies into the domestic slave trade. Although the cities were not directly involved in the production and marketing of cotton, they were indeed of crucial significance to the cotton economy.

Forced migrations inflicted unimaginable pain on Black families. Families in slavery provided emotional support and were oftentimes the only resort to bear the backbreaking work and humiliating existence as the property of somebody else. Enslaved women gave birth to an average of seven children. Some historians have claimed that the nuclear family was in the antebellum South as common among slaves as for Western Europeans, while others have remarked that the realities of slavery did not allow for this.[51] What is certain is that sale broke up thousands of families, separating children from mothers, husbands from wives, and sisters from brothers. Estimates suggest that during the time of the Second Middle Passage, every third marriage in the Upper South was destroyed because one of the spouses was transported away. An equal percentage of children were pulled apart from at least one parent.[52]

Enslaved people often anticipated an upcoming sale or a move and usually regarded this information as devastating.[53] Sale was a very realistic and constant fear of all enslaved people, and being "sold south" or "down the river" was a nightmare the majority of enslaved people in the Upper South worried about for either themselves or their loved ones. For enslaved Lincy, for instance, being sold was such a traumatic experience that the purchaser demanded to return her because he thought she was ill: "She is taken entirely senseless & struggles very hard," he wrote to the seller. She "will tear her clothes and bite her self & would hurt her self if she were not held & it takes four strong persons to hold her."[54] John Brown, who was walked south across the country to be sold, reported about a fellow slave, a woman named Critty, who died of grief on the route.[55]

In instances that enslaved people did not see separation coming or could not prevent it, there was often no way to reunite. Slave narratives and interviews with former bondspeople are full of accounts by people who mourn the loss of loved ones after years and even after the abolition of slavery. Carol Anna Randall, for instance, lost her sister in the slave trade: "It was de saddes' thing dat ever happen to me. Ma's Marsa tole my sister, Marie Robinson, 'Git yo' things together, I'm goin' to take you to Richmond today. I'm goin' to sell you. Ben offered a good price.' Lawd, chile, I cried. Mother an' sister cried too, but dat didn't help. Ole Marsa Robinson carry her 'way f'om dere. [. . .] I ain't never seen dat pretty sister of mine no more since de day she was sol'. Chile, it nearly broke my heart too, 'cause I love dat sister mo'n any of de others."[56]

Matilda Carter, who also experienced the sale of her sister, testified to the perpetual pain this inflicted upon her mother: "Mother never did git over dis ack of sellin' her baby to dem slave drivers down New Orleans."[57] Whereas the intensification of slavery was a development that affected all people who lived in bondage, the internal slave trade targeted primarily young people.

Planters who sought to establish themselves in the new western and southern regions favored young slaves of both sexes between fourteen and twenty-five years, yet generally more young men than women were required to do the physically hard work of cutting trees, draining swamps, and constructing paths—in short, to build a "Cotton Empire" out of the wilderness. The forced migrations to the Deep South assumed proportions so high in the era of the second slavery that Ira Berlin coined the term "migration generations" for those African American slaves who lived between the American Revolution and the Civil War.[58] And even this term does not nearly capture the dimensions of this harsh reality.

Contemporary observers not accustomed to the cruel realities of slavery were often shocked to see what sale did to enslaved families. In the 1830s, English philosopher John Stuart witnessed a farewell scene on the wharf in Charleston: "A slave ship from New Orleans was lying in the steam, and the poor negroes, handcuffed and pinioned, were hurried off in boats, eight at a time. Here I witnessed the last farewell,—thee heart-rending separation of every earthly tie. The mute and agonizing embrace of the husband and wife, and the convulsive grasp of the mother and the child, were alike torn asunder—for ever! It was a living death,—they never see or hear of each other more."[59]

Some planters moved south together with their slaves, or pioneered the founding of a new plantation with a selection of their slaves before summoning the rest of their households.[60] Most enslaved people, however, were ripped from their familiar environment and torn away from loved ones. In many instances, it was not purely economic considerations that determined which of their bondspeople a slaveholder would sell; this decision also had a personal dimension. William Grimes, a refugee to the North, claimed in his autobiography that "it is generally known that when a man sells a servant, he intends by that means to punish him, and endeavors to sell him where he shall never see him again."[61] Conversely, the threat of sale also functioned as a mechanism of controlling one's enslaved workers, but the odds of escaping sale were slim.

Family and kinship could be both a motivation for and a discouragement from escape, and the persistent threat of sale into the domestic slave trade made the preservation of family ties a more pressing concern than the struggle for freedom.[62] For a largely intact family on the plantation who would collectively suffer with the loss of one working member, escape could be construed as very selfish and harmful. Many enslaved people, moreover, chose family over freedom when they had the chance. Eighteen-year-old John Simmons, or John Pickling, from South Carolina decided against freedom and in favor of his family when he executed a successful flight attempt but later returned for his mother who was held enslaved by the same man as Simmons.[63] Frederick Douglass voiced such thoughts forcefully: "It is my opinion, that thousands would escape from slavery who now remain there, but for the strong cords of affection that bind them to their families, relatives and friends."[64] When family was broken up already, or friends sold away, potential runaways and their kin had less to lose. As this became increasingly common during the antebellum period, enslaved people, when anticipating sale, often saw running away as the only option to keep their families together. Broken families, because they made life in slavery even more unbearable, were a factor that exacerbated the urgency of running away.

AROUND THE TURN of the nineteenth century, economic considerations paired with new justifications of racial difference reconstructed American slavery. This "second slavery" absorbed more people into its merciless mills than ever before and all hope for formal abolition in the South vanished. The curtailment of manumissions negatively affected the possibilities of enslaved people to achieve a free status. But slavery did not only grow tighter, it also grew more intolerable as enslaved families, who constituted the cornerstone of social life and mutual emotional support, were increasingly threatened with destruction. Parallel to the expansion of slavery, slave sales and the internal slave trade triggered the flight of bondspeople who otherwise might have accepted their enslavement alongside their families for a little longer and rendered it an increasingly pressing enterprise. Yet, with the overwhelming majority of American slaves firmly in bondage, who were the men and women who were in a position to escape?

CHAPTER TWO

The Making of the New Fugitive Slave

In December 1856, Frances, or, as she called herself, Fanny, about twenty-six years of age, decided to abscond from the man who held her as his legal slave. It took William Taber, the slaveowner, ten months before he placed an advertisement in the *Charleston Mercury* to find his human property. He described Fanny as being "of a good height, brown complexion, rather sharp features; her upper front teeth gone, (but she may have false teeth to replace them, as she declared she would if she ran off,) talks like the North Carolina negros, where she was raised, but latterly has lived in Florida, has a pleasant expression, speaks slowly and deliberately, and altogether is a very likely girl." Taber informed the newspaper's readership that Fanny "has been seen about town, until within the last three or four months," and he believed that she was "harbored by some white person in the City [of Charleston]." In the ad, the slaveholder set a bounty of $100 on Fanny and an additional $50 "on proof to conviction of any responsible person who may have harbored her." This was a considerable amount of money, suggesting that Fanny was a valuable bondswoman to Taber. By January 1859, Taber had still not been able to get her back, although Fanny "has been seen often about the city" and the award had been raised to $300.[1]

Taber's short ad contains a great deal of valuable information that helps us understand who the men and women were that fled to southern cities. Taber speaks about the length of Fanny's absence, the color of her skin, her past, his own perception of her attitude, the involvement of third parties in her flight, and very importantly, her mobility. Examining the profiles of the people who escaped to southern cities reveals that features typically attributed to fugitive slaves—foremost, being male and being skilled—were not determinative of who ran away. Instead, it was about opportunities created by physical mobility, autonomy, and exposure to other people who were not slaves or slaveholders. The key determinant was knowledge of the broader world—mostly limited to the South—that became available to a growing number of enslaved people who worked independently as hired slaves, used new transportation infrastructures, or were forcibly sold away. Additionally and importantly, it was the profile of the enslaved themselves, their aptitude, boldness, and agency, that made slave flight possible for so many.

Gender and Mobility

Runaway slave advertisements and jail statistics leave no doubt that there was a gender imbalance within the runaway slave population of the American South; previous studies have underscored this. John Hope Franklin and Loren Schweninger evaluated over 2,000 runaway slave ads for the periods 1790–1816 and 1838–60 and concluded that the share of women was remarkably stable, namely 19 percent for both periods. Yet, there were some interesting regional differences between the five states they analyzed. In the early period, the percentage of women hit a high of 23 in South Carolina while in Louisiana they constituted 11 percent. In the later period, Louisiana had the highest percentage of female runaways (29 percent), and Virginia the lowest (9 percent).[2] Leni Ashmore Sorensen's analysis of the "Daybook of the Richmond Police" shows that women made up 24.7 percent of runaways suspected of being in that city between 1834 and 1844.[3] Judith Kelleher Schafer's statistics on runaway slaves in New Orleans in the year 1850 indicate that 31.7 percent were women.[4]

The two studies on Richmond and New Orleans are of particular relevance because they pertain to cities. There, women constituted roughly one-fourth to one-third of runaway slaves. These gender imbalances are remarkable, but the share of women was still large enough to give pause to the claim that the archetypal runaway slave was a man. When examining southern-internal flight, the presence of men was less prominent compared to other areas. When Silvey fled from Exeter Plantation in South Carolina at some point before 1854, she was first listed as absent in the record book before eventually disappearing from the ledger altogether in March 1855.[5] Based on Silvey's sex, it is statistically more likely that she sought refuge in an urban center in the South than leave the slaveholding states. Indeed, compared to the gender divisions of slave flight to the North and Mexico, in which over 80 percent and almost 90 percent were men, respectively, women were much more present in southern-internal escapes.[6] Southern cities, in comparison to other destinations, presented a particular opportunity for women who sought to free themselves by running away.[7]

Explanations for the generally lower number of women who escaped slavery have usually been attributed to their social role in the community. Various historians have claimed that as daughters, wives, and especially mothers, enslaved women held more responsibilities at home and were therefore more reluctant to leave their families behind.[8] This line of reasoning holds normative implications that enslaved men were less likely to make sacrifices for their families and children and portrays women as more caring and more engaged in their communities. Some enslaved women surely felt this sort of social pressure. Runaway slave ads featuring mothers that left children behind are rare. "Motherhood was central to enslaved women's concept of womanhood, their experience in slavery, and their resistance efforts," notes Amani Marshall.[9] Yet, contrary to these arguments that attempt to explain the lower numbers of women escaping, it can also be argued that bondswomen had even stronger incentives to flee. Women were given no preferential treatment in slavery, yet sexual violence in slavery was an additional danger to their physical and mental health.[10]

Flight from slavery, in contrast to the separation of families, was an active choice and it is wrong to assume that fathers had less desire to be with their families than mothers. Historians support this claim by showing how important and indeed prioritized kinship ties, families, and monogamous love was for enslaved women *and* men.[11] Yet, in the lives of enslaved people there were many factors that lay outside their area of influence, especially being sold away from loved ones. Many slave narratives display the pain of enslaved men of being separated from their families. Charles Ball, for example, lost his wife Judah when he was sold from Maryland, first to South Carolina and subsequently to Georgia. In the moment of hearing about his fate, "the thoughts of my wife and children rushed across my mind, and my heart died away within me." Ball constantly referred to his family throughout his narrative, expressing the sufferings of forced separation. After the death of his most recent master, he concluded that "my heart yearned for my wife and children, from whom I had now been separated more than four years." He broke free and returned to them.[12]

Without looking closely at the different situations men and women found themselves in, it seems too one-sided to claim that men saw it as less problematic than women did to be separated from their loved ones. At the same time, the majority of women did not have very good preconditions to escape. Men in the nineteenth-century United States enjoyed greater mobility than women. This held true for all men and women but had even more severe consequences for African Americans, particularly those in bondage. One's tasks and professions dictated their mobility level. The division of tasks was based on gender assumptions, which contributed to different experiences women had in slavery.[13] Plantation workers constituted the bulk of American slaves in the nineteenth century. They were mostly bound to their plantations and the nearby surroundings. Yet, looking at those employed outside of the fields, it becomes apparent that enslaved African Americans possessed different professional aptitudes, which furnished them with varying degrees of mobility and flexibility. More than anything else, mobility accounted for gender imbalances in slave flight.

Mobility was clearly related to jobs and tasks but it could also be achieved outside the realm of work. Moving for social and other nonwork reasons widened people's exposure to the outside world. But it was mostly men who officially as well as clandestinely visited spouses, lovers, and family members at different plantations, just like it was mainly men who drove carriages and delivered messages outside of the plantation. Enslaved women on the roads were therefore less common and more suspicious.[14] Through traveling between plantations, commuting from countryside to town, and moving within cities, many enslaved men and some women covered physical distances, which literally broadened their horizons.

In the 1960s, Malcolm X famously claimed that there was a distinction between field and house slaves. The house slaves had accommodated themselves in slavery because they realized that they were better off than the plantation hands. "He ate better, dress[ed] better, and he lived in a better house," Malcolm said, explaining why the house slave would not run away.[15] Although he was referring to the contrasting attitudes of Black Americans toward their oppression by White society in the twentieth century, his statement sheds light on why some people would want to flee slavery while others hesitated. Flipping his statement, it was precisely enslaved men and women who did *not* work in the fields who were in more advantageous positions for successful escape.

This speaks to differences between average field hands and a smaller class of more privileged slaves. Like Solomon Northup, who unsuccessfully tried to escape for twelve years, the vast majority of enslaved African Americans had virtually no chance to run away. Those who did have a chance met very specific criteria.

Broadened Horizons

The majority of fugitive slaves were between their late teens and late thirties.[16] Reckoning with their physical fitness to wage an escape attempt, their mental abilities to assimilate to the free population, their chances to find a job and make money for themselves, and the hope of having a family and seeing their children grow up in freedom, provided them with a window of about twenty years. Older bondspeople might not want to risk or upend their lives by running away. When northern journalist James Redpath asked an enslaved

man "if he did not think of escaping before" he was an old man, the man ab-
negated. "I wouldn't run the risk now of trying to escape. It's hardly so much
an object, sir, when a man's turned the hill."[17] On the other side of the spec-
trum, young children rarely escaped alone. Eight-year-old Marvin, who disappeared in New Orleans, and a ten-year-old girl with the name Nancy and a
boy called Henry of eight or nine years, who were believed to be hiding in
Richmond, were among the youngest documented runaways.[18]

In the decades before the Civil War, an enslaved American who was born
and died under the same master was almost an exception. Arthur, twenty-five
to thirty years old, was advertised as a runaway slave in 1821. Besides describing his physical features, including marks of the whip, wounds, and mutila-
tions, slaveholder Robert Martin from North Carolina included a history of
sales:

> [Arthur] was born in Maryland, and when about fourteen years of age,
> was sold to John or James M'Gill, in Wilmington, N.C.—by M'Gill to
> Blue—by Blue to Wm. Thomas, on Pedee, S.C.—runaway from Thomas
> and got back to Wilmington and passed as a free man for some time;
> at last was apprehended and put in goal, sold by order of Thomas in
> Wilmington goal to John M'Daniel of South-Carolina—by M'Daniel to
> Night—by Night to Alexander Bell—by Bell to me. Said negro may have
> obtained a free pass, or have been taken off by some evil disposed
> person. . . .[19]

Manifold sales were devastating for the lives of enslaved people who saw
themselves again and again ripped from familiar people and environments.
But new owners, new places, and the experiences of being removed also expanded one's networks and geographical knowledge. Very tellingly, in the
cases in which this information is included in the newspaper announcements,
41 percent of female and 30 percent of male runaway slaves had had multiple
owners in South Carolina.[20] It is likely that multiple previous ownership was
even more frequent than the mentions in runaway ads reveal.

The late historian Ira Berlin found that the runaway slave population did
not tend to include average field hands. Rather, he labeled them the "slave
elite," made up of mechanics, artisans, domestics, and drivers, and claimed
that they were "more skilled, sophisticated, and aggressive than the mass of
slaves."[21] At first glance, runaway slave advertisements support Berlin's claim
about the slave elite, as well as the very high bounties that enslavers set on
them. Professional training, mobility, strong mental capacities, and autonomy
turned enslaved African Americans into valuable property while simultaneously

increasing their chances of successful permanent escape. Contemporary observers understood this. The English traveler Marianne Finch found that
"those whom good treatment has rendered most fit for freedom, are the most
desired as slaves."[22]

Finch's comment seems particularly relevant to enslaved people whose
skills made them extremely valuable, like Isaac Wallace. Sometimes calling
himself Ezekiel, Wallace ran away near Baltimore in September 1817. "He is a
shoemaker by trade, and carried with him all his tools," stated his master, who
offered $100 for his return. And further, "he is a very good ploughman, and
excellent with the axe, scythe and cradle."[23] Likewise, it was worth $200 to
Dick's owner to get him back after Dick absconded in 1836. As "Dick is a brick
moulder by trade," he had a high value as a slave.[24]

Shoemakers and brick molders were common in runaway slave advertisements, as well as blacksmiths, sawyers, carpenters, caulkers, and waiters. Often,
not only their skills were mentioned but also the quality of their work, hint-
ing at the monetary value these people presented to their owners. Sam Howard, for instance, was an "excellent wood cutter"; Julis was described as a
"good sawyer, rough carpenter, and can work pretty well at the coopers
trade"; and Bennett Taylor's master thought of him as an "excellent black
smith and gun-smith."[25] Because these highly skilled slaves were so valuable,
we can assume that masters invested in runaway slave advertisements for
such people much more frequently than for other bondspeople of less monetary value. Because ads were expensive and posting them was an effort,
slaveholders were more inclined to place them for valuable slaves, of which
more were men. In this light, it is likely that, when women ran away, they
were announced in the papers less often and the share of women among the
southern runaway population was much higher than it appears.

Berlin is right in that higher-skilled slaves were well positioned for flight,
yet professional skills were not the main factor that gave enslaved people mobility. Indeed, enslaved southerners had a broad array of occupations that could
create mobility, including skilled *and* unskilled work. Ultimately, a broad horizon counted more than professional skills when it came to cementing networks and making plans to escape. Drivers, errand boys, woodcutters, and
vendors of all sorts did not need specialized skills to perform their jobs. However, an unskilled errand boy or an enslaved huckster could capitalize on the
mobility their jobs afforded them to get to the nearest city or to establish
important contacts. This was also true for women. Women who ran away
tended to be washerwomen, seamstresses, cooks, or servants, like Beckey, "an
excellent seamstress," who also "understands keeping a cake shop."[26] Although

not skilled in the actual meaning of the word, bondswomen specialized in certain areas of hand- or craftwork, and some amassed highly developed expertise in their roles.[27] Women and men with expertise often worked under less supervision and were regularly sent or rented out to other places. This increased their mobility, their circle of acquaintances, and their knowledge of the immediate and farther-flung world.

Plantation workers, whose actual work capacities often vanish in the records, could also have useful mind maps of the outside world. When they ran away, they sometimes were likewise considered very valuable by their owners: Jarrett, "an excellent hand on a farm" who fled slavery in 1817, found a bounty of $100 on himself.[28] An unskilled woodcutter who had a large radius of movement, like George William, could use his experience for a flight attempt. In 1800, William, who, in his owner's perception, "walks upright, is smooth spoken, but a great liar," escaped in Maryland and "took an axe and wedges with him: I expect he will go to cut wood, and pretend he is free," the slaveholder announced. William fled with another Black man whose name was Joshua Joice. He was "a free man, but he confesses to some of my people he was a slave and sold from the eastern shore to Georgia; and ran away from there to this country."[29] Joice was an example of a runaway slave passing for free and working alongside slaves. If he shared his knowledge with his enslaved coworkers about how to escape, get to a city, find work, and possibly forge a pass, they could use this information for their own missions. Getting to know such people was a huge benefit, and washerwomen or porters could likewise make useful acquaintances through their work.

Runaway slave ads speak volumes about the mobility of the absconded without reference to skills. For example, Nelson Duncan, a slave who fled from Richmond in 1837, had been a carriage driver and frequently drove from Petersburg, where he and his master resided, to Richmond. As such, Duncan acquired knowledge about routes and made contacts. Catherine, an enslaved woman from Manchester, Virginia, delivered milk to Richmond. She ran away in 1838.[30] Runaways did not always need firsthand knowledge and experience to escape. Through kin networks and exchanges of information, prospective fugitives could learn and benefit from the mobility of others.[31] When bondspeople lived close to roads, rivers, or towns, they could not only physically escape more easily, they were also in a better position to meet people who could provide them with information.

Urban bondspeople usually counted on greater autonomy and mobility than their rural counterparts, even when they lived with the person who owned them. House servants worked closely with the families they served and independently took to the streets to run errands, shop for groceries, and manage the housekeeping. Enslaved people working as personal servants traveled with their masters, amassing knowledge about interregional, inter-state, and sometimes even international contacts. Charlotte from New Orleans, for example, traveled with her master, Pierre Blancq, to Bordeaux, France, in 1820.[32] City slaves, furthermore, lived in a cosmopolitan, vibrant environment where domestic and international news, progressive ideas, and cultural events abounded. In South Carolina, 30 percent of women and 19 percent of men who were said to be runaways passing for free had lived in cities or towns before fleeing enslavement.[33] Frederick Douglass, who was sent from a plantation on Maryland's Eastern Shore to Baltimore, recalled that "going to live at Baltimore laid the foundation, and opened the gateway, to all my subsequent prosperity."[34]

The Hire System as Springboard

Many of the jobs that offered mobility were related to slave hiring. Connected to urbanization and industrialization processes, the hiring out of slaves to cit-ies and towns grew exponentially and became a central feature of urban slav-ery. Bondspeople, mostly men, who worked as hirelings, and especially those with professional skills, tended to be highly mobile. Slave hiring had existed during colonial times, but its expansion in the decades before the Civil War in towns and cities was striking: In the antebellum period, between 5 and 15 percent of the enslaved population were on hire, which increased in the run-up to the Civil War. In later decades, one-third to one-half of enslaved people were hired at some point in their lives, at least in parts of the Upper South. In the Lower South, fewer slaves were hired, usually below 15 percent, due to the lack of large-scale industrial enterprises and the dominance of mass plantations.[35]

Economist Claudia Goldin has calculated that by 1860, 62 percent of en-slaved men and 38 percent of enslaved women in Richmond were hired.[36] Richmond was the South's most important industrial city and enslaved labor was used in factories and plants. Although it was mostly men who were forcibly employed in these sites, small numbers of women labored there, particularly for a short period in the 1850s. Observing wage developments and changing demographics in the factories, historian Midori Takagi has claimed that when hiring prices for male slaves increased rapidly in the countryside, they were pushed out of the cities. Consequently, enslaved women who mainly labored in households were hired to work in the tobacco and cotton factories. While relatively brief and temporary, these new roles were liberating for women, claims Takagi. Living away from one's owner and in separate housing with other hired bondspeople created important networks and opened new geographies for female factory workers.[37] These experiences made running away a viable option for some enslaved women, and enabled others to support runaways in their efforts to escape bondage.

Hiring contracts for the forthcoming year tended to be negotiated between Christmas and New Year's Day, and offered opportunities both for urban slaves deciding to flee and for newcomers to arrive without causing attention, to get lost in the crowd, and to start finding work right away. Fugitive John Andrew Johnson targeted Christmas as a convenient time to flee from his South Carolina plantation to Charleston: "We all had three days' holiday at Christmas and I, therefore, fixed upon that time as most appropriate for m[y] escape." Johnson would blend in with the city's day laborers.[38] In Richmond, Lewis ran off on December 25, 1805, from the Washington Tavern. John Simmons absconded in South Carolina on Christmas Day 1855. He went to Graniteville by train to seek employment. John and his wife Mahala also left on December 28, 1859, and Fanny from this chapter's opening paragraph likewise absconded in December.[39]

Notwithstanding Christmastime as a popular time to run away, escapes took place all year. Dennis and Lewis from Richmond, both in their late twenties, were "employed in a tobacco factory for the last fifteen years, in consequence of which their finger nails are much worn from stemming and twisting tobacco." They ran away in August 1831. Both were described as generally dressing well and as having "carried away sundry clothing."[40] After fifteen years of working at the same site, Dennis and Lewis presumably knew exactly how they could disappear and who they could rely on to do so. Likewise, the owner of Lilytand, who ran away in Richmond in 1839, believed him to have "acquaintances working at almost every Tobacco factory in the place."[41]

Other bondspeople turned the tables on this strategy. An anonymous bondsman was hired out in Richmond in 1854, and while working as a hired slave "actually pretended that he was a free man and made a contract as such with some man of Richmond County to hire himself to him for a few month[s]" the year after.[42] This man made provisions for a future escape attempt pretending to be free. His long-term planning shows how complicated such an endeavor could be and how thoroughly he prepared for it.

In addition to bondspeople who were rented out by their owners, slaves throughout the South hired themselves out to others on their own time.

These men and women usually lived away from the supervision of their legal owners, arranged for their own occupations, decided autonomously on the place and duration of their work, and negotiated the payment with their hirers. One conservative estimate claims that 10 percent of all hired slaves in Virginia in 1860 were self-hired.[43] Yet, it is difficult to estimate the numbers of people who hired themselves out without the involvement of their owners because the practice came to be prohibited in all southern places at varying times. In the nineteenth century, it was generally illegal.[44] However, petitions and newspaper coverage show that legal codes forbidding self-hire were barely followed. For example, in South Carolina, where the law to curtail the self-hire of slaves was unanimously passed by both houses in 1850, a Charleston newspaper lamented a couple of months later that "it has completely failed. Not one slave less hires his time than before."[45]

Despite larger autonomy, slave hiring had a flip side. Kinship ties and social networks could weaken through dislocation, especially when slaves were hired out to distant places. Urban slaves could end up working in the countryside in mines or coalfields, or building canals. Some enslaved Virginians were even hired out to Florida where they were forced to build the railroads.[46] Harriet "Rit" Ross from Caroline County, Maryland, had nine children, of which two were sold and many others were hired out, among them Harriet Tubman. Those hired out rarely saw their mother.[47] Some masters were aware that hiring and lodging out meant separation from loved ones, which could lead to flight, and acted accordingly. In 1830, William Cox informed his boss, Virginia slaveholder William Cobbs, that he had hired out Stephen together with his wife. The rationale for hiring out a couple was that "under these circumstances there is no danger of his going of[f]."[48]

Aware of the opportunities that remote work offered, slaveholder Mary Spence summarized the inherent risks of hiring out one's slaves. When her husband died in the 1820s, the widow asked the Baltimore County Court for permission "to dispose of all these slaves at private sale" to avoid "the extreme inconveniency and loss she would sustain by being compelled to keep them." Spence saw a danger "if they are hired out and dislike their master [hirer], of their absconding from service altogether."[49]

Autonomy through Work

Self-hiring gave bondspeople remarkable autonomy. During an annual negotiation procedure in Richmond, traveler Robert Russell observed an enslaved man whose owner had furnished him with a piece of paper stipulating the apparently nonnegotiable price of $140 per year. The man, then, set out to find someone who would hire him. During the same occasion, Russell also studied a young female domestic servant in discussion with a prospective employer. She also had a fixed price set by her master, which was accepted by the hirer, a market gardener, yet they were negotiating other terms of the contract. The woman refused to work in the garden and was pleading for other privileges—"her friends and favourites" had to be allowed to visit her. Apparently eventually agreeing on this point, the gardener and the enslaved woman went to "visit her proposed home and see how things looked."[50] This woman seemed to be only limited by the hiring rate and independent in all other aspects of the work negotiation and relationship.

Equally autonomous was George Ingram. An 1824 runaway slave advertisement read, "a Negro Man, who calls his name GEORGE INGRAM [. . .] very black and likely," in his late twenties, "RUNAWAY From the Eagle Tavern." The subscriber, Fields Kennedy from Augusta, found it "probable he may endeavor to get to Savannah or Charleston. Has a written pass to hunt for a master, signed John D. Walker, with reference to the subscriber, and the price for him mentioned in it."[51] Ingram and the anonymous woman were not exceptional. Slaves who hired themselves out escaped the constant surveillance of their masters.

After years of working on their own and bargaining for wages and working conditions, enslaved men and women could grow remarkably bold. Slaveholder George Cox from Charleston offered a $5 bounty on Maria in 1803. "She had a ticket from me," Cox admitted, "authorizing her to engage in a place to work, which she told me she was previously promised. This is to give notice, that she is using that ticket as an imposition; and if she is engaged, or offers her services to any one, that she be taken to the Work House, as a runaway."[52] When sold to her new master, Maria tricked him into furnishing her with a ticket, with opened a door for her to escape from him. Only self-assertive, experienced people would dare to make such demands.

Many White people believed that the hire system rendered slaves' lived experiences too close to those of free people, and petitions by White city dwellers worrying that this practice decreased the value of slaves and befouled their character were plentiful. The *Charleston Courier* lamented the "unwillingness it produces in the slave, to return to the regular life and domestic control of the master."[53] The paper was right. Elizabeth Ann Yates, who resided in Philadelphia but had her business run by executors, had several slaves hired out in Charleston. At least two of them successfully camouflaged themselves amid the African American population there. In 1824, her son David wrote to Yates that "your servants Emma & Sally have not paid any wages for a long time I am trying to find out where they stay that I may make them pay wages."[54] Perhaps the two women had already crossed the very thin line between bondage and autonomy. Slave hiring divided mastery and thus weakened the absolute domination of the master-slave relation.[55]

Although many enslaved people understood that it was a "privilege", in Frederick Douglass's words,[56] to work as a hired-out slave in a city, they were very aware of the fact that they made good money because of their work—and could be making the same money for themselves instead of their owners. Runaway slave Charles Ball recounted that he once visited Savannah with his owner where he observed self-hired bondsmen: "In Savannah I saw many black men, who were slaves, and who yet acted as freemen so far, that they went out to work, where and with whom they pleased, received their own wages, and provided their own subsistence; but were obliged to pay a certain sum at the end of each week to their masters."[57] Yet, it was not only because of the earnings self-hired slaves had to cede to their masters that these people still knew and felt that they were enslaved.

Enslaved people with the broadest geographical mobility range were watermen and others working aboard vessels and boats. Washington, a bondsman from Richmond, "had been a waterman on James river for several years" before he escaped in 1837. His master offered $250 to get him back.[58] Later in the century, Black men came to dominate the steamboat economy. At any time in the 1850s, up to 3,000 enslaved and 1,500 free Blacks labored on Mississippi riverboats.[59] This kind of work obviously furnished them with a broad horizon, and many enslaved water workers enjoyed considerable autonomy. For example, John, who was born in New Orleans, ran away from the steamer he worked on, probably on the Mississippi River. And there were many more like him: A "large Negro Man," whose name is unknown, "with one hand cut off close to the wrist, speaks French and English," fled his slaveholder. "He has been running on steamboats on the Red river, but is supposed to be loitering about the city [of New Orleans]."[60]

The dimensions of the water business were immense. Almost all enslaved men who lived on the coast engaged in water-related jobs at some point in their lives. Next to a great many who rafted timber or went fishing, the traffic in the Tidewater, the coastal region of North Carolina and Virginia, was operated by enslaved ferrymen.[61] All these jobs held special importance for men, and African Americans were present in every niche of American maritime life. Enslaved and free, they worked on sailboats (and later steamships), schooners, and rafts as pilots, clerks, firemen (coal shufflers/stokers), and servants.[62] Working closely together, it was impossible to tell the legal status of these men.

Such was the case with John Scott, who generally did not act as an enslaved man. "I had seen him I was in the Dewitt Clinton last season & Knew him there. he was cook on board the Dewitt Clinton, he seemed to have no master he acted as he pleased & let himself on board any boat he chose," testified Solomon Lynethart, a free Black man, after Scott absconded.[63] Maritime and water life, due to its cosmopolitan nature and linkages to other Black Atlantic communities, was much less preoccupied with the legal status of men. Hardly restricted, seamen were able to make enslaved and free acquaintances over long distances.[64] People like Scott, who acted as free despite being enslaved, did not garner much attention, and close supervision of enslaved watermen was not feasible. Thanks to their autonomy, which was admittedly tainted by severe curtailments, hired and self-hired slaves had clear advantages when it came to flight. They basically could just walk away or not return the next day. If they were at sea, they could stay abroad.[65]

Depending on the agreements with their owners, self-hired slaves could benefit from a lead of some days, weeks, or even months. Escapes were common, and plentiful evidence shows how carelessly slaveowners behaved and how ignorant they sometimes were when it came to the opportunities a hire situation opened up for their slaves. James Lusk of New Orleans hired his bondsman Dennis out in 1847 as a cabin waiter to John Swon, captain of a steamboat. At the end of the steamboat season, Dennis did not return to New Orleans, having run away in St. Louis. Dennis was never seen again.[66] J. L. Marciaq's bondsman Jacko "was a runaway and had escaped from his master on several occasions." Yet, Marciaq still hired him out to work on boats on the Mississippi River, a task that included "running errands in towns while the boat was anchored." Unsurprisingly, Jacko made his escape.[67]

The hiring system, paired with widespread personal networks, made for a combination that created tempting opportunities for bondspeople considering escape. The New Orleans *Daily Picayune* summarized in 1859 that "the practice, so general in this city, of giving monthly passes to slaves, has proved injurious to the character and habits not only of those indulged, but to all those over whom they have influence. These passes make the slaves, for the time being, virtually free [and] furnish the means of concealment to any one who, to escape an irksome restraint, finally becomes an habitual runaway."[68]

A large number of people wanted in runaway slave advertisements had worked as hirelings at some point in their lives. Laban, a shoe- and bootmaker, fled enslavement in 1807. He had "followed the aforesaid business in

Richmond for several years, and is well known there" because he had been hired in the city during the previous two years.[69] Diana, who called herself Diana Todd, was "well known in the City [of Charleston], having attended at the parties with Camilla Johnson, from whom she was lately purchased." Sometime before her flight, Todd had hired herself aboard a steamboat.[70] Work that lacked the heavy supervision and regulation of plantation labor was a springboard for escape.

Toward a City

Fugitive slaves who gravitated to southern cities could be from rural or from urban areas. Urban slaves who absconded usually went to a nearby city or just stayed in the same place. In the latter case, they decided simply not to report to their owners anymore. Based on their experienced mobility and their strong networks, fugitive slaves in southern cities were overwhelmingly from the counties surrounding urban centers. Escaped slaves whose owners thought them to be in Richmond and for whom the police were asked to be on the lookout between 1834 and 1844 were in their majority from nearby Virginia counties and from Richmond itself.[71] Between 1841 and 1846, most runaways who found themselves detained in the city jail had fled from the neighboring counties of Chesterfield, Henrico, Hanover, King William, Goochland, and Caroline, and the city of Petersburg (see map 2.1, which highlights the most common places of departure).[72]

In Baltimore, many runaways were similarly from counties proximate to the city, while others came from the city itself or from northern Virginia.[73] Short-distance migration was a way to live a life outside the reach of one's master while at the same time maintaining ties to kin and staying close to the place considered home. Flight to the North, by contrast, was often a heartbreaking undertaking because those who moved left their loved ones behind, usually for good.[74] Charleston and New Orleans, more often than Richmond and Baltimore, attracted fugitives from a wider range of distances. New Orleans was by far the largest city in the Deep South, and often the only proper city in reach for a great number of refuge seekers.

It is important to keep in mind that slave flight was for some people not a one-time act, and destinations were not fixed end points of a short migration experience. For example, Pauladore, a "Negro Man," "commonly called Paul," of about fifty years, ran away from his master but had to remain on the move in order to balance his seeing his family, maintaining jobs, and avoiding cap-

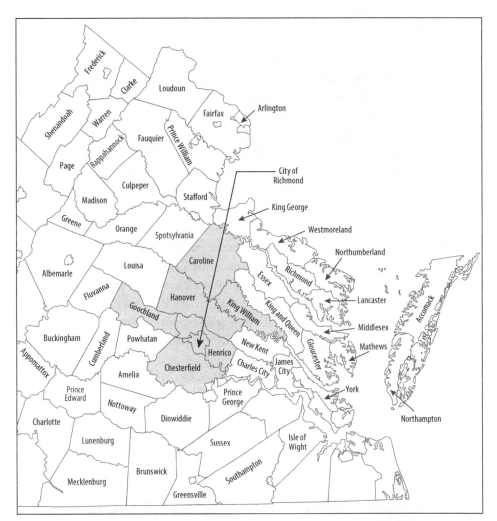

MAP 2.1 Origins of fugitive slaves in Richmond. Most runaway slaves sought in Richmond originated from the counties around the city. The map is based on Map of Virginia Counties and Independent Cities, Wikimedia Commons, September 15, 2009 (https://commons .wikimedia.org/wiki/File:Map_of_Virginia_Counties_and_Independent_Cities.svg).

ture. By December 1853, Paul had already been gone for fourteen months. Thomas Davis, who wrote the newspaper announcement, noted that since Paul "was brought up in the coasting business between this City [Charleston] and Georgetown, between which places he has been sailing for the last 30 years," Paul was "well known." Davis added that "Gen. R. Y. Hayne has purchased his Wife and Children from H. L. Pinckney, Esq. and has them now on his Plantation at Goose Creek, where, no doubt, the Fellow is frequently lurking, and may be much of his time in the City [Charleston], or sometimes in the neighborhood of Georgetown."[75]

Paul escaped slavery but strove to remain in contact with his family. Like him, many had the hope to be able to visit loved ones on the plantations where they lived, or meet them in the cities and towns. Therefore they often stayed close. Others who had escaped once also remained restless—by choice or by compulsion. There are a few sources that indicate that (mostly) male runaways moved back and forth between two or more cities and towns.[76]

The different geographies that surrounded enslaved people either facilitated or hampered flight to an urban center. It was much easier to move between cities and states that were part of the original thirteen colonies along the East Coast. The further west and inland one traveled, the sparser the settlement and population, which made it harder to blend into the crowd. City hopping in Mississippi, for example, where towns and cities were rather isolated, was much more complicated than in the Chesapeake region because Virginia was the only southern state in the antebellum era with a system of cities.[77] South Carolina was less densely populated than the Upper South but had more urbanized areas than the Gulf states. In the Upper South it was less challenging to gravitate toward the cities because the enslaved population of those states was relatively smaller and Black people who traveled on the roads and rivers raised less suspicion. In the Deep South, around half of the population was enslaved, while in the Upper South it was one-fifth to one-third.[78]

It was a learning process to detect the opportunities in one's environment. Mobile slaves often took a long time to learn about their surroundings before they actually made the step to disappear into them. Prior to an actual escape, enslaved women from Charleston's hinterland could spend years going to the city on a frequent basis to sell their self-grown produce, an activity integral to South Carolina's informal plantation economy.[79] There is no information how many times Catherine went to Richmond to deliver milk before she felt ready to not return to her owner.[80] These urban runaways typically did not raise suspicion when seen on the road or entering a city. As such, they could even travel openly, simply claiming the backseat on a wagon or taking a ferry.

Yet not everybody was in a position for long-term planning; others were forced to make more ad hoc escape attempts.[81] In the early nineteenth century and beyond, it was common to walk slaves in coffles to the places where they were to be sold. Eyewitnesses to these coffles stated that trafficked people were mostly chained in pairs, including at night during their rests.[82] While some displaced people tried to run away at the destinations of their forced migrations, others did not wait and broke free on the way.[83] Runaway slave Solomon Bayley recounted how he escaped from a slave wagon while on his way to be sold: "When night came and I walked out of the bushes, I felt very awful. I set off to walk homewards, but soon was chased by dogs, at the same house where the man told the waggoner he had taken up a runaway three days before. [...] I got down to Richmond; but had liked to have been twice taken, for twice I was pursued by dogs."[84]

Slave traders correctly suspected that the people they coercively removed from their loved ones would make attempts to get back home. As Charles Ball recalled, one of them, when entering South Carolina, "addressed us all, and told us we might now give up all hope of ever returning to the places of our nativity; as it would be impossible for us to pass through the States of North Carolina and Virginia, without being taken up and sent back."[85] As slavery expanded westward and into the Deep South beginning in the 1820s, Virginia, one of the oldest slave states, saw many of its slaveowners selling their human chattel to those markets. Richmond became one of the most important centers for slave sale and distribution, and slave auctions took place six days a week during the 1840s.[86] By the end of the antebellum period, they were open every day between nine o'clock in the morning and noon, and between one and five o'clock in the afternoon.[87]

Violet, thirty-two years old, and her daughter Mary, ten years old, were runaways who hailed from the departing regions of the internal slave trade. Their mistress, Mary Shirer from Charleston, claimed that "they are Virginia negroes, whither it supposed they will try to return. They took with them all their clothing."[88] If Shirer was right in her guess, the case of Violet and her daughter was one of the extremely rare ones in which a mother and her child attempted to return over large distances back to the Upper South. When the parents lived on two different plantations, children born into slavery usually lived with their mothers. In case of sale, infants also stayed with their mothers or were sold separately rather than forming a unit of sale with their fathers. Reinforced by the usually higher mobility of men, it is logical that it was mostly the husbands and fathers who tried to reunite their families by running away.[89]

A number of runaways were caught in flight and appeared in jail dockets and "Committed" ads.[90] In 1821, Peter was committed to the jail of Marlborough District in South Carolina. He said that he belonged to Mr. Samuel Stark near Camden and was on his way to North Carolina where he was bought. Together with Peter, Matt was caught. He confessed that "it was his intention to go to Norfolk, Va. from [where] he was bought when he was about 10 years."[91]

Long-distance migrants were significantly rarer than short-distance migrants, and the route was almost always from the Lower South back to the Upper South—the reverse direction of the Second Middle Passage. In very few cases, an enslaved person would also flee south- and westward in pursuit of loved ones; examples of this have only been found for men. Jim was one of them. Calling himself Jim Mason, he ran away from Alexandria, Virginia, in 1809. "A few days before his elopement, his wife (who was the property of a neighbor) was sold to a negro purchaser from the neighborhood of Nashville, Tennessee." His owner James Blake offered $100 to get hold of Mason again and "conjectured that Jim either pursued her [his wife] or that he went off by water and is now in one of the sea-port towns of the United States."[92] Likewise, Dick's wife was sold in 1838. After Dick's escape, his owner assumed that he had run from Kentucky to New Orleans, where she was then living, and tried to pass as a free man.[93]

The destination of migrants was seldom random, and neither was the route. Gaining geographical knowledge about the landscape of displacement was imperative. Some enslaved migrants succeeded at this, while others did not. John Brown, displaced from Virginia to Georgia, did "not recollect the names of all the places we passed through," yet he did recall the names of the major points of orientation like the Roanoke River, Halifax, and Raleigh, North Carolina.[94] Charles Ball revealed in his autobiography how he fought his way back to the Upper South, learning about the landscape and using the stars as orientation. He walked from Georgia to reunite with his enslaved family in Maryland, an undertaking that took him an entire year.[95]

Historian Kyle Ainsworth has speculated that with a two-week start, a runaway who did not intend to return to the home plantation could be within a radius of sixty to eighty miles of it if they were walking.[96] It is altogether possible, however, that fugitives moved faster. With freedom on the line, it is reasonable that a person could make ten miles a day, even if they just walked during the night. That would give a radius of 140 miles after two weeks.

Infrastructure mattered, too. The Mississippi River system facilitated the journey of fugitives from the riverine counties of Louisiana, Mississippi, Tennessee, Arkansas, Kentucky, and Missouri. During the 1830s, transportation between the Northeast and the Southwest by ship became increasingly common. Coast ships connected Virginia to New Orleans, from where river steamboats traveled to Natchez, Mississippi.[97] The part water and technology played in the forced migration and subsequent escape of enslaved Americans is illustrated by the account of Tom. He was brought "to the jail of the city of Norfolk as a runaway" in 1848 and described as "a negro man who says his name is TOM or THOMAS." Tom was about thirty years old, "a light bacon color, stoutly made, full face, bushy hair, has a very slight stoppage in his speech, and has been badly whipped." Tom told the jailer George Miller that "he was born in Middleburg, and sold in the city of Richmond, Va., to a trader and carried to New Orleans [aboard a schooner] some 20 years ago." There he lived with his owner, Mr. Necho, a Frenchman, "six or seven years, and thence escaped to Boston, where he has been following the water ever since until arrested here [in Norfolk] and confined in jail."[98]

Assuming that Tom's account was true, he was first displaced 1,800 miles down the East Coast and into the Gulf of Mexico. Later, he put 1,700 miles behind him by making his way from New Orleans to Boston. There is no information on how he traveled but it is likely that he covered a considerable part of the journey by steamboat over the Mississippi River. New technologies could enlarge the horizons of enslaved people, even against their will. Later, some of them had the chance to use these experiences to their advantage. Moreover, since mid-century the railroad had been a significant tool for traveling quickly and widely.

In 1858, an enslaved man was found dead trying to get away on a train: "A negro fellow belonging to Jno. N. Cummings was killed by the carrs at 41 station on saturday night last, It is supposed he was stealing a ride on the carrs going up and fell off."[99] Others, like James Matthews, were luckier. Matthews told that after being severely whipped while working in railroad construction, he escaped and climbed into a railroad car where he hid between cotton bales and went to Charleston.[100] By traveling by boat or rail, fugitive slaves made use of the same infrastructural developments that propelled the economy of southern slavery. Broadened horizons did not only provide the capacity to map the world differently, they also furnished bondspeople with a set of skills that helped them navigate the environment while fleeing.

A Porous Geography of Control

On their journeys, fugitives had to reckon with the intervention of their owners for whom their absconding could mean a real monetary loss. Frank Ball, a formerly enslaved man from Virginia, stated that bondspeople were perfectly aware of the financial consequences of escapes: "Cost a lot of money, it did, when you go git a runaway slave. 'Hue and Cry' dey called it, you got to put notice in de papers, an' you got to pay a reward to whoever catches the runaway."[101]

The amount of the bounty was an indication of both how wealthy a slave-owner was and how appreciated or financially beneficial the runaway was deemed. Advertisements that offered small awards like $5 or $10 must in this light not be read as a relative indifference on the part of the slaveholders to find their runaways but rather as a mirror into their limited financial means.[102] Slaveholders in the Upper South tended to be more willing to offer high rewards than in the Lower South. In Maryland, bounties of up to $400 for male runaways were not rare in the 1850s.[103] Rewards in newspaper notices also tell us about the difficulties in finding a runaway and the attitude of the slaveholders toward slave flight. Monetary remuneration for slave catchers often varied by location and increased if the wanted person was found outside the state or when retrieved from the North. When George Stewart, twenty years old, ran away from Baltimore County in 1852, the reward for him being taken in Maryland was $50. If "taken out of this State, and lodged in jail," the subscriber was willing to pay double the amount.[104]

Paying rewards and placing ads in newspapers was both a time- and money-intensive undertaking, especially when the ad ran over a long period and in several papers. The Baton Rouge *Daily Advocate*, for instance, charged the following advertising rates in 1857: one square cost $5 for one month, $7 for two months, $9 for three months, and $20 for twelve months. For two squares, the charge rose up to $9, $12, $14, and $30, respectively.[105] These were not the only expenditures. Besides rewards, slaveholders had to pay jail costs and travel costs to pick up their runaways, such as those borne by Dugald McCall, who in 1854 retrieved his slave Lewis from jail, which "cost me jail fees and other expenses $13.43."[106] For another runaway called Willis, McCall placed an advertisement to which he got a reaction a month later: "I got a letter from the tailor [jailor] in Vicksburg saying that he had a Negro of mine in jaile, and for me to come after him." Because Willis was being held in Vicksburg and McCall was in Tensas Parish, Louisiana, McCall had to travel there by boat. The expenditures of this trip included $10 for the passage, a $20 reward, and $10 in jail fees, adding up to $40.[107] Slave flight was an effective weapon to fight against slavery because of what it cost slaveowners.

Fugitive slaves could be actively engaged in making it as difficult as possible for their slaveholders to get them back. Many did not surrender to their fate without fighting. Some even went on fighting when all odds seemed to be against them. Pressly from Athens, Georgia, ran away in March 1852 and, as his owner stated, "although advertised in papers of Georgia and in one of the papers of the State of South Carolina and a reward of Fifty Dollars offered for his apprehension, no information was ever received." That same year, he "was arrested in the City of Charleston and lodged in the work House as a fugitive." Because he gave his name as Joe Brown, however, he was not claimed and consequently "sold pursuant to the requirements of the Ordinances of the City Council of Charleston."[108] Pressly decided to be sold into the unknown rather than return to his master in Georgia. He was able to do that because jailers had to rely on the statements of people committed as runaways. Surely, there was room to fact-check parts of the stories they told, but eventually it was up to the runaway whether they decided to reveal their actual origin.

John Hope Franklin and Loren Schweninger have claimed that a pattern existed for most slaveholders that they followed from the moment a slave fled to the placement of an advertisement in a newspaper. The first instinct was to wait a day or two to see whether the person would return voluntarily. The second step was to try to retrieve the runaway while they were still presumed to be close to home. At the same time, neighbors were notified and the slaveowners would start to pay attention to the capture notices in local newspapers. When an escaped person was not found in due time, slaveholders often engaged professional slave catchers with specially trained bloodhounds. If they remained unsuccessful, slaveholders would publish a runaway slave ad, but because this was expensive and time consuming, one-third of slaveholders waited to post ads until one month after the escape of a slave. One in ten waited four months or more to place one.[109] The reluctance to place newspaper notices suggests that slaveowners did not regard them as very efficient, which gave fugitives moving over longer distances a substantial lead.

Public announcements had consequences. A runaway slave ad was an open admission of failure for owners. George Washington, out of embarrassment, stopped advertising for his runaway slaves in his own name when he became president of the United States.[110] Even though economic considerations usually trumped ideology, a man who was not able to maintain control over his family and property weakened the social order and lost credit within society.[111] This aspect of southern values created further loopholes for people who depended on slaveholders' time and shame to give them valuable weeks and months to advance their flight.

Catching their masters by surprise was an advantage but it did not guarantee a flight without obstacles. In order to protect their property and their slaveholding way of life, planters organized patrols to supervise rural areas and prevent slaves from absconding. Slave patrols constituted a constant threat to runaways but planters had little interest in patrolling the roads themselves. Historian Sally Hadden has shown that men of higher social standing did occasionally participate in the patrols, yet decreasingly so as the antebellum period went on. Patrols also are suspiciously absent from autobiographies of formerly enslaved people, and the repeatedly enacted fugitive slave laws reflected the wishes of policy makers about how patrollers *should* behave rather than how they actually behaved. Moreover, patrols presented a visible debunking of the lie that enslaved people were happy and submissive.[112]

Inefficient mechanisms to retrieve fugitives were preceded by inefficient mechanisms of surveillance. The paternalistic view of slaveholders was not only a legitimization of the institution; many had actually internalized it. Without this changing attitude, the hire and self-hire of thousands of enslaved men and women would not have been possible. Both practices offered bondspeople opportunities to escape and to stay away. Because slave flight was not compatible with the paternalistic understanding of the master-slave relationship, slaveowners who considered themselves benevolent providers were often personally offended when their slaves absconded. They considered this act to be a deal breaker of the arrangements they made with enslaved people, which was—in their view—a mutually beneficial exchange of labor for protection and care. Fugitives could make use of this trust, a fact we can detect in runaway slave ads, in which owners expressed their grievance about slaves who "betrayed" them.

"Jack or Jack Ash, a gardener by profession was sold to a gentleman residing in Amherst county." The subscriber lamented that the "gentleman [...] permitted him to come down [to Richmond] last May, for the purpose of visiting his wife and relations, with a promise that his visits should be repeated frequently." In the mindset of slaveholding southerners, this was a major concession that should be rewarded with unparalleled gratitude. But Ash ran away, thereby harming the self-perceived clemency of the man who held him captive: he "thought proper to abuse this indulgence by not returning to his master."[113] In the master's worldview, Ash took advantage of an unusually generous treatment.

More often, southerners who published runaway slave ads could not make sense of the flight of their slaves. Slaveholders perceived people belonging to the "slave elite" to be privileged in comparison to "field hands" and were particularly surprised when they disappeared. Advertisements that mentioned that an enslaved person went off for no reason were common: Billy, for one, "absconded himself [...] without any known cause" from his enslaver in South Carolina.[114] The bondsmen Cyrus and Absolum, twenty-two and twenty-seven years old, ran off in 1814 "for some cause unknown" to their owner who had hired them in Long Island, South Carolina. He later filed a petition for compensation because they joined a gang of runaways and were killed by the slave patrol.[115]

The private conversation between the Virginians Lewis Stiff and William Gray in May 1842 speaks volumes about the different worlds slaves and slavers occupied. When Gray's slave Emanuel did not go back to Gray after leaving Stiff's house, Stiff wrote to Gray that he could not think of any reason why Emanuel should not return since he appeared to be so "pleased with his situation and so nice Satisfied with you as a master."[116] For a great many southern slaveholders, betrayal by their slaves was so unthinkable that they stressed the faithfulness and good characters of runaways even in the newspaper ads—after they had run away.[117] These reports demonstrate the performance enslaved southerners effected on a daily basis in order to mask their true intentions.

Contacts outside Slavery

It is difficult to gauge how challenging it was for fugitive slaves to take on a new identity in the slaveholding South. As political scientist James Scott has outlined, role-play by the subordinates did not only occur in acts of resisting but all the time.[118] People who lived as slaves had to wear masks at almost every encounter with White people. James Matthews narrated in his autobiography the day-to-day acting enslaved people displayed: "If we hated master ever so much, we did not dare to show it, but we must always look pleased when he saw us, and we were afraid to speak what we thought, because some would tell master."[119] Fleeing, in this context, was only the most expressive of many forms of resistance.

The issue of acting returns implicitly in many sources. A perusal of 200 runaway slave advertisements in North Carolina newspapers between 1820 and 1829 showed that sixty-seven people were suspected to be "lurking" with relatives and forty-eight to be passing as free persons.[120] Evidently, slaveholders often had an idea of the whereabouts of runaways, yet how did people degraded to the status of slaves manage to pass themselves off as free?

In the cities, they had to look unsuspicious and it was fundamental to change the visible markers of slavery once they ran away and decided not to come back. Runaway slave ads were full of assumptions and observations that escaped bondspeople had changed their clothes, taken apparel with them, or stolen attire of higher quality. For instance, Jules, who was arrested as a runaway slave in New Orleans in 1855, had a variety of clothing with him, suspected to be stolen.[121] Urban slaves had an advantage because access to additional clothing was less restricted than on plantations.[122]

The main distinction in clothing of enslaved people was not determined by where one worked (house or field), but between the workday and the Sunday clothes.[123] A Sunday dress or suit was a helpful tool to affirm one's new identity as a free person. Seaborn, "good looking and well made," of eighteen years, "took with him plenty of good clothes, blanket, a full Sunday suit, with silk hat, and patent leather shoes."[124] Andrew was dressed like a free man when he escaped enslavement in 1820. He wore a "drab colored coatee and gray cassimere pantaloons, but may change his dress as he took all his clothes away with him."[125] Dresses reflected social standing, and it must have horrified White Charlestonians to read an article in the city paper in 1850 that evoked a scenario in which "one of these very slaves will flaunt by the ladies in King-street more extravagantly dressed than they," referring to a bondswoman who absconded from her owner.[126]

Clothes that made a runaway slave look like a free Black person could be stolen, bought, or borrowed. But passing for free implied much more, foremost speaking and moving like a free person. Learning how to speak could be achieved by careful observation. Enslaved men and women could study the behavior of their masters and overseers or, if they had contact with free African Americans, absorb their manner of talking and acting. Over time, they could appropriate these traits. Joseph Holt Ingraham, an author from Maine, watched such a scene in Natchez, Mississippi. He accounted that on Sundays, Black men gathered in small groups "imitating the manners, bearing, and language of their masters." According to Ingraham, they were "astounding their gaping auditors 'ob de field nigger class,' who cannot boast such enviable accomplishments."[127]

When passing for White, merely looking like a White person was likewise not enough. Mary Jane, twenty years of age, could have been one of those who attempted to pass themselves off as a White person since she was "remarkably white for a slave." The problem, however, was that she did not sound like a White woman, according to her slaveholder who claimed that she, "when spoken to has the accent of a negress."[128] To flee successfully, and to subsequently be included into the Black urban communities, it was imperative to demarcate oneself from the enslaved population.

In general, nevertheless, lighter skin facilitated moving unmolested. After generations of racial mixing, the American South counted many men and women who were enslaved while their African heritage was not visible anymore.[129] Those slaves who had just been imported from Africa had hardly a chance to integrate into cities and towns. Their significantly darker skin color, the unfamiliarity with American culture, and language barriers impeded the success of such an endeavor. Nevertheless, African and African American slaves without prospects of passing for free also ran away, but their strategies varied. As a matter of course, African-born enslaved people not assimilated to American culture rarely sought to run to cities and other places where they were highly visible and in proximity to Whites.

For those who did, acting was everything. In 1833, Penny aka Henny, from 110 Church Street in Charleston, decided to move out of bondage. "She is a good looking woman, and so plausible as to deceive most persons unacquainted with her," stated the newspaper notice. A Black person received Henny's clothing before she disappeared, and she was thought to be harbored in the city.[130] Having a broad geographical horizon, experience doing things on one's own account, and engaging with other free people helped runaways "deceive" unacquainted persons and take on new identities.

In the 1840s, Durham Spalding sued captain George Taylor, clerk Mr. Twitchell, and other owners of the steamboat *Missouri* for $1,500 for carrying his slave Felix from New Orleans to St. Louis, where he disappeared. The defendants alleged "that a man did work his passage on board of the Missouri bearing name Felix but that he was a white man, or at least passed for such." They claimed that "no one could suppose he had any African blood; he would pass any where for a white man." Felix "was dressed like a gentleman, nor was there any thing in his manner or appearance, that indicated him to be a slave. There was no attempt to conceal himself."[131] Looking like a White person definitely helped but, more importantly, people like Felix and Mary Jane needed to play well-orchestrated roles.

Working alongside free people or living in a city offered ample opportunity to turn this theory into practice. William Grimes lived as a slave in Savannah, Georgia, between 1811 and 1815 and frequently attended meetings that often went so late that he reached his master's house at 10 o'clock at night or later and broke curfew. According to him, "the guard never attempted to meddle with me—they always took me to be a *white man*." The richness of his account is striking: "I have frequently walked the streets of Savannah in an evening, and being pretty well dressed, (generally having on a good decent suit of clothes,) and having a light complexion, (being at least three parts white,) on meeting the guard, I would walk as bold as I knew how, and as much like a gentleman; they would always give me the wall." Once, Grimes encountered two or three watchmen together. "I was afraid but summoned all my resolution; and marched directly on towards them." When, while walking past, he accidently brushed one of them, "they immediately turned off the walk; one of them spoke and said we ask your pardon sir."[132] Walking like a free person, wearing adequate clothing, and retaining one's composure in delicate situations were essential qualities to possess.

Acting became more challenging when runaways chose not to pass as free but as self-hired slaves. This was often the best option in Charleston.[133] Although the daily lives of enslaved and free Black people bore many resemblances, passing as free and passing as a self-hired bondsperson were different experiences. In Baltimore, where African Americans were prima facie considered free, settling down, starting a family, and building a life worked relatively well. Passing as slaves required much more organized effort. When renting a room or an apartment, the owner could ask for a written permit; when questioned about one's master, a convincible story had to be constructed, and if runaways had children with them, a way had to be been found to keep them from enslavement. The written documents required for slaves in particular had to be constantly renewed, and surely some fugitives passing themselves off as hired slaves dared not to remain in their living and working spaces for very long. In short, passing for a slave might have required an even more sophisticated planning and support networks than passing as free, at least in the long run.

To this end, possessing a pass or freedom papers was instrumental. Passes were usually written by slaveholders to grant enslaved persons the right to visit somebody, run an errand, hire themselves out, or live on their own. They could be restricted to a few hours, days, months, or even a year, like an example from Charleston that reads: "My Boy Mack has my permission to sleep in a house in Bedon's Alley, hired by his Mother. This ticket is good for two months from this date. Sarah H. Savage. Sep^ber 19th, 1843." See figure 2.1).[134] Watchmen were instructed to arrest Black people who were on the streets without passes, but even without possessing one, it was possible to get away. George Teamoh was in Norfolk when he was stopped by a constable who demanded to see his pass. When Teamoh told him that he had lost it, the watchman said "you must go to jail." In a maneuver to keep himself from being arrested, Teamoh pretended to be "afflicted with small-pox" and the constable shied away from touching him.[135]

Freedom papers were documents African Americans could obtain if they were born free, manumitted, or otherwise released from slavery in conformity with the law. Usually, they had to register their status with the municipal or county authorities and were given a copy of said register. This document included the name, (approximate) date and place of birth, and a physical description. It was affixed with the seal of the respective court and included the signature of the clerk or a high-ranking person in charge. It is not always clear

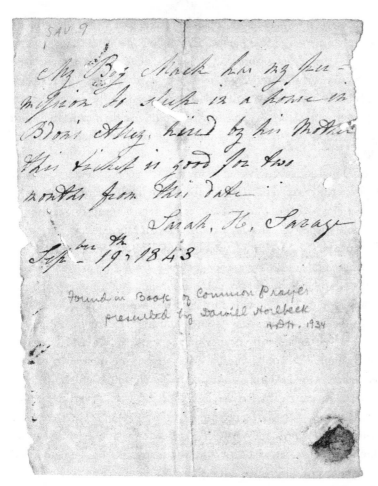

FIGURE 2.1 Slave pass, Charleston, 1843. Handwritten slave pass by a slaveholder to allow enslaved Mack to sleep in a certain place. This furnished Mack with great leeway. "Sarah Savage. Slave Pass, 1843," Charleston Slave Passes, Mss 0034-040, College of Charleston Libraries, courtesy of Special Collections, College of Charleston Libraries (https://lcdl.library.cofc.edu/lcdl/catalog/lcdl:5531).

whether the reference in a historical source is to a pass or free papers. When Pompey Jackson absconded from his enslaver in 1840, the public was informed that Jackson "can read and likely may get forged papers to travel with."[136] To move over short distances, he only needed the written permission of his owner. To permanently pass as free, official freedom papers were helpful, yet from this short ad it remains unclear which of the two Jackson acquired. The former was relatively easy to forge while the latter required more sophisticated efforts.

There were several ways to obtain a piece of paper that would allow one to travel freely or to pass as a free person. Evidence is plentiful that men and women of all legal statuses and skin colors falsified passes for enslaved Americans to run away. Moreover, many Black city dwellers could read and write, and reports have survived of urban slaves reading the newspaper.[137] Essentially, everybody who was able to write could use their skills to forge a pass, yet it was important to be able to imitate the writ, style, and language of a slaveholder.

Frederick Douglass had always felt motivated to become literate so that he could one day write his own pass. He "continued to do this until I could write a hand very similar to that of Master Thomas."[138] John Thompson mentioned that he was once suspected of having written passes for three fellow slaves who escaped because he "could write a tolerable hand."[139] Louis Hughes lived on a plantation where none of the slaves ever got a pass from their master "but the slaves did visit in the neighborhood, notwithstanding, and would sometimes slip into town at night." A fellow bondsman, Tom, who was planning his escape, "had in this way seen the pass of a neighboring slave to hire out; and it was from this he learned the form from which he wrote his, and which opened his way to freedom."[140] Mobility and knowledge outside one's own narrow circle opened access to new information and to people with useful skills.

Official freedom papers were forged less often, yet it was nevertheless possible. Joe Sutherland, an enslaved coachman, accompanied his master to the county courthouse where his son worked as a clerk. Sutherland secretly became literate and wrote passes for other bondspeople. By "going around the court everyday Joe forged the county seal on these passes," as his fellow slave William Johnson remembered.[141] An enslaved man named Ben, who ran away from the District of Columbia in 1825, could "write a pretty good hand, and no doubt has copied the papers of some free man," the newspaper ad read. His master even had "reason to believe he stole the Stafford County seal and attached the impression of it to his papers."[142] This way, Ben could furnish counterfeit papers with official seals. In a curious case, slave refugee Dennis, who lived disguised as a free man with the name William Mayo, was tried for helping three slaves abscond. The freedom papers under which he passed for free were apparently so convincing that the Court of Fredericksburg applied the sentence for free persons and sentenced Mayo to ten years in the penitentiary.[143] When freedom papers were forged, it was often difficult for those involved to judge their authenticity.

In other instances, slaves even stole the papers of other African Americans, which could bring the latter into great trouble.[144] More often, free people passed the originals on to others who used them to get out of bondage. Newspapers frequently published advertisements by free Black residents claiming to have lost their freedom papers.[145] Many must have given them to slaves. A bondsman named Tom was believed to have used the papers of a dead man, James Lucas, to pass himself as the deceased.[146] Finally, slaveholder Henry Burns advertised for his escaped slave George in 1852 in New Orleans after having received a hint that George might have arrived "9 miles below the city, on Wednesday morning last, from steamship Ben Franklin." Burns claimed that George was in possession of "what purported to be free papers, dated some 17 years since, made in another State, and corresponding nearly with his appearance."[147]

As early as 1796, Maryland introduced a law that proposed a fine of $300 for free African Americans convicted of handing freedom papers to slaves. In 1818, free people who enticed a slave to run away or assisted or harbored them on the run faced up to six years in prison and could be forced to pay a financial recompense to the respective owner. In 1849 this law was sharpened, stipulating at least six and a maximum of fifteen years for the same offense.[148] Other southern states passed similar ordinances. As lawmakers recognized, many of the strategies that allowed runaways to succeed would not have been possible without the enslaved having connections to free southerners.

AT FIRST GLANCE, the significant portion of the enslaved population who came to possess high mobility and flexibility refutes Stephanie Camp's observation that captivity as the essence of slavery did not end when the nineteenth century dawned.[149] Their escapes took place at a time when American slavery was becoming tighter and more repressive. But it also became more variegated, and a small fraction of the enslaved population broadened their horizons through work, autonomy, and mobility, thereby getting to know the world and forging important contacts for their endeavors. Broader knowledge of the world came to be available to a growing number of enslaved people over the course of the nineteenth century as slave hiring became more widespread, new infrastructures increased mobility, and the interstate slave trade displaced ever more people.

Slave flight in the South, regardless of gender, was mostly the outcome of preexisting mobility and not necessarily bound to formal occupational skills. This way, women were, like men, able to expand their knowledge and personal webs of acquaintances. Fanny, from the opening paragraph of this chapter, was raised in North Carolina, had lived in Florida for some time, and had escaped from South Carolina. Her geographical knowledge and life experience extended across at least three southern states. Despite the fact that the vast majority of southern urban fugitives were men, women played a much more significant part in this type of slave flight compared to those who escaped out of the slaveholding South. They were better equipped to navigate southern cities of refuge.

With runaway slaves all over the South, the geography of bondage had many more cracks than hitherto assumed. Slaveholders saw that their bondspeople escaped in ever larger numbers. Yet, they insisted on hiring them out and sending them around. The mobile ones among the enslaved took these opportunities and became the new fugitive slaves. The great downside was that these actions were against the law, and runaways who stayed in the South could not assert any legal claims to freedom. Therefore, it was all the more important that they had allies.

CHAPTER THREE

Receiving Communities, Illegality, and the Absence of Freedom

The curtailment of manumissions, the spread of slavery, and the expansion of the domestic slave trade were severe setbacks for enslaved southerners, yet for those who sought to remain in the South, one new development contained a silver lining. To be able to stay within the region, fugitive slaves needed cover, and the substantially growing free Black population in southern cities, foremost Baltimore, was able to provide it. The lure of nearby cities with African American communities to blend into was a significant pull factor for enslaved people contemplating fight. Urban Black communities varied greatly from city to city, yet they loomed like beacons on the horizon for fleeing slaves.

"The free people of Baltimore had their own circles from which the slaves were excluded, [yet] the ruling of them out of their society resulted more from the desire of the slaveholder than from any great wish of the free people themselves," claimed Frederick Douglass's daughter, Rosetta Douglass Sprague, in 1900, pointing to the social division between those legally enslaved and their free counterparts of the same skin color. She also acknowledged that the chasm could be overcome: "If a slave would dare to hazard all danger and enter among the free people he would be received."[1]

Explicitly prohibited by law, aiding and harboring fugitive slaves was a punishable offense, and it was not a given that fugitive slaves could find refuge among free Blacks. Certain kinds of solidarities and institutional resources had to be mobilized to turn cities into hospitable places for fugitives. Black families contained both legally enslaved and free members, and shared social and political experiences bound people of African descent together, regardless of their legal backgrounds. But what exactly was the situation— legal and otherwise—of Black people in southern cities? After all, their conditions shaped the prospects of fugitive slaves of their lives outside of bondage. Looking closer highlights how the African American population was not neatly divided into enslaved and free but distinguished along many different axes, including a variety of legal statuses. With illegality not limited to men and women who fled slavery but affecting the southern Black population more broadly, it is the "absence of freedom" that helps illuminate the Black experience in southern cities.

Black Cities

Fugitive slaves needed anonymity and invisibility. To achieve this, they relied on a group of people that were more numerous and among which they did not attract attention. Free Americans of African descent not only consti-tuted a visible contradiction to the justification of slavery, but by the turn of the nineteenth century their communities were, according to Ira Berlin, for the first time in American history "large enough and dark enough to camouflage large numbers of runaways."[2]

This held true for southern cities more than anywhere else. Manumitted slaves and free Black Americans in general were disproportionately drawn to urban centers compared to other ethnic groups. The city authorities of Pe-tersburg, Virginia, raised alarm as early as 1805, warning that "Large numbers of free blacks flock from the country to the Towns." In a petition, they sought the General Assembly to restrict "the residence of free blacks, if practicable, to the Counties or places in which they were born or liberated."[3] Apparently, this did not happen because the numbers of Black urban residents further swelled. In the Upper South, one-third of free African Americans came to live in the urban areas while in the Lower South, over half of the free Black popu-lation lived in cities.[4]

The main reason for this internal Black migration was that Black people were barred access to land due to money and politics.[5] As a group, African Americans generally had considerably less money and property than White people. Purchasing land was for the vast majority a financial impossibility. Additionally, they encountered political barriers. An 1831 petition from Virginia complained about skilled slaves present in several trades. Proposing a law to prohibit the apprenticeship of all people of African descent, the petitioners argued that White mechanics were driven out of employment and from the state entirely "to find in the west an asylum where he [they] will be appreci-ated according to his [their] Honesty, industry and ingenuity."[6] What these petitioners made sound like a devastating disadvantage for White mechanics in reality pointed to an alternative to city life from which Black people were blocked. The lands in the West, violently taken from native communities by the United States government, were exclusively sold or granted to Whites.[7] Free Black southerners had, with few exceptions, little choice of residence besides cities and towns.

Ever growing, the urban Black populations were fundamental to reducing the detection of runaway slaves. Urban demographics of particular cities de-termined whether an unfamiliar Black person would be assumed to be a slave or free. Baltimore and Charleston were historically embedded in a network of East Coast seaport cities that depended on commerce while fueling their respective hinterlands through marketing and distribution. Baltimore, a modest town during the eighteenth century, became a thriving commercial city. Situated on the northern border of the southern states, Baltimore's location on the western shore of the Chesapeake Bay provided the city with a protected harbor, proximity to Pennsylvania, and, later, a strategic position in the growing rail network. In 1800, it had a population of 26,900. It grew to be the second-largest American city in 1830, 1840, and 1850, and was the fourth largest in 1860, with 212,000 inhabitants. It had the most spectacular growth of all southern cities, with free African American residents increasing in number from 2,700 in 1800 to 25,700 in 1860. Including 2,200 slaves, Baltimore counted nearly 28,000 people of African descent.[8] Its urban slavery evolved from a mechanical, proto-industrial labor force to a largely domestic labor force for those who could afford it.[9] By 1860 most Baltimore slaveholders owned but a single slave,[10] and from around 1830 onward, chances were increasingly slim that a Black person one would meet on the streets was enslaved.

While mono-agricultural slavery entered its next round, slavery in the cities developed differently. In the early nineteenth century, it still showed growth, but from the mid-antebellum era onward, the trend drastically declined. Charleston and New Orleans, where slavery started to decrease after 1830 and 1840, respectively, are representative. Baltimore's slavery, which was never very strong, dropped after the first decade of the nineteenth century. Richmond was an exception to the southern picture. There, the number of bondspeople grew continuously until the Civil War.

In most urban places in the Upper South, the free Black population was significantly larger than its enslaved counterpart, with Richmond again forming a deviation. Richmond was not a direct seaport city. It owed its rise to its location on the James River, about sixty miles from the coast, channeling products and goods between Virginia, North and South Carolina, and the District of Columbia, Maryland, and the North. With its large manufacturing operations and factories, it developed into the South's most important industrial site.[11] Considerably smaller than Baltimore, Richmond counted an enslaved population that markedly outstripped the free Black population at all times. By the eve of the Civil War, Virginia's capital had 38,000 inhabitants, of which 14,400 were African Americans. Some 11,700 of them were enslaved.

This gap between free and enslaved African Americans had not always been so large, but as the nation edged toward the Civil War, Richmond's demographics looked similar to Charleston's. Both cities had played significant

FIGURE 3.1 View of Richmond, c. 1860. The image gives insight into the city beyond the city center and the often-depicted Capitol Hill, riverside, and surroundings. Mathew Brady, "View of Richmond, Va" (1860–1865), War Department, Office of the Chief Signal Officer, National Archives at College Park, Still Picture Records Section, Special Media Archives Services Division (NWCS-S), U.S. National Archives and Records Administration (https://commons.wikimedia.org/wiki/File:View_of_Richmond,_Va_-_NARA_-_524454.jpg).

economic and cultural roles in the colonial era and beyond, but Charleston was even more dominated by its port than Richmond. The city funneled the produce of the hinterland plantations—mostly cotton—out of the country and nourished itself with the output of slave agriculture. Although other cities in the Lower South were also growing rapidly, the institution of slavery was much more firmly entrenched in Charleston, and manumissions occurred much more selectively and sparsely. As we saw in chapter 1, manumissions had laid the groundwork for the expanding free African American population in the Upper South around the turn of the century. Consequently, regions further south had relatively smaller free Black populations and more enslaved city dwellers. By 1860, Charleston counted 40,500 inhabitants, of which 17,100 were African Americans and only 3,200 of whom had free status. The likelihood of meeting a free Black person was small.

By the mid-nineteenth century, the Black populations in southern cities were so significant that they were often remarked upon by visitors. In 1842, Traugott Bromme, a German author of guidebooks seeking to increase German migration to the United States, warned of an insurgence by free Blacks because "their number outstrips in some cities that of the whites."[12] The Swedish writer and feminist reformer Fredrika Bremer observed in 1850 that in Charleston, "negroes swarm the streets. Two-thirds of the people whom one sees in town are negroes or mulattoes. They are ugly, but appear for the most part cheerful and well fed. In particular one sees fat negro and mulatto women [. . .]."[13] About Richmond, journalist Frederick Law Olmsted likewise recounted that "among the people you see in the streets, full half, I should think, are more or less of negro blood, and a very decent, civil people these seem, in general, to be."[14]

Contemporary travelers were likewise astonished by the large numbers of Black people they saw in the streets in other cities of the South. Historians have often downplayed such observations by claiming that African Americans were simply more visible than Whites in public urban spaces because of the distinct nature of their work, which was often performed on the streets and in public places.[15] Yet it should be noted that throughout the antebellum period, the Black populations of the major southern cities were large by any standard.[16]

When New Orleans became part of the United States in 1803, American immigration and the investments that came with it drove the city toward an intense phase of modernization and growth, with a dramatic population increase that rivaled Baltimore's expansion. Louisiana, admitted to the Union as a slave state in 1812, had an insatiable demand for enslaved workers until eventual abolition put an end to it, while urban slavery in New Orleans started to decline after 1840. By 1860, 168,700 people lived in New Orleans, making it the largest city on the Mississippi River, and the sizes of the free and enslaved Black populations were not all that different: New Orleans registered 10,900 free Black and 13,400 enslaved residents (see table 3.1). When a New Orleans resident saw a person of African descent, the statistical odds that he or she was a slave or a free person were more or less the same. This made the efforts of runaway slaves a little less complicated because White people did not hold property claims on Black people who were not slaves. Female runaways, moreover, had a slight advantage over men because in all cities except Richmond, Black women outnumbered Black men. Women's overrepresentation as urban slaves, discriminatory manumission patterns, and the higher mobility of men that allowed many of them to migrate to the North, accounted for this gender disparity.[17]

TABLE 3.1 Free African American, enslaved, and total urban populations, 1800–1860. Populations changes of the cities of Baltimore, Richmond, Charleston, and New Orleans.

		1800	1810	1820	1830	1840	1850	1860
Baltimore	total	26,500	46,600	62,700	80,600	102,300	169,100	212,400
	free Black	**2,700**	**5,700**	**10,300**	**14,800**	**18,000**	**25,400**	**25,700**
	enslaved	2,800	4,700	4,400	4,100	3,200	2,900	2,200
Richmond	total	5,700	9,700	12,100	16,100	20,200	27,600	37,900
	free Black	**600**	**1,200**	**1,200**	**2,000**	**1,900**	**2,400**	**2,600**
	enslaved	2,300	3,700	4,400	6,300	7,500	9,900	11,700
Charleston*	total	20,500	24,700	24,800	30,300	29,300	43,000	40,500
	free Black	**1,000**	**1,500**	**1,500**	**2,100**	**1,600**	**3,400**	**3,200**
	enslaved	9,800	11,700	12,700	15,400	14,700	19,500	13,900
New Orleans°	total		17,200	27,200	46,100	102,300	116,400	168,700
	free Black		**5,000**	**6,200**	**11,900**	**19,200**	**10,000**	**10,900**
	enslaved		6,000	7,400	9,400	23,400	17,000	13,400

Boldface font highlights the most relevant population group of this book.
*Since 1850, including Charleston Neck
°Since 1852, including Lafayette
Source: U.S. Bureau of the Census, Population of the 100 Largest Cities and Other Urban Places in The United States: 1790 to 1990, https://www.census.gov/library/working-papers/1998/demo /POP-twps0027.html, January 8, 2019; Population of Virginia—1810, http://www.virginiaplaces.org /population/pop1810numbers.html, January 8, 2019; U.S. Bureau of the Census, *Aggregate Number of Persons within the United States in the Year 1810* (Washington, D.C., 1811); Population schedules for the Territory of Orleans of the Third Census of the United States, 1810, 468–70, and for Louisiana of the Fourth Census, 1820, II, 193, in Paul Lachance, "New Orleans in the Era of Revolution: A Demographic Profile," paper for symposium *Revolution et Contre-Revolution a la Nouvelle-Orleans et dans le Monde Creole*, sponsored by the Services Culturels Français de la Nouvelle-Orleans, Ambassade de France, 20th Annual Meeting of the American Society for Eighteenth-Century Studies (April 1, 1989), 3, https://ruor.uottawa.ca/bitstream/10393/34115/1/Profile%20NO%201989.pdf, January 8, 2019; Kennedy, *Population of the United States in 1860*, 191; J. D. B. DeBow (ed.), *The Seventh Census of the United States: 1850. Embracing a Statistical View of Each of the States and Territories, Arranged by Counties, Towns, etc., Under the Following Divisions ...* (Washington, D.C.: Robert Armstrong, 1853), 221, 339; U.S. 8th Census, 1860, *Population of the United States in 1860; Compiled from the Original Returns of the Eighth Census* (Washington, D.C.: Government Printing Office, 1864), 214; J. L. Dawson and Henry William DeSaussure (eds.), *Census of the City of Charleston, South Carolina, for the Year 1848, Exhibiting the Condition and Prospects of the City, Illustrated by Many Statistical Details, Prepared under the Authority of the City Council* (Charleston: J. B. Nixon, 1849), 10.

With both the free and enslaved Black populations in southern cities substantial and growing, fugitives from slavery could move relatively unnoticed
in their midst. However, free African Americans, as a group, did not exactly
look like their enslaved counterparts, and Black people were far from homogeneous. Cultural factors varied from city to city in the Lower South, and influenced the ways in which free and enslaved people lived there. For example,
New Orleans's social composition was more akin to Caribbean societies than
to American places and would remain so over the course of the antebellum
period.[18] Interracial relations between White men and Black women dated
back to French times, and in the nineteenth century, "mulattos" (people of
mixed race) were strongly represented among Louisiana's free non-White
population. They were lighter-skinned than the population held in bondage,
and remained that way after the Louisiana Purchase.[19]

What emerged in New Orleans and in other parts of the Lower South was a
society based on three ethnic groups: White, mulatto, and Black, in the order of
their social standing. Charleston contained a small community of light-skinned
Black people that called themselves "brown" in order to explicitly demarcate
themselves from the enslaved population, which was considerably darker.[20]
Charleston's distinct cultural environment with nuanced color lines, greater
levels of amalgamation, and a White society accustomed to artisans of African
descent offered more security for mulattoes than in other cities. A South Carolina senate meeting from 1859 voiced the opinion "that the free negro had as
much right to have his property protected, as he had to hold property." The
House of Representatives agreed that "although it is an anomalous class, and
though it may be that gentlemen will say that we are not to know free negros,
we, as legislators, find free negros, and we are bound to protect them."[21]

These considerations reflect the status of an intermediate caste of "free people
of color" and the interest of slaveholders to keep them as allies against slaves and
poor Blacks. Despite the fact that free Blacks were often accused of enticing
slaves to abscond, wealthy Whites in the Lower South also recognized their strategic value. Alfred Huger, who hailed from a slaveholding family in Charleston,
stated in 1858 that there was "no better intermediate class in the world than the
free colour'd people in this city." Free Black people were "our natural allies, tho
they can never be our Equals." "They work faithfully and more economically
than those [White men] who would supplant them [. . .], are easily managed and
controul'd," Huger claimed, and added that they "are disenfranchised forever . . .
yet paying their taxes with punctuality and humility."[22]

White southerners like Huger felt that free Black people who enjoyed an
extent of wealth were grateful for their position in a racist society and were

therefore less problematic than Whites because they did not make political demands on them. Furthermore, by allying with White slaveholders, they split the Black population, which would prevent insurrections. "Elite people of color," who were more in number in the Lower than in the Upper South, remained among themselves, linked their families through intermarriages, and pursued their businesses like White people, including their treatment of slaves.[23] And slaves they did own, especially in New Orleans and Charleston, while their family networks did usually not include slaves. Given that these linkages were the most important connections for runaway slaves to gravitate to a certain place, wealthy free Blacks were hardly connected to runaways.

Skin tone was less important in the Upper South. Whether lighter or darker skinned, runaways' chances for blending did not differ that much. Due to manumission schemes that were less discriminatory in gender, skin tone, and status than in the Lower South, the free Black population in the Upper South was considerably darker in physical appearance. Courts in Virginia and Maryland did not distinguish between Blacks and mulattoes and law dictated that everybody with at least one-eighth of African descent was a "negro."[24] When the bondsman Essex ran away from Richmond in 1840, for example, he had a better chance to pass for free in Virginia and Maryland than further south. Essex, "of a dark brown, approximating black" complexion, did not look like the majority of free Black men in a place like Charleston.[25]

Without knowing much more about other visuals, manners of talking, language, dressing, and behavior, enslaved people with darker hues of skin could more easily succeed at passing for free in the urban Upper South. Despite the fact that the free Black population did not form a homogeneous group, its mere existence made it a desperately needed community for runaways to join, and fugitive slaves gravitated to southern cities because of the possibility for attaining anonymity.

Increasing Pressure

Besides often succeeding in going unnoticed, what perspectives did fugitive slaves have among Black urban residents? Once free African Americans had grown so visible that Whites could no longer pretend to ignore their existence, they increasingly faced racial discrimination in their communities. In a society that defined freedom through slavery and justified slavery with race, free people with Black skin were a visible contradiction to southern notions of race and freedom. White southerners came to see free Black people as a threat, both to the institution of slavery and the social order. Additionally, urban free Black communities were constantly accused of enticing slaves to abscond and of aiding, sheltering, and harboring them. Their lives, as a consequence, became harder.

Free Black women and men were considered by law to be persons, not property like the majority of the members of their racial group. Nonetheless, free African Americans were socially seen as members of a low caste, a circumstance that drastically limited their societal, political, and economic fates and fortunes.[26] Yet, the official legal status of free people of African descent was unclear. As historian Martha Jones has observed, former bondspeople and their descendants were neither slaves nor aliens nor free White people (the only classifications public jurisprudence allowed for) and their status essentially presented a "juridical puzzle" to contemporaries. The American Constitution obscured the status of free Black people by simply not mentioning them.[27]

The legal fuzziness was a mirror of societal confusion: free Black people should not even *be* in the United States. The American Colonization Society (ACS) was the institutionalized form of this desire. Formed in 1817, it dedicated itself to sending African Americans to the west coast of Africa, with state branches that were much more active and successful in the Upper South than in the Lower South.[28] Whites who supported colonization were driven by the wish to expel Black people and the idea that they were better off in Africa. The anomaly of their existence was in the word: "Free people of color" or "free negroes," as nineteenth-century Americans classified freeborn and manumitted Black people in census records, tax registers, administrative documents, and public communication, were terms to describe the exceptional condition of persons of African descent who were *not slaves*. Legal texts addressing slaves as "Negros and other slaves," implied that all Black people were slaves, and the ACS, even more bluntly, stated that "the position of every 'free person of color' in the United States" was that of a "'slave without a master.'"[29]

In the antebellum South, the Black population came to converge more because both free and enslaved African Americans were increasingly treated like they were one group. As a result of the rule of whiteness, which was visually coded, laws were designed that stressed the similar treatment of slaves and free Blacks in punishment, and demarcated Whites from Blacks, regardless of the latter's legal status. Slave codes became Black codes, and Black people who had gained a free status were increasingly forced to endure the same treatment that White society had formerly reserved for slaves. One of the most extreme examples was that after 1858, free Blacks in Maryland could be sold for crimes.[30]

With the growing free Black population, White Americans were concerned about how to exert control over them beyond the master-slave relationship.

They designed guardianship laws, as in South Carolina, that foresaw that Black people needed White sponsors to vouch for their character. In theory, the guardianship was extensive and legally binding for all free Black men above fifteen years of age. It stipulated a written attestation to the "good character and correct habits" as well as a registration of the guardianship with the city clerk. No White man would have ever accepted this official relation with somebody he did not know.[31] In practice, the guardianship laws, while enacted in 1822, grew to be more and more neglected until many free African Americans were not even aware of their existence.[32] After all, personal acquaintance with Whites was a much more secure backup to prove one's free status than a piece of paper. This was also true for fugitive slaves. The longer they remained in one place and the better they were known, the lower the chances that somebody would think that they were slaves. The balancing act was to get to that point.

Legislative restrictions varied from state to state and emphasized political and judicial exclusion. In most states, persons of color were not allowed to vote, to testify in court, or to sit on juries. They were not allowed to freely travel, assemble, or marry Whites.[33] In Virginia, the division between White and Black punishment was particularly strong. Virginia's Black code of 1859 was the most comprehensive and systematic attempt to regulate the conduct of Black people. Moreover, Richmond's courts were increasingly preoccupied with offenses that involved the crossing of the color line,[34] such as miscegenation and other forms of interracial mixing.

Free Blacks were compelled to carry freedom papers and to register their status, a measure that was designed to prevent slaves from passing as free. Already in 1800, Gabriel Prosser's alleged coconspirator was witnessed to have complained that he could not visit his wife since it was very difficult for a Black man to travel, because "the white people had turned so comical, a man can't go out of his house now but he is taken up to be hanged."[35] After the failed rebellion, the situation for Black people predictably worsened. Legally, any White man could at any time and place check the identity of any non-White persons he encountered.[36] If the latter could not identify themselves, they would be beaten up, or they could be brought to jail where further investigation about their persona took place. Documentation was, hence, increasingly important.

Throughout the South, it was the legal obligation of Black people to prove that they were not slaves, and inability to do so could lead to enslavement and sale.[37] The only exemption that levied the burden of proof on the accuser instead of on the defendant took place in Maryland in 1817. Due to the high number of its free Black population, the state, despite great opposition, relieved Black people of the burden of proof to verify their legal liberty and instead assumed all of them to be free unless proven otherwise.[38] Nevertheless, the lives of free African Americans did not improve. Instead of "upgrading" slaves to the status of free Blacks, Whites placed both groups on the lowest rung of the social ladder. Furthermore, legally free Black Americans who were believed to be runaways continued to be jailed in the state.

The undefined legal status of free people of African descent informed how a life outside slavery could look for fugitive slaves. Historians largely agree that freedom took on very different meanings for different societal groups given the pluralist society of the antebellum United States. After the Revolution had already "revealed the contradiction," the Declaration of Independence of 1776 formulated freedom as a universal right, a rhetoric that did not pass by enslaved people without noticing. According to Eric Foner, enslaved people considered themselves as individuals deprived of the very right of personal liberty and self-determination. More concretely, what bondspeople desired as freedom was a life free from the whip and sexual abuse, control of their own family affairs, maintenance of kin ties, access to education, and the ability to keep the fruits of their own labor.[39] Often, the only way they could achieve this was by running away and living illegally among other Black people in southern cities.

Free urban African Americans were not under the control of an individual master but were heavily restricted by public law and surveillance. Although there was a degree of legal protection, White violence against free Blacks was rarely sanctioned. Moreover, Black children were barred from public education, and teaching Black southerners to read and write was in many states prohibited. Yet, a great many African Americans received education in Sunday schools organized by church congregations, secretly in states that did not allow for this.[40] Importantly, Black people did keep their wages and earnings, and so did fugitive slaves who succeeded in breaking free from enslavement. But this was hardly real freedom in the sense of civil and political rights, and there were other mechanisms that restricted the lives of Black southerners in a way that it was free African Americans whose lives actually came closer to the experiences of illegal fugitives, rather than the other way around.

An Illegal Population

Municipal authorities themselves were often far from certain how many people of African descent lived in a city, let alone what their exact status was.

As early as 1820, Virginia governor Thomas Mann Randolph admitted in a speech to the House of Delegates that "the actual relation of numbers between the free citizens of the state, and that distinct and inferior race so unfortunately intermingled with them, must necessarily remain somewhat longer undetermined."[41]

In Louisiana, the chaos was even more intense because the federal government had, firstly, no idea about the population volume of the Territory of Orleans when it purchased the land in 1803: "It is impossible to tell with any exactness the number of free Males from 18 to 45 in the different Settlements," was the official announcement from Washington.[42] Secondly, during the immigration wave of Black and White Caribbean migrants in the early nineteenth century, New Orleans's government was incapable of impeding or controlling Black persons from coming to the city.[43] In 1805, the mayor recognized his impotence to control and even to distinguish between their status as free or unfree persons: "Many worthless free people of colour or persons calling themselves free arrive here daily without our being able to prevent it, or to drive them away after they have come."[44]

The confusion was aggravated when different southern states passed a series of laws at different times in hope of curtailing the free African American population. In 1806, Virginia was the first state to require all newly emancipated slaves to leave the state within twelve months.[45] The law remained virtually unenforceable since many, if not most, emancipated slaves simply refused to leave.[46] It could be argued that the ordinance was thus a dead letter. However, the meager execution rather meant that its impact was felt on a different level. Instead of reducing the free Black population, it criminalized and, indeed, illegalized all newly manumitted slaves. In the sixty years to come, the ordinance created a significant illegal population of free Black people throughout the state—legally emancipated but illegally residing in Virginia. They could not register their status with local or state authorities and had no documentation to prove their free status. The number of these illegal free African Americans reached well into the thousands and must have stood in considerable contrast to the official census data.[47]

Maryland's free Black population also became partly illegalized, a process that occurred on various levels. From 1824 onward, manumitted slaves were required to pay a $1 fee to receive a certificate of freedom by the clerk of the court.[48] Those who could not afford the dollar could not prove their free status without major efforts. In 1832, another law was enacted that required slaves manumitted from that year onward to leave Maryland.[49] Legislators, who had watched the effects of the 1806 Virginia law for a quarter century

and eventually copied it, knew that it would not work the way it had originally been envisioned. It was nevertheless enacted with the side effect of creating a large population of undocumented people who were stripped of any
legal rights. Louisiana passed a similar statute in 1830.[50]

Contrary to the official census data that divided the Black population into
two categories, free and enslaved, this evidence calls for a more nuanced picture including additional classifications (see table 3.2). There were, firstly, persons of African descent who were born free or legally manumitted, who were
registered with the authorities as such, and possessed certificates to prove
their freedom, and were therefore de jure and de facto free. Most historians
think of all de facto free Black people in this category because this is how they
appear in contemporary sources. However, there were more scenarios in
which people could be living as if they were free without having a legal basis.

Based on the concept of illegality, there were, secondly, many freeborn
people of African descent who for a variety of reasons did not possess free
papers (for instance, because they could not pay the fee, did not renew them,
or had lost them) or were not registered. These people were legally free but
lacked the documentation proving their status when mistaken for or suspected of being runaway slaves.[51]

Thirdly, there were those who were manumitted in conformity with the
law but resided in the state illegally. William Stebbins from New Orleans, a
free Black man, was arrested in December 1858 for "having no evidence of
freedom, and supposed to be a runaway." Stebbins "proved his freedom, but
at the same time showed that he is in the State in contravention of law, and
was discharged, with a due notification to leave the State within 60 days."[52] In
1838, citizens of Berkeley County (now West Virginia) realized exactly this.
They warned that many emancipated slaves did not emigrate and called attention to the deficiency of the code since sister states had likewise enacted
laws to prevent free Blacks from immigrating.[53] With no viable destination
and a lax execution of the law, it is logical that Stebbins and others in his situation did—and could—not leave.

Many southern states had banned Black people who were not enslaved
from entering since the early nineteenth century, but these policies largely
failed. South Carolina introduced this legislation in 1800; Maryland followed
in 1808.[54] Louisiana enacted a similar code in 1807, but because it was neglected, it was reintroduced in 1830 requiring the expulsion of "free negroes of
other States from its territory who had entered after 1825." From 1838 onward,
it was "modified so as to allow all free blacks in the State" under the precondi-
tion that they registered themselves and posted a bond, but this law also

TABLE 3.2 Composition of the free African American population.

1. Born free or legally manumitted, with proper registration and freedom papers
2. Born free or legally manumitted, without proper registration and/or papers
3. Legally manumitted, illegally in the state residing
4. Illegally immigrated
5. Illegally manumitted
6. Fugitive slaves

→ *de facto* free, yet undocumented / illegal

remained "rarely enforced." And so, free Black people grew oblivious about it, as the press came to realize.[55] These men and women, who migrated to another southern state in contravention of the law, constituted a fourth group of illegal free Black people.

A fifth group of illegal free Black residents was created by complicating or prohibiting manumission. In South Carolina, for example, manumission was only allowed with the permission of both the state House of Representatives and the Senate after 1820, which was such a high obstacle that practically no slaveholder pursued this path.[56] Instead, they continued to conduct manumissions without legal approbation. The extent of illegal emancipations is made clearer by the fact that in 1850 only two bondspeople were officially manumitted in the entire state of South Carolina.[57] Two years prior, Judge John Belton O'Neall, justice of appeals at law, wrote that the prohibition of manumissions of 1820 had "caused evasions without numbers,"[58] reflecting the ignorance of the state regarding the dimensions of the phenomenon.

Most of these illegalization processes were top-down measures, but not readily recognizable as such. Some Black southerners, however, had good reason to actively seek illegality. The inability or refusal to pay capitation taxes was presumably the strongest motivation to dodge the official registry. Capitation taxes were high. In Charleston, free women of African descent between eighteen and fifty were required to pay $5 per year. If they were between fourteen and eighteen, the fee was reduced to $3. Meanwhile, men between sixteen and twenty-one years of age had to pay $5. Afterward they were charged $10 until they turned sixty.[59] This was an additional burden to the $2 annual tax levied on Black residents by the state of South Carolina.[60] Seen in this new light, the head taxes, which were much higher for men than for women, might have been a strong reason for the dramatic sex imbalance within the urban free Black population. Whereas the female-male ratio was nearly even when looking at young residents, it shifted to almost two to one when full capitation taxes were due. The lower wards of Charleston counted sixty-eight women between fourteen and eighteen and an equal number of men between sixteen and twenty-one in 1858. In the same year, 341 women above eighteen paid head taxes in comparison to only 181 men older than twenty-one. In the upper wards and in the following year, the numbers were similar.[61] The annual tax of $12 constituted a serious obstacle to making a living and it seems that a great many free Black men tried to avoid paying it. Not paying taxes could maneuver legally free people into a situation in which their freedom became very fragile. Although risky, a condition of undocumentedness was for many Black residents one less financial burden to bear.

Fugitives from slavery, the sixth identified group, were far from being the odd ones out. They camouflaged themselves among a population which, in large part, likewise could not afford confrontations with the city guards, police, or other hostile people who could question their identity. They were illegals among other illegals.

Legalization Strategies

Similar to fugitive slaves, free people of African descent with an undocumented status had to act very carefully. The city of New Orleans, for one, intended to "imprison strange negroes or colored people [...], should they be unable or unwilling to give such an account of themselves as shall be satisfactory to the police," former enslaved John Brown recalled, emphasizing that this regulation was "especially oppressive to the free coloured people."[62] If they could not prove that they were not slaves, they had to avoid authorities at any cost, could not seek legal ways to protect themselves from injustice and abuse, and were in danger of re-enslavement. Despite the heavy weight of tax payments, these people had good reason to try to decriminalize their status. And so, great numbers of legal petitions to the Virginia governor asked for exemptions from the law of 1806 with the intent to legalize the petitioners' residency.[63]

Lunsford Lane was one of many trapped in the paradox of emancipation. After saving up a considerable amount of money, in 1835 he was able to purchase his freedom. Five years later, while making plans to buy his wife and six children, Lane received notice that following the statutes of North Carolina, he was in the state contrary to law and had to leave within twenty days in order to avoid prosecution. With the help of White friends and employers who vouched for his good character, Lane decided to petition to remain in the state. His wish was not granted, and he had to depart from Raleigh and his family in 1841. Aptly expressed, his autobiography includes the subtitle *His Banishment from the Place of His Birth for the Crime of Wearing a Colored Skin.*[64]

For Black families, it was even more important that the woman prove her free status. If she was suspected of being a slave at any point in the future, all her children would likewise be officially regarded as enslaved. Tellingly, in Richmond, many Black people claimed to be the offspring of freeborn mothers when they asked for registration, even though they were children of former slaves who were emancipated after 1806 and remained in the state contrary to law. For example, when Monroe Jordon, about seventeen years old, was apprehended, it turned out that he did not possess a register. The Hustings Court decided that he was the son of a woman who was released from slavery after 1806. He was to be hired to pay his jail fees, and afterwards registered, but had no right to stay in the Commonwealth.[65]

The same strategy worked more successfully if undocumented residents had White people to vouch for them. In 1852, Charlotte Coleman had such a relation with a White woman who testified to her freedom, and Coleman was included in the registry as a free person: "It appearing to the Court, by the testimony of Tabitha B. Peterson, that Charlotte Coleman, a woman of colour, was born free in Chesterfield County, it is ordered that she is registered in the office of this court." In a different case, Clement White, a White man, testified the same for a Black woman called Mary Ann King.[66] If a respectable White person corroborated a Black person's account, illegal residents had a chance to legalize their status.

Elvira Jones from Richmond obtained her freedom by working hard and saving enough money to purchase herself and her two children from their master Samuel Carlisle. Jones not only acquired the means to buy three persons out of slavery, but her earnings also allowed her to become the owner of a small house in the suburbs of Richmond. Moving up and achieving modest property was unusual, yet possible, for freed slaves and Jones, emancipated after 1806, was an example of a manumitted woman staying in the state of Virginia illegally. Importantly, she had a personal relation to a White man called Samuel Harris who managed the receipt of the money for her emancipation and the conveyance of the house she purchased.[67] Yet, many Black people did not have these sorts of connections with White people, and those who dared to submit a petition represented only a small fraction of illegal free Blacks; granted petitions to remain in the state were the exception. For most illegals, and especially refugees from slavery, it was safer to keep a low, anonymous profile.

Fugitive slaves were much less likely to have a relation with a White resident, but for undocumented residents—and perhaps even runaway slaves—being able to produce tax receipts over a couple of years could serve as a way to legitimize their nominal freedom. This strategy was the opposite to the "voluntary" illegalization intended to avoid tax payments. While some historians have suggested that Black people could easily make these payments, in reality it was not that simple.[68] There was a constant danger that, after the death of their legal owner, they could be exposed or they could be seized for possible debts.

The account of Joseph Elwig from Charleston is a case in point. His father, Peter Elwig, bought him and his two brothers in 1823. Because it was after 1820, Peter Elwig was not able to officially manumit his sons and so they grew up as undocumented residents. Like his father, Joseph became a carpenter and started operating a shop in the city when he was 26 years old. He paid "free Negro capitation taxes" and city taxes, and married a free Black woman. Joseph Elwig led the life of a regularly free Black man but in times of uncertainty, his situation risked turning dire. When Peter Elwig became ill, he sold Joseph to Joseph's wife, Rebecca, to protect him from de facto enslavement.[69] Joseph Elwig's case shows, on the one hand, that it was indeed possible to achieve a certain level of security by paying head taxes. On the other hand, it also illustrates the fragility of this condition and the constant danger that could be triggered when circumstances changed.

There were more cases like Elwig's. In 1843, George Lucas, a free Black resident of Charleston Neck, directly north of the city of Charleston, purchased his three daughters. Also in Neck, Nelson Richardson bought his wife, Ann, in 1849. And in 1853, Georgianna Alston from the city of Charleston purchased her husband, Thomas. In these examples, the nominally free managed after a couple of years to convince the tax collectors and census takers of their free status. In the case of Nelson and Ann Richardson, this strategy also worked for their children.[70] With persistence, patience, and luck it was possible for undocumented people to gradually join the official ranks of the free Black population. This bottom-up process of legalization contrasted sharply with top-down illegalization practices. Yet, the breadth of the former was much smaller.

We can only speculate about how likely this was for runaways from slavery and their offspring. It is certain that a great many fugitives, the majority of whom were in their fertile years, had children after their escape. Did, for instance, Cicily Page succeed at passing her children off as free persons? The "first rate seamstress" was advertised to the police by her owners from Williamsburg, Virginia, seven years after she had left them. She had successfully blended in with the free African American community in Richmond and was assumed to have two children.[71] Between 1800 and 1820, nearly 600 African Americans applied to the courts in Baltimore for legal certificates of freedom.[72] It can be assumed that a number of them were illegal residents, including runaways, who dared to try to legalize the status of themselves and of their children.

In many cases, it was entirely unclear whether a Black person was born free or in slavery. Rivan Mayo, for one, was in 1855 registered as a "free man of color" in Chesterfield County, Virginia. This was confirmed by the clerk of the court. His mother appeared to be freeborn, as the correspondence between a slaveholder and his agent reveals. Yet, Mayo was claimed as a slave in Kentucky.[73] Mayo could have been freeborn indeed, or he was a fugitive slave from another state. Given that he did not enter the Negro Register before he was twenty-three years old, both scenarios are plausible.

Although it cannot give us a precise understanding of the size of the illegal Black population in antebellum southern cities, the evidence suggests that African Americans were aware of their precarious legal status, and that those who considered themselves able, stepped forward to better their condition. The majority of Black southerners, however, did not have strong connections with Whites, could not afford to make strategic tax payments, and could not improve their reputation by becoming property owners. Those with an illegal or undocumented status were as far from being free as people who escaped slavery and hid in southern cities.

BALTIMORE, RICHMOND, CHARLESTON, AND NEW ORLEANS attracted and absorbed large numbers of runaway slaves and unregistered free Blacks. The close links between free and enslaved African Americans impacted both groups. While it offered opportunities for fugitive slaves, it negatively impacted the situation of those with a legal free status. Conversely, these developments influenced, and eventually restricted, the aspirations of runaway slaves, and the spaces of refuge they could find remained fragile. Joining a population that, to large extent, likewise had an illegal status, they could not hope to achieve legalization by assimilating to them. Not only were they vulnerable to retrieval and re-enslavement on basis of the rule of slavery in the South, becoming part of the free Black population did also not automatically entail that fugitives were seen and treated as nominally free people.

The illegal status of thousands of Black southerners made all of them vulnerable and constituted a constant threat to their lives outside of bondage. Illegality was what fugitive slaves decided to run to, and marked the lives they could find in the South. Consequently, the worlds of free illegals and fugitive slaves did not diverge that much. All these groups were exposed to discretionary policing, extralegal violence, and civil disability before the law. This shared discrimination and vulnerability worked as a connector between free and enslaved Black southerners because nobody Black ever truly exited slavery or attained full freedom in the South. Real freedom was not to be found.

CHAPTER FOUR

Navigating the City

Because of their lack of distinction from other Black southerners, any random African American that one encountered on the streets of southern cities could theoretically be a legal resident (enslaved or free), a runaway slave, or a free Black residing illegally in the city. At first glance it was usually impossible to tell, a situation aggravated by a general disorder in the streets of antebellum cities. In such opaque places, how did fugitive slaves know where to go? How did they navigate urban spaces, contact allies, find places to hide after dark, and socialize?

The physical layout and residential geographies of Baltimore, Richmond, Charleston, and New Orleans varied. Yet in all places, particular racial and ethnic demographics marked off certain spaces as more congenial for fugitives than others. Without disregarding the risks and dangers involved, new modes of urban segregation worked favorably to create "Black spaces" in the cities. It was to the advantage of fugitive slaves that a large number of illegal and undocumented city dwellers already depended on these geographies. In 1859, an editor for the New Orleans *Daily Picayune* warned that "a perfect system for mutual protection exists here among this class of [the Black] population, rendering New Orleans one of the safest of hiding places for runaway slaves."[1] Despite these opportunities, fugitives had to be alert, as surprise encounters could always happen: smaller parts of the Black community were not on their side, and policing of the lower classes grew tighter over time. Cities were not perfect places of refuge, even as they were natural beacons for fugitives and other illegals.

Ties and Solidarity

Upon arrival in a city, runaway slaves seem to have had clear ideas about where to go. In a city that was continuously changing and attracting new residents, visitors, commuters, and suppliers, it was relatively easy to hide, and fugitive slaves made use of their (often) extensive networks to do so. An important factor of urban life, particularly in commercial and growing cities, was that the streets were always swamped with new people. Benjamin Moore Norman considered New Orleans such a thriving destination for business and travels that he compiled a guidebook to the city in 1845. He speculated that around 20,000 businessmen were in New Orleans during business season alone, which exempted the hot summer months. Besides them, 300 riverboatmen streamed into the city monthly during half the year.[2] Joseph Holt Ingraham witnessed that plantation slaves were allowed to visit Natchez, Mississippi, on Sundays, adding to the presence of Black people in the streets.[3] Antebellum cities were messy and chaotic and overwhelmed by a constant influx of newcomers. This was a welcome environment for fugitive slaves and others who, according to the laws of the time, should not have been there.

In the southern states, the rate of urbanization was significantly lower and slower than in the northern states, but towns were nevertheless steadily growing. From 1830 onward, American cities expanded dramatically, in absolute size, relative to the overall population, and in number. Baltimore, Richmond, Charleston, and New Orleans were major cities in their respective regions as well as in the South as a whole. Cities were modern and exciting. For many urban slaves, it was unimaginable to live anywhere else. Bella could have been one of them. A February 1835 newspaper ad stated that the bondswoman, thirty-five to forty years of age, "absconded herself [from Charleston] in November last, under the pretence that she did not wish to go to the country."[4]

For runaway slaves from the countryside cities offered never-before-seen impressions, and southern cities had cultural activities for non-White people unimaginable even in the North. In Richmond, Black people went to amusements alongside Whites. There were dances and theaters and on Sundays, they gathered to game and drink.[5] The most exciting city for visitors and foreigners alike was probably New Orleans. It offered cabarets for free and unfree Black people, and they could join the yearly celebrations of All Soul's Day, Christmas, New Year's Eve, the Twelfth Night, and Mardi Gras.[6] Whether it was the unique composition of its inhabitants—"White men and women, and of all hues of brown, and of all classes of faces, from round Yankees to grizzly and lean Spaniards, black negroes and negresses, filthy Indians half naked, mulattoes curly and straight-haired, quadroons of all shades, long haired and frizzled," as Benjamin Latrobe summarized in 1819—or the rich supply of exotic food, New Orleans was extraordinary.[7]

Although runaways moved clandestinely, the popular image of a fugitive arriving in a city in the middle of the night, shirking the night watch, and waiting for the light of the day in a back alley was surely the exception. Most men and women who escaped slavery and went to southern cities to stay had been there before and knew where to go. James Matthews mobilized his knowledge of and contacts in Charleston before he escaped there. His work as a carriage driver had taken him to Charleston before, so he "went to the tavern where I used to stop, when I carried eggs and peaches and other things to market." In the following days, Matthews "slept on some hay under a shed in the tavern yard."[8] The tavern owner or employees at least condoned his presence there at night; perhaps they even supported him actively.

The majority of those planning a flight to a city, and especially after arrival at their destination, were taken into a solidarity network of kin and acquaintances. The hope of slaveholders to keep free and enslaved people apart in the cities waned as slavery tightened its grip in the South. Free and unfree Black populations were closely interconnected, a phenomenon that varied by place, yet remained constant and buttressed by kinship ties in both slavery and freedom. Newspaper announcements about runaway slaves thought to be harbored by free family members are countless throughout the antebellum era. In 1805 Jack Ash ran away, and thanks to his wide network his master William Rose was unsure about where to look for him. In his fifties, Ash was considerably older than the average runaway. Rose advertised that "he is well known in and about the city of Richmond, Amthell, in the County of Chesterfield, where he has a number of free connections, and in the neighbourhood of Williamsburg—Tis very certain that he is lurking about one of the above places, most likely Richmond, where he has a free woman for a wife."[9]

In 1832, Nelly was believed to be harbored by her husband in Charleston.[10] And in 1840, $100 was set on catching Ellick, eighteen years of age. He called himself Alexander Brown and absconded from Jefferson County, Virginia. His mother lived near Baltimore and his sister in Baltimore, and so his owner believed that Ellick had gone there.[11] The strategies that Ash, Nelly, and Brown applied are known as network-mediated migration or chain migration. It is characterized by the knowledge on the part of those who are about to migrate, already have ties at the destination, and know that they will be helped upon arrival, often via offers of information and encouragement on arrival.[12]

Such slave networks contradict the theories of sociologist Orlando Patterson; though he contributed a great deal to understanding the essence of slavery and his approach to defining slavery as social death provoked numerous scholarly debates. He emphasized the loss of identity and absolute isolation, which produced total powerlessness on the side of bondspeople.[13] As the networks of fugitive slaves show, however, his theory is more useful for the moment of capture and enslaving, rather than in the context of fugitive slaves in nineteenth-century America. After generations of captivity in the Americas, the majority of enslaved people were born into social communities. These dynamics were strengthened by the fact that already before the

Revolutionary War, American-born slaves outnumbered those born in Africa.[14] Enslaved people in the United States, and particularly the mobile slave population, were far from isolated, passive, and immobile, and oftentimes not even tied to a specific plantation or a single master.

As we have seen in earlier chapters, network-mediated slave flight worked particularly well in the Upper South. The Chesapeake Bay had been one of the earliest sites of African American slavery, and by the antebellum period, 200 years after the first enslaved Africans put their feet on soil that would later become the United States, many enslaved families had been rooted in this region for several generations. Family networks were firm and extended over rural and urban areas. As enslaved families were increasingly broken up and a significant number of slaves experienced a higher mobility and more varied employments, these kin networks expanded.[15]

When the threat of sale loomed, relatives and friends became extremely active supporters of runaways. The domestic trade of slaves dealt a heavy blow to Black communities, and it might have motivated them to cling more to each other and to see family as an important safety net, both in economic and psychological aspects. Additionally in the Upper South upward social mobility was almost unachievable for any person of visual African descent, which led to the strengthening of horizontal solidarities and a degree of "racial unity."[16] These constituted convenient preconditions for men and women who needed useful contacts to escape.

Even people with weak personal networks had the opportunity to join with others who were in a similar situation. Slave refugee Charles Ball, for one, experienced the solidarity of a stranger who furnished him with valuable information to escape just because they were both from the same region in Virginia. Their common birthplace and sufferings as displaced slaves united them.[17] And Willis Hodge, a Black man born free in Virginia, accounted that he would have protected a runaway slave at gunpoint: "I had been taught by my parents that it was far more honorable to suffer death than to betray one that had run away from the slave-holders, be the runaway bond or free man."[18] Black people often supported each other, and urban runaways could rely on their close and extended personal contacts to find shelter.

Runaway slave advertisements reveal that, as the nineteenth century progressed, more and more enslaved people had relatives who lived in cities. Contrarily, in the late eighteenth century, few ads had mentioned the family relations of the runaways in Baltimore.[19] Increasingly, masters began to give information about the personal contacts of the absconder and, in numerous cases, also on presumed employment. Charles A. Pye, the legal owner of twenty-year-old "rather handsome" Watt, who left him in March 1816, announced a reward of $100. "He has some relations at Mr. Foxall's, in Georgetown, and a free brother in Baltimore, where he will probably endeavor to reach. It is likely he will have a pass, as some of his relations read and write."[20] With the number of Black city dwellers increasing and urban slavery in Baltimore shrinking, city contacts were often free people. As early as the 1830s, free Black inhabitants outnumbered the city's enslaved residents by more than 10,000, which meant they had more ability to shelter and aid runaways.

Into the Underground

Not all fugitives, however, had friends and family in a city. Runaways who were new to a city had to make up their minds about where to go first. Architectural historian Rebecca Ginsburg has directed our attention to the "Black landscape," stressing the different geographies and knowledge used by rural Black people. Essentially approaching the Black landscape as a counter-geography, she has argued that Whites knew surprisingly little about this other world because it was spiked with markers that were unintelligible to them.[21] Such alternative geographies existed also in cities with critical numbers of Black inhabitants.

Even without knowing people personally, fugitives could look for Black people congregating in public spaces. They were disproportionately present in markets, squares, back alleys, docks, churchyards, and elsewhere in cities. Places and events where many people crowded together allowed clandestine people to inquire about shelter, food, allies, and work. Mid-February was "the week of the Charleston Races, a season of much dissipation," wrote slaveholder William Read to his brother Jacob in 1800. Suspecting his brother's runaway slave Hercules to be drawn to the spectacle of the horse races, William informed Jacob that "I have got some persons looking out for your Hercules, as I think he is in or about this City, + that would be a very probable place to meet with such villains."[22] The same spectacle, horse races, attracted Lewis to Richmond from Chesterfield, Virginia. When he absconded in 1806, his owner thought Lewis would "attempt passing as a free man, and will attempt to make his escape to Norfolk by water," yet the owner also informed that "he was seen in Richmond during the Broad Rock Races, dressed in black" and added that "it is probable that he is still lurking about there."[23]

New Orleans had a special meeting place for Black people that did not exist in other southern cities: Congo Square, located just outside the original city walls "below Rampart street, with St. Claude on the rear, and St. Ann and

St. Peter streets on its sides."[24] Since 1812, it had been a public space constituting a centralized congregation spot for enslaved people. Prior to that, urban
slaves assembled throughout the city. The Sunday afternoon gatherings focused on dancing, singing, and musical performances and had social, cultural, economic, and religious meanings to those who participated.[25] The
Daily Picayune recommended Congo Square to visitors to the city. It had
the appeal of a tourist attraction that was markedly different from mainstream
American culture. An editor wrote: "The scene is novel, interesting, and
highly amusing. In various parts of the square a number of male and female
negroes assemble, dressed in their holiday clothes, with the very gayest ban-
dana handkerchiefs upon the heads of the females, and, accompanied by the
thumping of a banjo or drum, or the squealing of a greasy cremona, perform
the most grotesque African dances." Being attracted to and simultaneously
repelled by what he perceived as African aesthetics, the editor described the
most distinguished person at Congo Square, as of a "particularly killing
appearance. [. . .] the very *beau ideal* of a master of ceremonies."[26]

Filled with enslaved people, Congo Square was a site to find allies sympa-
thetic to the fate of a runaway. While slaveholders surely also thought of looking there for their escaped property, only a few would have dared enter the
area and expose themselves to a mass of Black people. Moreover, the participants dressed differently than during the work week, and a colorful head rag
or a newly acquired Sunday suit led runaways blend in with the crowd. The
markers that helped them seek out alternative geographic options were not
visible to people not privy.[27] They could include hand gestures; marks on
houses, taverns, and walls; signs in alleys; passwords; specifically tied handkerchiefs; or items arranged on a window sill. It is impossible to know how
exactly fugitives found their way in the cities, but with adequate information
it is likely that they could approach possible allies, drop code words, or simply walk into the right tavern.

Runaways needed the support of others when they arrived as well as when
they planned to escape from a city. A friend could walk past the courthouse
or post office to check for handbills or announcements of whether a runaway
was actively wanted in a given place.[28] Runaways could find sympathizers in
the grog shops of lower-class neighborhoods, such as Neck and the northern
edge of the city in Charleston, and, in New Orleans, the Second District just
beyond Canal Street.[29] Taverns in East Baltimore, with often dual function of
brothels, brought together lower-class residents and newcomers.[30] Fugitives
frequently arrived at taverns after their flight from outside the cities, where they
affirmed existing networks, forged new connections, or simply socialized.

While we often think of taverns as male spaces, they also served as networking sites for women. In November 1843, the Richmond police were looking for "Rebeca belonging to Jns Smith[,] Gingerbread Colour[,] tall and slim." She had "been in the habit of washing in the back of the Bell Tavern" and it is altogether possible that she established ties there that helped her escape.[31] Because police and slaveholders would look at such places for runaways, it happened that John Robertson—who was originally committed to jail for want of his freedom papers but the Henrico County Court later decided that he was a runaway slave—was caught at the same Bell Tavern where Rebeca would later work before her escape.[32] When Martha, twenty-eight years old, was sold from Richmond to Charleston in 1844, it only took her three months in a new place to forge strong enough ties to people willing to aid her in her escape and concealment: "She was seen the night after she went away in a house occupied by negroes, on Boyce & Co's wharf," the newspaper announcement claimed.[33]

For reasons of solidarity and camouflage, fugitives joined Black people who were driven out of the White public space and into illegality. Clandestine life occurred in back alleys, shops, and taverns, often at night. Alcohol was consumed and illegal card games like faro were played, mixing members of the lower classes of all races, ethnicities, and legal statuses. In Charleston, "six negros were arrested in a house on Savage-street on Saturday night, while engaged in gambling. Two of the negros were recognized as runaways, who have been absent from their master's service for several weeks."[34] Reports like these were common in southern urban newspapers, pointing to both the interconnectedness of legally and illegally free Black people and the fact that fugitives were often discovered by engaging in activities for which Black people—but not White people—were criminalized.

Enslaved people officially needed authorization from their owners to purchase practically everything, a statute that came to be extended to free people, who had to secure permits from the municipality. Free Black Baltimoreans, for example, were criminalized when they bought firearms, dogs, or liquor without a license.[35] One of the most dramatic censure practices regarded education. In the South, people of African descent were not only excluded from public education, but schooling was actively prohibited. In Baltimore, institutions such as Black schools and benevolent societies had to operate clandestinely and were frequently shut down. Recognizing the close connection between a barred access to education and the maintenance of inequality, Virginia was particularly hostile to Black education and African Americans in Richmond had to study in secret places. It was a similar situation in Charleston but schools were sometimes allowed under close regulation.[36] Seeking out a Black school led fugitives to people who were accomplices in actively contesting a racist, discriminatory system, and connected two types of resistance.

Beyond those who planned on staying in southern cities, many other fugitives used them as a waystation for their migration north and remained a couple of weeks or months. William Anderson, who also helped other enslaved people escape, tried to use New Orleans as a point of departure for his escape to the North: "My plan at this time was to write myself a pass down to New Orleans, and when I got there, to take a ship to New York or Boston."[37] Caroline Hammond was, together with her mother and father, first harbored by a White family in Baltimore "who were ardent supporters of the Underground Railroad," before being smuggled into Pennsylvania.[38] While most allies' networks were informal and sporadic, at times runaways could make use of more organized structures such as the Underground Railroad, which also extended its reach into the urban South.

Meeting points where Black activities occurred were usually located in alleys or were hidden venues altogether. Many buildings were constructed in a way that their residents were protected from outsiders' views. When cholera broke out in Baltimore in 1849, its origins were traced back to "some free negroes, whose houses were only accessible by narrow alleys running into St. Paul street."[39] In essence, then, the places where runaways gathered in cities were already refuges for other Black people that lived there.[40] Urban slaves used these spaces to seek relief from work, obtain a degree of privacy, conduct secret business, or have love affairs. Likewise, free Blacks used Black geographies to do whatever they wanted to keep secret from Whites and public view. In Richmond, a policeman "detected a secret door in the partition" of a confectionary shop without a license in 1853, "and opening it, found it led to a narrow passage. Passing through it for some distance, he came upon a large bar room [...]."[41] The policeman had detected a small sliver of Richmond's hidden underground.

Slaveowners were often clueless about the secret activities of their bondspeople. Some, however, were aware of their clandestine lives, as one slaveholder wrote in a Charleston newspaper: "How many of us retire on a night under the impression that all our servants are on the premises, and will continue there till the morning. And how often is it quite the reverse, especially with our men servants, who are wandering to and fro all night, or are quietly esconced in some dark retreat of villany, exposed to all sorts of vices and temptations, alike destructive of their morals and their usefulness. It is thus that some of our best servants become *cast-aways*."[42]

That these meeting places were an open secret to those who wanted to know becomes clear when reading that even Frederick Law Olmsted knew about them when he was just visiting Richmond for a short time. He wrote: "A great many low eating, and, I should think, drinking shops are frequented chiefly by the negroes. Dancing and other amusements are carried on in these at night."[43]

While New Orleans officially allowed free Black people to "give a ball or any other party," when more than ten people attended, "they shall apply to the judge of the Parish [for] his permission." Enslaved people were also allowed to join, under the condition that they obtained a written permit from their owners.[44] With these practices and allowances, New Orleans was the most liberal place for people of African descent. In the other cities, the efforts to keep enslaved and free Black people separated were stronger. The more room there was to mingle, the easier it was for runaway slaves to escape to the city.

In general, White city residents saw Black people as a necessary evil, which meant that they were at times relieved when they did not have to confront them. Not seeking out control over them also meant being able to temporarily ignore their presence and the accompanying fear they harbored toward Black people. In urban clandestine places, camouflaged among other African Americans, fugitive slaves were not necessarily invisible, but rather, in Katherine McKittrick's words, "'imperceptible' social, political, and geographic subject[s]".[45]

Urban Segregation

Despite not being easily recognizable, urban refugees typically tried to avoid Whites. To this end, they depended on the cover of the urban Black population not to raise attention. Their endeavors were facilitated by the social and physical developments of nineteenth-century cities. Distinct from the full-blown, top-down racial segregation of the twentieth century, many studies do not recognize racial segregation as a phenomenon of the antebellum era.[46] In those days, urban segregation was class-based, yet these modes likewise created Black spaces over time.

This was especially visible in Richmond and Baltimore. In the early nineteenth century, free and enslaved Black people generally lived scattered over the cities. As the decades passed, more and more visitors observed not only the poor living conditions of African Americans, but increasingly also the spatial division between Black and White.[47] By mid-century, housing patterns in Baltimore and Richmond were slowly reorganized as Whites who had the money for new homes that met the new, modernized urban standards flocked together in certain areas. For Baltimore, this included the western part of the city or uptown. New luxury houses emerged around the cathedral; on Charles Street; Madison Avenue; Bolton, Hoffman, and Preston Streets; and on Lexington Street near Pearl. Mount Vernon and Bolton Hill were home to the upper classes and their servants (the latter often living in nearby alleys).[48]

White native-born mill workers and industrial workers dwelled close to the mills or wharves to the east (Canton), and the mostly White construction workers of the Baltimore & Ohio Railroad Company lived on Mount Clare in the southwest. Skilled workers had houses in Oldtown, along the Jones Fall, Gay Street, Penn Avenue, or Frederick Road. Black people usually lived apart from White native-born workers, in precarious neighborhoods that also absorbed the recently arrived (mostly Irish and German) immigrants, like Fells Point, the industrial area of Spring Garden, the middle ring, or the perimeter wards. Prior to mid-century, a concentration of Black people could be found in several of the narrow streets that ran north to south, like Happy or Star Alley.[49] (See map 4.1) Runaways were often believed to be in poor areas with significant Black populations. Nineteen-year-old runaway James Harris, with a "very large mouth [and] thick African lips," could have used his private and work-related network to conceal himself in Fells Point, where he had lived prior to his sale. His new owner therefore believed him to be "lurking about that part of the city" in 1842.[50]

Richmond had an inner section occupied by industry and commerce. The James Falls to the southwest of the city powered the ironworks and flour mills while tobacco manufacturers settled in the southeastern part.[51] White people who could afford it moved away from the riverbank and up the hills into neighborhoods on higher ground. From the 1840s on, enslaved and free Black city dwellers increasingly crowded together in the northwest and along Shockoe Creek near the docks, tobacco factories, foundries, and train depots. They were not alone; poor workers of all races and backgrounds lived there.[52] Other lower-class neighborhoods were Oregon Hill, directly above the Tredegar Iron Works; the dock area of Rocketts; and Fulton, Port Mayo, Mount Erin, and Butchertown (a neighborhood of Shockoe Valley). Enslaved tobacco workers who were permitted (or forced) to secure their own boarding lived in brick dwellings in the African American neighborhood of Shockoe Bottom. Free Black people owned or rented shacks in narrow back alleys in neighborhoods such as Bacon Bottom and Jackson Ward.[53]

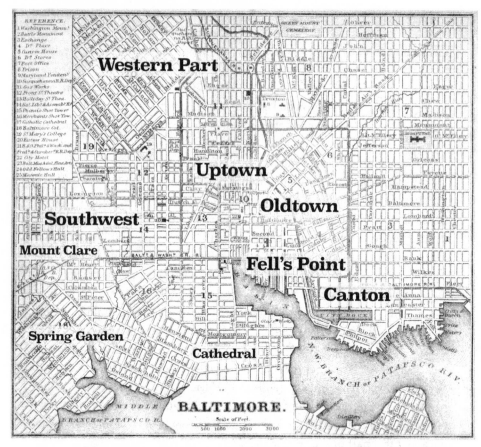

MAP 4.1   Baltimore, 1848. City map showing size and density of Baltimore. Class-based, and partly race-based, residential segregation started to manifest in the nineteenth century. "Baltimore, Maryland 1848," *Appletons' Hand-Book of American Travel* (New York: D. Appleton and Company, 1869), courtesy of the University of Texas Libraries, University of Texas at Austin (https://legacy.lib.utexas.edu/maps/historical/baltimore_1869.jpg).

Wealthy people moving outside of the city center marked the reversal of long-established patterns. Earlier, they had lived within the inner ring while less well-off residents occupied the periphery. With innovations in transportation, these norms were turned upside town. By mid-century, carriages became widely accessible and city dwellers with money could afford to take the new streetcars and omnibuses pulled by horses; the middle classes went with hack drivers. But it was not only changes in transportation that created these new residential dynamics: the industrialization of cities, which included craft

TABLE 4.1 Population of Charleston wards, 1824. Whites, enslaved, and free black residents of Charleston wards.

Ward	Whites	Slaves	"Free Colored"	Total
1	2,322	2,598	**133**	5,053
2	2,157	3,379	303	5,839
3	3,517	3,394	522	7,433
4	4,361	4,481	**650**	9,492

Boldface font highlights entries of special interest that are discussed in the text.
Source: *Charleston Courier*, August 7, 1824.

shops and residences fading from the highly visible main streets, was an even stronger force.[54] Employees and workers had to follow their work sites out of the center because they depended on living within walking distance from them. Because White people moved away from poor and Black people more often than the other way around, the segregated residential patterns that emerged in the late antebellum decades were dictated by White mobility.

These findings suggest the beginnings of residential segregation—not of street blocks and neighborhoods but of smaller sections of a neighborhood or single streets that were marked by wealth, race, ethnicity, and origin of their inhabitants. Free Black people in Charleston were concentrated on Nassau, Henrietta, America, and Line Streets. North of Calhoun (the division between Charleston and Neck), they clustered along Coming and east of Meeting Street.[55] Free African Americans rarely lived south of Calhoun Street, but sometimes enslaved people dominated a street block. For example, in Clifford's Alley, west of King Street between Queen and Clifford, sixty-six slaves and one White person lived in wooden houses.[56]

The racial distribution by residence in Charleston was already uneven in the early decades of the nineteenth century. Table 4.1 shows the population of Charleston's wards divided according to race and legal status in 1824. In Ward Four, for example, 6.9 percent of the residents were free Blacks, compared to 2.6 percent in Ward One. If fugitive slaves went to Ward Four, they blended in with a free population that was in relative numbers 2.7 times larger than in Ward One. Because Black southerners held a minimum of legal rights, at times this even resulted in an advantage for those hiding and those who helped them because police could not always enter premises of free African Americans freely. Police first had to issue search warrants before they entered the house of a free Black woman in 1837 and a free Black man in 1838 who were under the suspicion of harboring runaways in Richmond.[57]

Urban segregation was also linked to a desire to relegate frowned-upon practices and criminalized persons to the margins. Toward mid-century, for instance, increasing restrictions against prostitution tried to outsource this practice to less reputable areas of cities.[58] Bawdy houses and grog shops were natural refuges for runaway slaves because illegal activities often took place there. Newspapers wrote that some sold alcohol without licenses, while others were involved in human trafficking.[59] Brothels also served enslaved men. In a New Orleans case, involving the White brothel keeper Alice D'Arthenny (alias Constance La Farbe), "Recorder Bright found that the charges of keeping a disorderly house or brothel, and of offending against public decency by consorting with the slave Sam, were fully made out."[60]

Likewise in Charleston, involvement of enslaved men in "disorderly houses" was so common that in 1821 the city council ordained that free Black persons and slaves were not allowed any longer to act as musicians in "public Dancing Room[s]."[61] Although White society and authorities regarded interracial sexual contact with horror, the top-down measures to move brothels and prostitution to less well-off parts of the cities worked in the opposite direction. With Black-run businesses particularly targeted, these places turned into more convenient contact points for runaways, who could remain out of view there, unlike in more strictly controlled parts of the city. And indeed, Black women in Baltimore more often managed bawdy houses in back alleys and less frequented streets.[62]

While spatial segregation was not good for business because it was White clients who brought in the money, it did benefit Black people's autonomy. Enslaved city dwellers, too, had advantages. It was not only the hireling system that rendered the daily lives of some bondspeople very close to those of free people but also the fact that some were able to live on their own. While prohibited by law, it was a common practice throughout the urban South. Sylvia, who, at fifty-five, was considerably older than the average fugitive, had enjoyed great autonomy before she was sold. In Charleston, she had been working and living alone, and being forced to change her life and to comply with the close supervision of a new owner could have been the reason for her escape in 1840. The ad read: "She has been in the habit for several years of selling about the streets and lately has been living in the yard No. 9 George street, where she hired a room."[63]

Larger southern cities had two main types of housing for enslaved people. In the first, more common scenario, enslaved servants lived with their owners, and in the second, they had external boarding. When they lived with their owners, they either slept in the same house, in the attic, in a small room, on the floor, or in an outbuilding of a town house. These outbuildings were attached to the back of the master's house and provided maximum supervision of enslaved people. When, however, constructed as a separate building in the rear, for example on top of the kitchen, servants more often had their own entrance, which was usually out of sight from the street. Slaveholders with more than two slaves usually preferred a detached solution if they could afford it.[64]

In 1801, John Francis Delormes claimed that "two of his Negro girls" were "enticed away from him." After offering a reward of $50, he "received information that they were harboured, concealed & locked up in one of the outhouses of George Reid" in Charleston. Delormes "then made application to a Magistrate of the said city who delivered a Search warrant to an Officer to Search the Premises of Said G. Reid in which my property was found locked up in a Room & concealed under a bed." They were sheltered "for nearly two months."[65] Since the runaways were found in the outbuilding, they must have been hidden by an enslaved domestic or laborer of Reid's.

Because urban space was limited and increasingly expensive, proper town houses gradually gave way to multistory buildings in some parts of the cities. Buildings were subdivided into different residences and could contain three separate dwellings on three stories.[66] An architecture that provided degrees of protection from outsiders' views enabled enslaved city dwellers to become accomplices in aiding fugitives from slavery. Mary William, for example, the bondswoman of John G. Cocks in New Orleans, was in October 1853 "arraigned before Recorder Winter, on the charge of having for some time past, secreted and harbored the runaway slave Harrick, the property of C. V Burterbire, at her house in St. Paul street, between Gravier and Perdido streets."[67]

Lucy, "commonly known by the name of *Lucy Bee*," about forty years old, absconded in Charleston from her mistress who lived at 76 Broad Street. The mistress believed her to be "accommodated or secreted by the domestics in some family, or probably may be harbored by free persons of color." Although Lucy was described as looking noticeable ("fat and stout, with broad shoulders, short neck, small hands and feet"), was well known in the city, and "has frequently been seen by her acquaintance," she was already missing for seven weeks when the advertisement was published.[68] Slaveholders knew about the dangers of boarding-out slaves harboring runaways. The *Daily Picayune* wrote in 1859 that slaves in New Orleans, "without going more than a few squares from the residences of their masters, they have, in many instances, found security in the lodging places furnished by those who live under the protection of passes, for months."[69] Some enslaved people made a business out of "renting rooms to other slaves."[70] Slaveholders were torn between the desire for physical distance from Black people and the necessity to control their slaves. Yet, those who did not belong to the most prosperous class regarded their enslaved workers sleeping in the hallway as almost as annoying as the slaves themselves, and pushed them to seek residence elsewhere in the city.[71]

Depending on the location and the price of rent, tenements evolved in the cities where enslaved and free African Americans chose to live among themselves, and Black districts emerged on the margins of the cities or close to industrial and commercial districts. If their dwellings were not multistory buildings, they were small, wooden structures.[72] When census takers came along, it was often unclear to them who lived in these compounds, and often they would simply count them "without recourse to owners"; the names of the masters were not included in the records.[73]

In 1856, segregated housing had become so pronounced in Charleston that its grand jury dedicated a report to it. The jury noted that in what previously had been Neck, there were now "rows of buildings constructed expressly for and rented to slaves and persons of color; in these negro rows as many as fifty to one hundred negros, or persons of color, are sometimes residing, shut out from the public street by a gate, all the buildings having but one common yard, and not a single white person on the premises." This living situation basically violated the prohibition of assembly at all times, the jury complained,[74] a welcome invitation for Black men and women to engage in criminalized activities and with criminalized people, including fugitive slaves.

An Imperfect Social Distance

New Orleans was far less segregated than Richmond. With slavery playing an important role and the intermingling of Whites and mulattoes being stronger there than anywhere else in the United States, emphasis was put on social distance rather than physical separation from dark-skinned free Blacks and slaves. Whites increasingly tried to demarcate themselves and the spaces they inhabited from those occupied by Blacks. Interaction between the two races was socially acceptable only on a master-servant basis; otherwise they essentially lived in two different worlds.

While least pronounced in New Orleans, social distance between people of African descent and Whites expanded throughout the South and elsewhere in the nation. If wealthy Whites had to live in the same cities as Black people and poor Whites, they reasoned, at least they should mark off their living and leisure areas from their undesirable neighbors. As a consequence, free and enslaved Blacks were excluded from taverns, restaurants, hotels, hospitals, and cemeteries. The Richmond Negro Code, for one, determined physical locations like the capitol where "slaves [were] not to Walk or be in."[75] In short, the nineteenth century marked the advent of city planning, which resulted in more structural exclusion of people whom developers sought to keep out of sight. Hand in hand with increased spending of public money on exclusive areas and recreation sites like parks and cemeteries came an unwillingness to support those parts of the city not of interest to the managers of tax money. The unequal division of resources between poorer and wealthier streets, neighborhoods, and wards worsened the living situation for the lower classes. For those who profited from city planning, it was a small step to link the disastrous sanitary conditions in certain parts of the city to the character of the people living there.[76]

The popularity of cities was tempered by a dark side: the generally lower life expectancy compared to rural areas. In nineteenth-century urban America, the larger the city, the higher the mortality. Pollution, unpaved streets, garbage, horse droppings, and dust, waste, and emissions from factories threatened the health of urban residents.[77] Near the Richmond factories, slave housing ranged from "nearly uninhabitable to tolerable, at best," Midori Takagi has found.[78] Frederick Law Olmsted observed during his travels in the South that the city was compactly built between "some considerable hills" and lying among "a dull cloud of bituminous smoke."[79] Free Black and White laborers sometimes lived in worse conditions than the enslaved. Slaveholders wanted to make their slaves and society believe that Black people were worse off in freedom than in slavery, and some reports on the housing situation of free Black people indeed supported this claim.

From the 1830s on, European immigrants diversified the urban populations. Although mainly concentrated in the northern states, those who did migrate south generally went to cities. These dynamics made the social composition of the urban centers more ethnically and religiously diverse. In 1850, Charleston counted a White majority for the first time in its existence, with about 20 percent of its residents being born outside of the United States. In New Orleans, foreign-born residents composed about 40 percent of the city's population.[80] While earlier migrants from the Caribbean, who were often slaveholders, had arrived with money, the majority of the newer immigrants were poor. In the cities, they inhabited the lower-class neighborhoods, where people of African descent also lived.

Charleston, despite its small size, was clearly stratified. In 1838, an ordinance was passed to prevent the erection of wooden buildings in the city. In

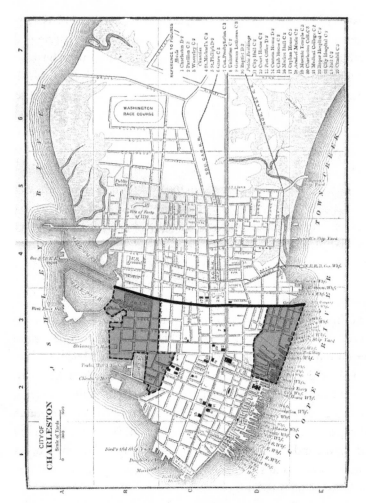

MAP 4.2 Charleston according to the exemptions to the prohibition to erect wooden buildings, 1857. The areas in Charleston where the upper-middle and upper classes resided were strikingly small. Map is based on Charleston 1885, *Appletons' General Guide to the United States and Canada, Part II. Western and Southern States* (New York: D. Appleton and Company, 1885), courtesy of the University of Texas Libraries, University of Texas at Austin.

order to prevent fire, it stipulated that only brick or stone was to be used and the walls had to be of a minimum thickness. Violation of this ordinance called for fees between $500 and $1,000.[81] As a consequence, people of lower socio-economic status could no longer afford to build or buy houses in the city. In 1857, this ordinance was loosened, allowing residents to erect buildings within twenty days of its enactment, and structures were exempt if they were located "south of Calhoun street, and east of that portion of East Bay street lying north of Market street, or to the west of Legare, Savage, Franklin, or Wilson streets, or of that portion of Smith street from Beaufain to Calhoun streets."[82] Map 4.2 shows the areas on the margins of the city where the erection of wooden buildings remained permitted (marked in gray). These were streets were the lower classes lived (Calhoun Street is marked in thick black). It is striking how small the remaining areas are, comprising neighborhoods where the upper middle and upper classes resided, and where city authorities and police had most stake in patrolling and supervising.

Physician Thomas Buckler reported that in Baltimore, families crowded themselves into tenements infested with vermin. Frederick Law Olmsted noted that "very dirty German Jews [...] are thickly set in the narrowest, meanest streets, which seem to be otherwise inhabited mainly by negroes" in Richmond.[83] Public boards of health were formed in American cities to control epidemics such as cholera, typhoid, and diphtheria. Yellow fever and cholera plagues were reported in all cities, but New Orleans was struck hardest, hit by yellow fever epidemics in the 1820s, 1832, 1847, and a most destructive one in 1852, which left thousands of people dead. Although yellow fever, in contrast to cholera, hit White city dwellers more severely than Blacks, the life expectancy of the latter was in general lower, as was the percentage of children born to parents of African descent.[84]

Despite hardening color lines and the entrenchment of White supremacy, people of low socioeconomic standing often mixed. "I am struck with the close cohabitation and association of black and white—negro women are carrying black and white babies together in their arms; black and white children are playing together," reported an astonished Olmsted from Richmond.[85] The urban space facilitated interracial contact. A White man called William Nelson was arrested in Charleston, "Drunk and Rioting with Negroes in Calhoun Street." Because the police could not really believe that a White man would assembly with Black people in this way, his case was "turned over to [the] Magistrate for investigation as to whether Nelson is a white man or not."[86] For the lower classes themselves, however, this interdependence became obvious to many at a young age, as recognizable through a teenage Frederick Douglass trading bread with hungry White children for teaching him to read. As Douglass claimed, they would then console him when he shared his sadness about being a slave, which "used to trouble them."[87]

Evidence of White men and women supporting runaway slaves is plentiful enough to give them a space in this narrative of networking and resistance. When Mary ran off in 1822, the newspaper announcement described her as "very neat in her person." The subscriber claimed to "have lately been informed that Mary is harboured by a White man residing near Rantoles Bridge [South Carolina]."[88] Since Black women were more numerous than men in most southern cities and European immigrants skewed male, it is not surprising that White men and Black women intermingled in the integrated neighborhoods. Traugott Bromme, a German traveler, wrote that poor German immigrants lived disorderly lives in New Orleans and often "fell already in their first summer victim to their own debaucheries." They lived "outside of marriage, or keep negresses of which many have four to five children."[89]

Rarer were relations between White women and enslaved men, although in 1860, officers in Charleston arrested a White woman by the name of Ann Catherine Moore and a "negro boy" called William "who arrived that day [Friday] by the Savannah Railroad from Savannah. They were lodging at a private boarding house in Queen-street. On communicating with Savannah, it was ascertained that the boy had been a runaway for the last five years from his mistress, Mrs. N. RAHN, residing about thirty-five miles from Savannah." Attesting to the much more beneficial contexts and opportunities for interracial couples in New Orleans, the editor informed that "it is supposed that the pair were travelling to 'Dixie's Land,' where they could live with less liability to interruption than at Savannah."[90]

Trying to live "with less liability to interruption" was seemingly also the idea of "a runaway negro and a white woman" in New Orleans in December 1852. They "were last night arrested by the police of the Third District, being found together under the Port Market." The paper reporting this case tried to calm its surely excited readership by assuring them that "such occurrences are very rare."[91] But still, they occurred, and three years later, the media covered the account of two White women who lived "in unlawful connection with a negro Wm. Jackson, who claims to be free but who is believed to be a runaway."[92]

Slaveholders knew that free people could be involved in the disappearance of their slaves and that sometimes these helpers were White. A furious slaveholder set the enormous bounty of $1,000 "for the apprehension and conviction of him who gave my servant boy GEORGE Free Papers, and induced him to quit my service." George's owner inquired about "gentlemen" who were on the same train from Columbia, South Carolina, to Aiken, in which George had traveled with a White man who gave his name as John Tyne. George, now eighteen years old, "had been waiting on the table in Clark's Hotel the last ten years" and was seen in Charleston only a few days after he left Columbia. He was suspected to go to New York or Boston but "a boy answering his description has been seen in Mobile."[93]

Clearly, it was more concerning when a White person aided runaway slaves than when a free Black person did the same. Prince, who "from an indolent habit usually wears a beard upon the upper lip, and a point of the chin," went off in January 1832. In August of the same year, an announcement promised $25 if he was apprehended and taken to the workhouse in Charleston, $50 if harbored by a Black person, and $100 if proven that it was a White person.[94] When Lucy absconded, her slaveholder offered a reward of $50 "on proof of her having been harboured by a responsible person."[95] "Responsible person" meant a White or free Black person who could be held accountable by law.

Sometimes, interracial networks contributed to the aid of runaway slaves. In the case of Betsy and the four-months-pregnant Fanny, both twenty years old, who escaped with two "very fine children," it appears they were aided by a White man. Yet, the runaways were also "suspected to be accompanied by a very tall black Woman, sometimes called Nancy, and sometimes Mary," and her husband Isaac or Henry. Fanny and Betsy were "well known in Charleston. [. . .] Nancy and her husband are believed to be old runaways."[96] White people could support fugitives in ways different from Black people because they could pass them off as their servants. They were able to help them flee, could support them on the run, traffic them, and harbor and employ them at their destinations. However, they could not provide a receiving society for them as a whole. Here, the African American populations were of particular importance.

Church Networks

Social distance between the races extended into the spiritual sphere. Systematically excluded from White society, African Americans organized themselves independently, through ideology, religion, benevolent societies, social spaces, and sometimes schools. Baltimore's Black community established its own religious institutions quite early. There, free African Americans had their own official places of worship since the early nineteenth century. The African Methodist Bethel Society was founded in 1815, and by 1860, there were sixteen Black churches and missions in Baltimore with at least 6,400 registered members who worshiped in their own fashion. This relative autonomy allowed preachers the liberty to interpret the Bible in a way that did justice to Black people's struggles.[97] Family separation and the legal, social, and political shadow of slavery were shared experiences among many Black southerners, both slave and free. Could runaway slaves count on religious support in their fight to resist enslavement? After all, Black communities in different places interacted with each other through churches. The African Methodist Episcopal Church of Baltimore, established in 1816, was connected to the ones in Philadelphia, Charleston, and New Orleans.[98]

Black people who fought against racial persecution and injustice were often affiliated with the church. In the northern states, independent African American churches and societies took a leading role in fighting for Black rights. Institution building was the cornerstone of Black abolitionism and a distinct "black public sphere" gave birth to alternative discourses.[99] Unlike in the North, these alternative currents could hardly have been exhibited publicly in the South. The question of whether Black churches and independent denominations nevertheless helped enslaved southerners in their escapes is therefore difficult to assess.

What is known is that class leaders (of small groups of church members) of the Black Methodists and Baptists in Charleston used church funds to purchase and manumit enslaved people. These practices were discovered in 1815 and the churches were put under White surveillance.[100] In the northern states, Black activists were mostly church members, which points to a connection between Black congregations and abolitionism, which extended into the slaveholding South. *Walker's Appeal*, for example, a pamphlet distributed throughout the American North and South calling for Black resistance, was, when imported south, handed over to Black preachers in port cities.[101] The African American community would likely know about abolitionist networks and individuals, and a fugitive slave asking questions after church services could find the right person to approach.

Whether the resistance efforts of church members indeed extended to aiding fugitive slaves cannot definitively be answered on the basis of archival sources alone. The silence of the archives is unsurprising, given that these institutions and organizations had to keep a very low profile in order to successfully operate. Supporting slave flight, harboring a slave, or using contacts in church networks to assist with slave resistance required secrecy. Under no circumstances would information on these illegal activities have appeared in minutes or other records.

White southerners were watching. Ironically, Whites first forced Blacks out of social spaces, including the religious sphere, and then came to see them as threats because they lost supervision over their activities. Yet, the increasing independence that Black people created in their communities and institutions did not mean that they were left in peace. Churches operated autonomously, but Whites viewed Black religious services with suspicion. Suspicion translated into panic when Black people occasionally decided to stand up against repression. In 1822, the Denmark Vesey conspiracy shook Charleston. Together with another wirepuller called Gullah Jack, Vesey was a member of the African Congregation, which was formed in Charleston and their church built in Hampstead, a suburb of the city. White people did not attend the meetings of the church.[102]

Historiography of the late nineteenth century lamented the suppression of the African Methodist Episcopal Church in Charleston after the discovery of Denmark Vesey's conspiracy because "being an independent ecclesiastical organization, it gave the idea and produced the sentiment of personal freedom and responsibility in the Negro."[103] African American churches indeed offered a separate space for Black people to follow their own agendas and to create a Black counterculture. As historian Gregg Kimball has argued, the labelling of new institutions as "African" gave Black people, regardless of their legal status and place of birth, a feeling of unity.[104]

Nat Turner, who led a rebellion in Virginia in 1831, was involved in the church as a preacher. Although the rebellion was put down after a few days, White Virginians became panicky and passed a law in 1832 prohibiting "slaves, free negroes and mulattoes [. . .] from preaching, exhorting, conducting or holding any assembly or meeting for religious or other purposes." Black Richmonders reported two years later that, as a consequence, "many coloured human beings are interd like brutes, their relatives and friends being unable to procure white Ministers to perform the usual ceremony in the burial of the dead." Capitalizing on the opportunity that was opening up, the petitioners asked for authorizing "free persons of colour, as well as slaves, to perform the ceremony usual on such occasions by white ministers, provided they obtain a License for that purpose from the Pastor of the Church to which [they] respectively belong."[105] It seemed to work. Some twenty years later, Frederick Law Olmsted observed a "negro funeral procession" in the city with six hackney coaches, six well-dressed men on horses, and twenty or thirty men and women. "Among all there was not a white person."[106]

The views of churchgoing Whites toward their Black brethren greatly varied across the South. In Richmond, the First African Baptist Church (FABC) was founded in 1841 as an African American branch of the mixed First Baptist Church, from which Black people were increasingly excluded by White members. The church was located across Broad Street from Capitol Square, from where Black Richmonders were banned.[107] The division into a White and a Black branch had reverberations for Black people that increased their self-confidence and autonomy. Since the Bible taught them that God was omnipotent and omnipresent, Black Baptists could address God directly without the mediation of Whites.[108]

The membership of the FABC in Richmond grew from 2,100 in 1843 to 3,300 in 1860, and the construction of the second, third, and fourth African Baptist churches soon followed.[109] Over time, Black Americans grew more assertive. In 1852, Black Baptists stood up and left the church building while Judge Oneal of South Carolina, a White man, was lecturing on temperance, which apparently displeased them. Oneal "gave offence, by sundry expressions, to the congregation, as was painfully evident by their murmurs, + by their leaving the house in large numbers!!"[110] The increasingly segregated spheres of Blacks and Whites might have been desirable for Whites, but they were even more beneficial for Blacks. It allowed them to form their own parallel society, with organizations and institutions that replaced official jurisdiction and provided safety nets for runaway slaves.

Like all people, runaway slaves depended on a close-knit, supportive social community, not only for their escapes but also for the lives they needed to build afterwards. Likely some of them found community in Richmond's First African Baptist Church. In the minute book of the church, several names appear of persons whose legal status seemed to have been unknown to the institution. In 1848, William Jackson passed away, reported as a free man with a question mark next to the word "free," suggesting that he was passing for free but had no papers to prove it, or that the church otherwise had cause to doubt that he was indeed free. In the following year, the legal status column next to Maria Frances Myers's name, who was baptized that year, was simply left blank—church elders either did not ask about her official situation, or they did not wish to record this information in their registry.[111]

The incomplete information in the church register is suspicious, revealing that church members had unclear or dubious backgrounds. They could have been legally and illegally free women and men, slaves, and very likely also runaways. The boundaries between enslaved, illegal, and free status in the urban South were so blurry that not even the church, whose very existence fueled Black resistance and community, knew about it. How, then, would city authorities know which Black people they found on the streets were free and which were runaway slaves?

Policing

The disarray, anonymity, and dynamism of growing cities constituted beneficial conditions for newcomers to dive into. In 1844, Armstead Meckins ran away in Richmond "on friday night last [and] he has been seen every day since."[112] Even when slaveholders were sure that their runaways had gone to a particular city, they often failed to catch them. Different from rural areas, where privately organized patrols were the norm, in urban spaces, city governments held the claim to maintain law, order, and tidiness.[113] Whereas in the country-side, "the security of the whites" depended "upon the constant, habitual, and instinctive surveillance and authority of all white people over all black," as Frederick Law Olmsted observed,[114] in the urban context, the authorities took on the matter of social control. The increasingly centralized organization and regulation of populations even permeated the practice of slave hiring, which created a vacuum of responsibility filled by a public system.[115]

Runaways, who observed the environments in southern cities, saw that public systems of control were weak because they were unable to accommodate a heterogeneous public. New Orleans' diverse cultural, ethnic, and political composition brought administrative challenges that at some point became seemingly untenable. On the one side stood the Francophone community consisting of New Orleans Creoles and foreign French originating from France, Haiti, and other Francophone places, as well as immigrants from the Caribbean and Latin America. Being united by their Catholic faith, they formed the majority of New Orleans residents until mid-century. Anglophone Americans stood on the other side. Mostly drawn to Louisiana by business endeavors and mainly Protestant, they were the dominating commercial force.[116] In 1836, responding to ongoing ethnic disputes, the city was divided into three separate parts, "granting to the three municipalities the exclusive privilege to pass or have executed all the public laws or regulations within their respective limits."[117] This included policing.

By the early nineteenth century, city guards resembled militias who, in cities with high shares of enslaved residents, were agents of slave control. In the following decades, policing in the United States developed from an informal and communal watch system to a state and local police force system. Yet, due to the division of New Orleans, it still did not have a united organization in the city.[118] The question arises of whether undocumented persons had a harder time because it was easier to efficiently control a smaller, limited space than an entire city, or whether it was beneficial because they could easily slip from one municipality over the demarcation line into the next where the watch of the former was not responsible.

In 1840, the First Municipality reorganized its police and designed a distribution plan according to which the night watch was to patrol the streets of the sector and the suburb Trémé. Map 4.3 shows the First Municipality, located between the Second Municipality on the left and the Third Municipality on the right. Zooming in to the First Municipality (map 4.4) shows the

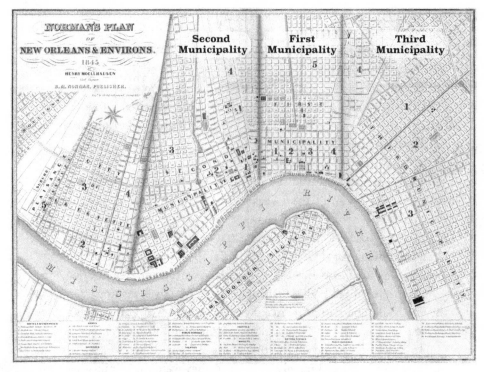

MAP 4.3 New Orleans with three municipalities, 1845. Between 1836 and 1852, the city of New Orleans was divided into three municipalities. Henry Moellhausen, *Norman's plan of New Orleans & environs, 1845*, engraved by Shields & Hammond (New Orleans: B. M. Norman, 1845), Library of Congress Geography and Map Division (https://www.loc.gov /item/98687133/).

patrolling plan of the night watch, with thirty-four privates in the First Municipality up to Rampart Street (marked in thick black and corresponding with today's French Quarter). In the suburb Trémé, north of Rampart Street, the vigilance was more relaxed, with patrolling only taking place along the vertical streets and ending on Villeré or Robertson Street (in one case further up on Roman Street). In Trémé, thirteen watchmen were on duty during the night. The daytime police consisted of ten men for the First Municipality and three for Trémé, of which one remained at the fort and two "scour[ed] the suburb."[119]

This was a relatively well-drafted plan to secure order and to detect possible agitators and in general people who breached the nocturnal curfew—at least on paper. Clandestine people in New Orleans heard and saw that the watchmen were often asleep during their shift.[120] Police work was exhausting. In New Orleans, the shifts usually lasted twelve hours for seven days a

MAP 4.4 First Municipality and Trémé, with patrolling plan of the night watch in dotted lines, 1840. The patrolling plan of the night watch of the First Municipality was thorough, but only on paper and only in the most central part of the city.

week. From 1836 on, the constables were hardly supervised by a higher-ranking officer during their shifts. Men who worked as police for longer than a year were an exception; many did not show up or neglected their duties.[121] Emphasizing this point, a local paper reported that one could walk "at night two miles through the most thickly populated portions of New Orleans without encountering a single watchman, and more especially that this can be done night after night at different hours."[122] Based on the ineffectiveness of the patrol system, the low commitment of watchmen, and the split responsibilities over the city, it was possible for fugitive slaves and other Black people to move about New Orleans day and night.

In 1852, the three municipalities were again consolidated into one city, and the neighboring town of Lafayette was incorporated, too. The Anglo-American contingent had allied with German and Irish immigrants and was now dominating politics.[123] Runaways from slavery remained an integral element of the usual crime patterns of the city, whether divided or not. The police report of New Orleans on a regular December morning informed that Recorder Genois' Court was that day occupied with seventeen cases of vagrancy, disorderly conduct, runaway negroes, and so forth, "which were hustled up by the police last evening." The *Daily Picayune* wrote that "none of them were of sufficient interest to be worth narrating."[124]

With Charleston not establishing its police force until 1852, New Orleans a year later, and Baltimore in 1857, runaways and all other persons living in these cities largely escaped the regulation, watch, and punishment of a centralized municipal police department. Richmond did open a formal law enforcement agency in 1807, but the organization, with few watchmen, was ineffective.[125] Under the watch system, with constables patrolling during the day and night watches operating after sunset, policing institutions were only partly financed by the public and semi-bureaucratic at best. Policemen tended to be either volunteers, fee retainers, or part-time employees without economic security, and the informal watches and constable systems were insufficient to control disorder in the rapidly expanding cities—foremost drunkenness and prostitution, which became uncomfortably visible in the urban public spaces.[126]

Fugitive slaves had the hardest time in Charleston, which commanded the strictest policing system.[127] This was due to its small size and the natural limitations of the peninsula it was built on. Boundary Street was the city's demarcation to Charleston Neck. It was renamed Calhoun Street when Neck was incorporated in 1850. Fortunately, runaways could swerve into this historical hiding place before that time. This was widely known already in the late eighteenth century. "Charleston Neck, by its vicinity to the city, is rendered so extremely convenient a place of refuge for runaway negroes, &c. to commit thefts and robberies both in and out of the city," lamented a local newspaper in 1788.[128] In the nineteenth century, things did not improve for Charlestonians concerned about Neck. In October 1822, enslaved Ben, Glasgow, and Peter ran away from a plantation on the Wateree River in central South Carolina. Two months later, "they were since seen in Charleston Neck, and are supposed to be lurking about the Plantations, 12 to 14 miles on Ashley River, Dorchester Road, Charleston Neck or Charleston."[129]

In 1845, a resident of Neck called for more police regulation there because Charleston's city police were pushing out criminals from the city and into Neck, which was infamous for its "defective organization." He lamented that Neck was "situated in the immediate juxtaposition with a city where an active and vigilant police is ever in operation, and from which all suspicious and mischievous characters are speedily routed out." The problem for White Neck residents was that they did have a night watch but there was no guardhouse in which to store offenders. And so, patrollers usually "immediately punished and discharged" the Black people they encountered.[130] For fugitives who were discovered and rounded up, this often had no long-term consequences.

The importance of suburbs for fugitive slaves can hardly be overestimated. In the antebellum era, Black people moved further outside of the cities' limits. Richmond's western and eastern suburbs were not official parts of the city and it is unlikely that the night watch ever went there. New Orleans' *faubourgs* (suburbs outside the city limits) had a weaker security than the city center. Other southern cities faced similar dynamics. A newspaper reported in June 1845 that "the suburbs of Mobile are said to be infested by large numbers of runaway negroes." This exact wording was used a month later to refer to the situation around Natchez.[131] Police did often not feel responsible for suburbs or more remote neighborhoods because the centers were what concerned those who gave the orders.

Equally beneficial for urban runaways was that they were often not the main preoccupation of city authorities. White residents were more tumultuous than slaves and free Blacks due to riots, gangs, incendiaries, and uproar on election days. City governments were weak and inefficient and failed to regulate their heterogeneous citizenry throughout the country.[132] Additionally, when taking over Louisiana, the Americans not only inherited an ethnically diverse population but also a maroon problem.[133] Spread all around New Orleans, lingering near plantations where they stole food, and occasionally entering the city's suburbs, Louisiana's maroons were usually armed and did not hold back when encountering people who minded their presence. Newspapers made sure that New Orleans residents were aware of them.[134] Compared to maroons, who were a constant threat to the valuable plantation economy, urban runaways appeared much less harmful because they presented a one-time loss for their owners and relied on keeping a low profile and staying out of trouble.

Getting involved in slave flight, moreover, could bring problems for police, for example, when interference occurred against the will of the slaveholder. In Richmond, Billy, a slave of Thomas Massie, was taken up for not having a pass and, according to the police, resisted his arrest and caused a disturbance on the streets. Siding with his bondsman rather than with the police, "Massie said he would sooner believe his man, than the watchmen, who were a set of worthless lazy fellows, who would take up occasionally inoffensive servants, merely to show they did something."[135] Indeed, the owners of slaves and public authorities often collided about the manner in which to handle runaways in the cities. Yet despite all deficiencies, police and night watches did present a danger to fugitives and illegals. Jail ledgers with pages of names of Black men and women arrested for being runaways from slavery bear witness.

Always on Guard

Fugitive slaves had to stay alert. One of the highest risks of discovery was to be recognized by a familiar White person. This happened to Elihu, who legally belonged to William Cochrone from Natchez. When Cochrone's father died of cholera while on a trip with Elihu to Albany, Louisiana, the bondsman "availed himself of the opportunity to gain his freedom. About four months since he shipped on board the Adrian as a cook, since which time he has been sailing to this port [Natchez], where, through a friend of his master, he was discovered and caused to be arrested."[136] In 1830, while living in the area of Baltimore after having run away, Charles Ball was recognized by his former mistress's younger brother and recaptured.[137]

Over time, more and more runaways appeared to prefer hiding out with free Blacks, enslaved acquaintances, or other more distant nodes in their networks rather than with family members. Masters knew about the family situations of their slaves, as often did relatives, White business partners, and neighbors, who would not know every field hand but were familiar with those bondspeople who were the most mobile. Slaveowners had information about their slaves' kinship ties in cities, knew their names, and often even places and street names where runaways might try to hide. Precisely for this reason, the closest relatives were not always the best choice to seek permanent refuge with because masters would know where to look. James, whose owner knew that his mother lived at the cotton factory on the canal in Richmond, believed him to be there in 1840, and he was caught two weeks later.[138] Professional networks became more relevant and may over time even have outstripped the importance of kinship ties in providing refuge.

The dangers inherent in urban flight stemmed from the fact that runaway slaves hid among the very people who were the targets of social control. Men, and to lesser extent women, of African descent were often arrested for offenses like disturbing the peace or vagrancy. Black Americans became criminalized for actions that did not qualify as offenses for White people. Called "status offense," this phenomenon refers to crimes that could only be committed by persons of a certain legal status, for instance, slaves or people of African descent.[139] The state of Virginia designed over seventy capital crimes only Black people could commit. Besides the laws that allowed for the enslavement of Black people who moved into a state or returned from a trip outside of a state, free African Americans could be sold into slavery for crimes for which Whites were punished significantly less harshly. Very common was the crime of insolence toward White people that only people of African descent could commit.[140] When the spaces of Whites and Blacks overlapped, it was up to the Black person to move aside. Frederick Law Olmsted gave an account of this when he observed Black Richmonders literally giving way to Whites.[141]

Those in power implied that crime and disorderly conduct were the outcomes of a "biologically criminal, riotous, and intemperate group of persons located at the base of society," as sociologist Robert Lundman has claimed, with alcohol consumption being the trigger of these troublesome conducts. This "dangerous class" consisted of lower-class Whites, European immigrants, and free African Americans, and was therefore easy to identify.[142] One of the worst-case scenarios was to have "white men, free men of color and slaves [. . .] play together at cards, or at any other game." This got punished draconically in New Orleans.[143] Under no circumstances did slaveholders and defenders of slavery want to create the impression that slaves could be part of the drunk and ill-tempered underclass that threatened the public order in the cities. Drunk runaway slaves on the streets, as reported by the press, could not be tolerated.[144]

Yet, visibly inebriated runaways were very exceptional. Under normal circumstances, they held a strong interest in maintaining low profiles and sought to avoid police because the risk of arrest was strong, even when they were not explicitly targeted.[145] And so, while runaways did everything they could to remain undetected, the Charleston police was busy picking up drunken White men and drunken slaves from the streets, both of whom were more numerous than sober runaways.[146] Fugitives knew that causing attention, like being out at night, could lead to discovery. In 1856, Charles, a slave to Mr. Barker, was arrested in Charleston at nearly midnight.[147] Another bondsman, Moses, was found "Drunk on East bay & Tradd Street." He must have raised attention since he was taken up half an hour before curfew.[148] Likewise, a great many runaways were captured either early in the morning or at night close to curfew, making these two times of the day the riskiest to be outside. If possible, many Black Americans adapted their behavior. The hostility of White law and the undocumented status of many made them cautious when being in the streets. Those illegally free had to keep their heads down and live an unsuspicious life.

An unassuming profile was essential to maintain before all people who were not within a runaway's inner circle of allies. Historian Anthony Kaye has argued that runaways were suspicious of other slaves, and vice versa, and that solidarity was unreliable.[149] Although betrayal appears to have been less frequent in cities than in the countryside, it also happened that urban fugitives were betrayed by Black people, whether free or enslaved. Mary, a runaway from South Carolina, returned to Charleston from where she was sold in 1824. In Charleston, she lived with a White woman and was reported to the authorities by a Black woman.[150] Likewise, Lucy or Lucy Bee lived at least seven weeks as a runaway, a time during which she "has frequently been seen by her acquaintance" who also must have reported her to her mistress.[151] Outside New Orleans, a light-skinned Black man called Bambou was passing for free and cutting wood together with some maroons. Alexis Bougny, a free Black man, denounced them to the authorities and Bambou was taken up and jailed.[152]

These events speak to the ambivalence that could reside in Black communities. Besides personal motives like jealousy, rewards, fear, or job competition, cities housed an emerging Black middle class that was critical of gambling, drinking, and lower-class activities easily perceived as criminality. The First African Baptist Church in Richmond, for instance, also took on the function of social control and replaced official jurisdiction when the matter was about minor offenses. Robert Johnson was summoned to answer a charge on gambling, Peter Robinson and Ned Harris were excluded for adultery, and William and Wellington Hawkins were charged with visiting a "low house when dancing was going on," as were two other male members.[153] This self-policing was another challenge for runaway slaves to navigate.

The criminalization of Black Americans and illegal residents was ironic because they very likely committed fewer crimes than Whites did.[154] Yet, they were more often arrested for minor offenses, unlawful acts that counted only for Black people, and they were more readily found guilty. Historian James Campbell has demonstrated that in Richmond, slaves were taken into custody more than twice as often as Whites, and free Blacks twice as often as slaves in the 1850s.[155] In Baltimore, a free Black man was sold to a Georgia trader for theft. His legal counsel described the situation: "We know [...] that some men are so prejudiced ag[ain]st people of colour so that they are ready to lay hold of the <u>slightest</u> evidence ag[ain]st them and convict when outhg not to be convicted."[156]

In a few cases, it emerged at trial that free Black culprits had in reality a different legal status than assumed and were actually runaways. Because their disguises were successful, they received sentences for free Black people.. Hetty, for instance, escaped her slaveholder around the turn of the nineteenth century, went to Baltimore, passed for free, and was years later convicted of theft, for which she was sent to the workhouse for eighteen months.[157] In 1824, Maria Dickson aka Charity Riggs was tried and convicted as a free Black woman for stealing bedding, china, and muslin, and sent to the penitentiary of Maryland. Three years later, her owner John Chambers proved with the help of a witness that Dickson was his absconded bondswoman.[158]

Free Black Americans were legally discriminated against and criminalized for a variety of behaviors and activities. Being a visible contradiction to the justification of slavery as well as a constant—active and passive—enticement for bondspeople to break out of enslavement, they found themselves the targets of continuous rejection and suspicion. In the late 1830s or early 1840s, for example, the dances at Congo Square in New Orleans ended or became strictly regulated, which severely curtailed the freedom of assembly and movement available to the city's free and enslaved Black population. In 1845, a visitor recalled the Congo Square as "the place where the negroes, in olden times, were accustomed to meet to while away the cares of servitude,"[159] implying that these events belonged to the past. A newspaper article of the same year, however, reported that "thousands of negroes" congregated there the previous Sunday because a couple of weeks prior "an ordinance was passed restoring to them their ancient privilege of resorting thither, and thither they now repair in countless throngs."[160] Probably, the Sunday activities were continued with irregular frequency until 1862, albeit under the supervision of police.[161]

IT WAS NOT ONLY PEOPLE of African descent who consciously crafted spaces for runaways to navigate; Whites also inadvertently contributed to this. Indeed, many different players and dynamics were involved in the creation of hospitable spaces: the negligence of authorities, the solidarity of Black people, and the rhythms of urban development. Fugitive slaves sought shelter in all those places where Black people were living, and moved within all the spaces where Black people were moving. Through the right information, allies, and knowledge, they learned how to navigate Black spaces in their cities of refuge. They lived within Black communities, formed social ties with

Black people, and went to Black churches, where they were married and buried. Thanks to increasing spatial and social segregation, thousands of illegal city dwellers could remain in their own circles with basic services provided by the lower classes. There, they could live without being detected.

Over time, the legislative framework as well as the supervision in cities grew tighter. In 1859, the pastor of the FABC in Richmond "complained that often of late the deacons were absent from the public worship + it was told that in consequence of increased stringency in police regulations it was dangerous to attend to any business of the church at night."[162] After every real or perceived threat to White dominance, legislation became stricter. It mostly affected the assembly of Black southerners, including their worship, burials, and social activities. Ironically, more control from above translated into less control from within as White people increasingly retrenched from Black people and the spaces they inhabited.

The limitations faced by the free Black communities and everybody who joined them were a severe setback with regard to the lives runaway slaves could find in southern cities. As the illegal status of so many Black city residents backfired, collective control, illegalization, and criminalization gave beacons of refuge a bitter aftertaste.

CHAPTER FIVE

Finding Work, Remaining Poor

The lives of fugitive slaves in the cities across the South did not only take place in clandestine social gatherings, segregated churches, and after dark. Fugitives needed to work to survive, and if the cities to where they escaped could not provide access to employment, they were not long-term refuge options. But where did they find work? After all, they had occupations before leaving slavery and many were skilled and highly mobile. The best-case scenario for men and women would have been to be able to capitalize on their skills acquired under slavery. However, in antebellum cities, finding a job that was tied to one's specific occupational expertise was only in very exceptional cases feasible.

Runaways were aware of this even before they decided to make a bid for freedom. Thanks to their mobility and their broad social networks, they were informed about the conditions and opportunities in the cities. Many of those who later fled to Baltimore, Richmond, Charleston, and New Orleans had already been there and had firsthand knowledge about the landscape of work. Why could they in most cases not make use of their often advanced skill sets, and what kind of work could they really hope for?

Antebellum urban labor markets were coded by race and legal status. This had consequences for fugitives from slavery, who, being Black and undocumented, were adversely affected by both codes. Women were especially impeded in their search for economic independence by a strong division of urban labor by gender. And so, fugitives encountered an array of obstacles to finding a job that corresponded to their skills. When they arrived in a city, they had to be able to decipher coded working areas and worksites in order to navigate the spaces that the labor markets offered. These codes were dynamic and developed over time, generally to the disadvantage of people of African descent. Yet, fugitives seemed to have an understanding of where to work to earn enough money to survive and remain anonymous in the city.

Besides the economic position of free Black Americans, which was generally worsening, the fugitives' presence in the labor markets worked to their further disadvantage despite being facilitated in the first place by their solidarity and the possibility to camouflage among them. Free African Americans forfeited even more of their already severely restricted leeway by counting among their group large parts of illegal and, hence, powerless workers. Due to legal restrictions and discrimination, Black workers had to toil harder and, in competition with lower-class Whites and European immigrants, accept lower remuneration. This kept the overall wages low and provided capitalist employers with the cheap workforce they wanted.

The Racial Coding of Labor

The volume of the runaway population in southern cities depended on the relative and absolute size of the free and unfree Black population and on the opportunities the labor market offered. Since the majority of absconders attempted to pass as free persons in the South, they aimed to find work in those occupational sectors in which free Black Americans were represented. Generally speaking, in terms of artisan skills and White competition, employment prospects for free Black men were better in the Upper South than in the northern states, and superior in the Lower South to the Upper South.[1]

Looking more closely, race organized labor differently from place to place. Whether an occupation was coded White or Black depended on many factors, including demography and customs. In most southern cities, the lives of free Black people were interwoven with urban slavery. This overlap occurred on social, economic, and professional levels since Black people shared certain jobs and professions that—varying from place to place as well as over time—were regarded as suitable only for them. Deprecatingly labeled "nigger work," many of these jobs were carried out by both free and enslaved Black people. Most of them comprised menial, servile, dirty, or distasteful occupations and Black people on average received less salary than Whites; barbering and butchering are examples.[2]

Historian Ira Berlin has argued that while Black-coded work reinforced damaging racial hierarchies, it could also offer job protection for Black people, especially in those regions where slavery was strongest because it discouraged White people from competing with them for these undesirable jobs. Consequently the differences between skilled workers of African descent in the Upper South, where slavery was weaker, and the Lower South, where it was stronger, were remarkable. One-third of Richmond's free Black men were skilled in 1860, compared to almost 80 percent in Charleston, where they composed a fourth of the city's carpenters, 40 percent of its tailors, and three-quarters of millwrights.[3] Additional large numbers of free Black men worked as painters, barbers, butchers, bricklayers, shoemakers, and blacksmiths.[4] People of African descent with the highest economic standing were in Louisiana.[5] Essentially, New Orleans was the only American soil that provided economic opportunities for people of African descent.

The geography of Black occupations in southern cities dictated the economic integration within their borders. Seamstressing, for instance, was a job for Black women in Charleston but not in Baltimore.[6] Tailoring was a male Black occupation in Charleston, but not in Richmond.[7] Because they did not want to raise attention, prospective fugitives who worked in sectors where Black people were overrepresented had an easier time fitting in after their escape. Those who formerly engaged in occupations where their skin color was conspicuous might have been advised to switch jobs. If an enslaved tailor from Charleston decided to escape to Richmond and start a new life there, he might want to consider employment as a factory worker instead, where there were higher concentrations of Black workers.

In Richmond, skills in construction, shoemaking, carpentering, plastering, and barbering were in high demand.[8] A runaway trained in one or more of these trades who could convincingly pass as a free man could find a decent job in this city. After all, it was the human capacities of enslaved people's bodies and minds that made them valuable to their owners, and many of the professional skills they possessed were also wanted elsewhere. In 1836, the Richmond police were informed that "Mr Benjamin Wallers man Humphry runaway from Mr Thomas Mayberry of Rockbridge County whom he was hired to this year." Humphry, besides being a hired slave and a "good coarse Shoe maker," also had networks with free Black people in the city: "His wifes father lives in Richmond[,] a free man of colour name[d] Jonathan."[9] Humphry possessed the skills to find employment, the experience of mobility as a hired slave, and personal contacts to seek support.

The factories in Richmond were even better places to look for a job. Labor was always in high demand and employers did not seem to care where it came from or what the status of their workers was. Richmond's focus on production and manufacturing attracted large numbers of free and enslaved men to the booming city. Half of the Black male workforce worked in factories such as paper mills, ironworks, flour mills, and tobacco manufactories on the eve of the Civil War. Tobacco was a labor-intensive business that relied on a variety of workers with differing skills. Besides tobacco factories, there were numerous warehouses where tobacco was lodged before export. In 1820, 760 people worked in 20 tobacco manufactories; in 1850, 1,400 people were employed in 19 factories. During the 1850s, both the number of manufactories and laborers who worked in them rose nearly threefold, with 80 percent of people working in tobacco being enslaved men.[10]

In ironmaking, a large industrial sector in Richmond, blacksmiths were constantly needed.[11] Enslaved Billy likely had promising employment prospects when he escaped from his owner Jeremiah Hoopers in King William County in 1835. Having "a Scar on the Side of his neck produced by the cut of an ax & a good Blacksmith by trade said man is Suspected to be about Richmond."[12] The fact that subscribers felt the need to include this information in the search notice demonstrates that they reckoned with the possibility that fugitives would indeed try to apply their skills in the cities to which they escaped. If Billy found employment, he would be able to make a decent living as a blacksmith.

That being said, race and legal status tended to trump skill set, although the importance attributed to those factors often varied according to a particular work site or individual employer. The famous Tredegar Iron Works in Richmond was one of the city's largest employers and expanded in the 1850s to supply hardware to railroads and mills in Cuba. In the early 1840s, White artisans dominated the factory landscape, and Billy would not have had a chance at employment if he sought it in there. His chances would likewise remain slim later, when Tredegar's manager Joseph Anderson began experimenting with enslaved labor, because he meticulously monitored his staff at all times.[13]

Typically, fugitives had to carefully weigh the risks of pursuing a particular job and how employment in any given industry might affect remuneration, visibility, and mobility. In South Carolina, free Black people were very urban with a focus on artisanal occupations.[14] It is unlikely, though, that highly skilled runaway slaves in Charleston attempted to find employment as barbers, blacksmiths, or carpenters because people working in these trades often operated their own workshops and depended on White customers for business. Charleston's free Black community was so small and the number of those in skilled jobs was even smaller so that every newcomer trying to integrate there would have attracted attention, although the level of risk depended on the distance from one's master and the reach of the latter's network.

Seabourn, who spoke French and English, is also a case in point. His owner, H. Stackhouse from Tchoupitoulas Street, New Orleans, offered $100 for his arrest in 1848 and announced that "he is supposed to be across the Lake or in the vicinity of Pass Manchac cutting wood." Believing to know the behavior of his slave, Stackhouse informed the readers of the paper that Seabourn "is somewhat of a circus actor, and when a little tired of work will no doubt attempt to pass himself off as a circus performer." Apparently, the slaveholder was wrong and Seabourn resisted the temptation of earning quick money by performing for an audience. Five years later, Seabourn was still at large: "He is somewhat of a circus actor," claimed the ad, sticking to the same strategy to find him, "by which he may easily be detected as he is always showing his gymnastic qualifications."[15] Yet, it is likely that Seabourn never exposed himself this way.

Self-hired slaves, free Blacks, and undocumented men and women passing as one or the other had to stay alert and flexible to make ends meet and to adapt their strategies to the changing surroundings. Work was, moreover, not steady for most people. When laboring as a slave in the shipyards of Norfolk as a caulker, there was not always work for George Teamoh and he took on a variety of other jobs aside: "When not in their [the shipyard owners'] service, I was found at the common labor of carrying grain, lading and unlading ships freighting Rail Road iron, and, perhaps there is no species of labor, such as may be reckoned in the catalogue of Norfolk's history but I have been engaged at."[16] Following every opportunity that opened up could mean the difference between being able to pay the rent or not.

The casual sectors, where one would not know today if they were employed again tomorrow, met runaway slaves' need for wages by offering them low-level employment. These jobs did not correspond to the profile of often highly mobile and experienced runaways.[17] Runaway slaves migrating to southern cities were aware of the opportunities the labor market offered and poorly paid jobs were almost always available, especially in port cities beginning in the 1820s. From that time on, demand for laborers for the construction of roads, canals, houses, and ships, and for dock work grew extensively due to increasing commercial and trading activities.[18] Stepney from Columbia, who had been absent for at least eight months when the ad was placed in 1820, was "of a smiling countenance," and could have made it as a bricklayer in Charleston, his owner believed.[19] This was also an option for those who escaped in the Upper South. Baltimore, the fastest-growing city featured in this book, had approximately 600 houses built per year in the 1830s; in 1851, it was 2,000. The 1850 census registered 1,400 brickmakers in the city of Baltimore and Baltimore County, most of them of African descent.[20]

With high urbanization rates and a decline in the relative demand for skilled work, the demand for menial and unskilled labor soared. New urban residents needed houses in which to live, clothes to wear, and food to consume. Streets had to be cleaned and maintained, dikes repaired, new canals dug, and rail tracks placed. Flexible, dilative labor allowed employers to hire and fire workers on short notice, according to their daily needs. Dock

FIGURE 5.1 Dock work in New Orleans, 1853. Southern ports were busy and stevedores were always ready to load and unload incoming and outgoing ships. Hippolyte Victor Valentin Sebron, "Bateaux á Vapeur Geant, la Nouvelle-Orléans 1853," oil on canvas, 58 inches x 82 inches, courtesy of Newcomb Art Museum of Tulane University, Gift of D. H. Holmes Company.

workers and stevedores, for instance, could be hired the minute a vessel got into port. The challenge for refugees was to read the landscape of labor to decode the particular permutations of race and legal status in a given city (see figure 5.1).

The seasonal job market in the Lower South also offered opportunities for runaway slaves. Hundreds of White laborers from the North migrated south for the winter months and departed again in spring, leaving vacant jobs behind them ready to be filled by Black workers. In New Orleans, Whites fled the city during the summer months when residents tended to fall ill with yellow fever, and fugitives who were familiar with this cycle knew that jobs were likely to be found then. In the spring and fall, Virginia slaveholders often hired their bondspeople out to Richmond and other cities to work in industries located there.[21] Conversely, this also meant that in some months of the year, competition was particularly dire. Economic fluctuations also determined job availability and migration patterns. After the crisis of 1857, for example, the movement of unemployed workers from the North to the South soared.[22] This made life harder for the lower classes, and harder still for the Black lower classes.

Although many jobs were coded Black, the large share of White laborers meant that manual and menial occupations were often not limited to people of a specific racial group. In fact, most of these jobs were carried out by Whites, simply because they came to be more numerous in many cities, including Baltimore.[23] In railroad construction Black people sometimes worked alongside Whites because it was more efficient to employ free Black and White workers than slaves.[24] In the event of accidental death, employers did not have to reimburse owners for loss of property, and because the death tolls were relatively high, slaveholders were discouraged from hiring their slaves out to the railroads, which were desperate for labor.[25] This opened up spaces for fugitive slaves in need of work. In fact, most industries in the South, including the lumbering, mining, and salt industries, were of an extractive nature and therefore located outside of city centers. This made it even more challenging to satisfy the high labor demands.[26] In Virginia, the press reported on a railroad worker named Quintus or Terry "who has lived here for four years without a register, stated that he was employed by the Central Railroad Company."[27] Whether Quintus was residing illegally in the state as a free Black or a runaway is unclear, but his case illustrates that it was perfectly possible for any group of illegals to find work without showing any sort of register or freedom papers. Work sites that were too dangerous for slaves were an option for runaways.

Tobacconists in Richmond, railroaders in Baltimore, and other industrialists and employers in Charleston and New Orleans were first and foremost businessmen. Their goal was to gather enough workers to make their businesses run and to pay them as little as possible to gain the highest profits. They knowingly employed illegal Black residents and they did not pay attention to whether some of their employees were actually runaway slaves. It is likely that some might have taken advantage of the vulnerable situation of their illegal employees to exploit them even more. Others simply did not want to know. Turning a blind eye was the most common and helpful support for them.

How to Find Work

The racial coding of certain occupations structured the search for work, but it does not illustrate what people *did* to procure employment. In the majority of cases, the subtleties about *how* to find work are lost because they do not show up in historical records. Seth Rockman, in an attempt to reconstruct hiring processes in Baltimore, has speculated that information was obtained through observation and informal communication.[28]

Early January was usually the time when self-hired bondsmen and -women roamed the streets of southern cities looking for contracts for the new year. Around Christmas and well into January, manufacturers closed businesses, and free and enslaved workers were increasingly found on the streets, both celebrating their days off and negotiating the terms for the following year. This was a welcome opportunity for fugitive slaves to blend in with the Black community and to establish important business connections. Robert Russell, a British visitor, observed this in the mid-1850s, stating that "Richmond was at this time literally swarming with negroes, who were standing in crowds at the corners of the streets in different parts of the town."[29]

When looking for work, runaways had to be careful to avoid detection. A convincing story and other people to back it up were fundamental prerequisites. While January was the most convenient time to blend in with the job-seeking crowd, it was not the only time that that runaways could find work. Many cities contained specific places where day laborers gathered to wait for recruitment. These spots could be ordained by the municipal government or developed organically. This was also connected to the organization of slave hire. New Orleans and Charleston, for example, set clear rules regarding the hiring of unskilled slaves, including places where they could go to get hired by the day, the daily lengths of the service, and sometimes the wages.[30] In Baltimore and Richmond, by contrast, slave hire was less regulated by city authorities, and instead occurred through private negotiations, also involving brokers.[31]

Fugitives in search of work understood where to go to seek work and how to avoid detection. After fleeing enslavement, James Matthews went to Charleston. Being able to read the racial and regulatory landscape of labor in Charleston, he included detailed information in his autobiographical account on how finding employment as an enslaved laborer worked: "I went down to the stevedore's stand and waited there with the rest of the hands to get work. By and by a stevedore came along and asked if I wanted work. I told him yes. He said come along, and I followed him on to the wharf, and worked with a good many others in stowing away cotton in a vessel."[32]

Whatever they decided to do, most illegal workers—fugitive or otherwise—needed the help of others to find work. Historian Calvin Schermerhorn's research sheds much light on how enslaved people operated as networkers, driven by their need for patrons. While Schermerhorn focuses on White supporters, urban fugitive slaves built similar networks based on their reliance on free Black supporters not just for shelter but to create pathways for them to employment. Social networks provided access to security, goods, information, allies, and even status, and reputation as a reliable worker was useful to get frequently hired.[33] Free people of African descent played a distinct role in these networks. Not only did they have jobs in which they could lobby for the inclusion of a newcomer, free Blacks offered daily services like food and accommodation to enslaved workers.

Like Matthews, John Andrew Johnson first fled to Charleston before leaving for the North on a vessel. His account on laboring in the city is similar: "I joined a gang of negroes working on the wharfs, and received a dollar-and-a-quarter per day, without arousing any suspicion."[34] Apparently, it was a feasible endeavor to go to the docks and activate the sympathies of other Black men by talking to them. This must have happened regularly as petitions from rural slaveholders lamented that their runaways were hired in Charleston to load vessels at night.[35]

Evidence suggests that many men indeed attempted to work as common laborers. To succeed, they needed information about the internal infrastructure of Black work and about strategic locations. George Teamoh, an enslaved man from Norfolk, Virginia, wrote in his autobiography that in 1853, his wife, Sallie, was brought to Richmond together with their youngest child and stored in the slave pen until they were sold. Teamoh wrote his own pass and went to visit them. Since he intended to "remain a few weeks," he had to find a job, which apparently was not a problem: "I sought, and found employment during a few days," Teamoh wrote, and he added that he started working at a dockyard at the Richmond Basin as a common laborer.[36] Working on the docks was a frequent occurrence that connected the experiences of fugitive men in all four cities. People usually knew that these were the places where casual work was to be found. When they were in Baltimore, they went to the harbor; in Richmond to the docks on the James River where the Basin was one of the major loading stations; in Charleston to the port in the east; and in New Orleans to the levee at the Mississippi River.

The New Orleans levee was an active construction project that needed maintenance all year long and the demand for laborers never slowed, which was very convenient for Black men who needed work. Enslaved Jim, twenty-eight years of age, "stout and muscular, with sullen expression of countenance," was in October 1855 absent from his owner (which was a firm) in New Orleans for already four months. "The negro was seen in the lower parts of the city on Saturday and Sunday last, and is no doubt lurking about the city," read the advertisement, and that he "has been seen twice on the Levee during the last month."[37] The levee itself also functioned as a recruitment site and it was common for captains to send out mates or stewards to fill their crews with men laboring on the New Orleans levee, among them many runaways.[38]

Terence was a New Orleans local who in May 1850 was "taken into custody" together with Jackson and William, "for working by the day on the levee without badges." While Jackson and William were in all likelihood hired-out enslaved men, announced the paper, Terence was "supposed to be a runaway." Terrence legally belonged to Mr. Duplantier, a tobacco inspector, who resided on 33 Dauphine Street in New Orleans.[39] There is no information about what kind of work Terence did for Duplantier but it appears that once he stopped laboring for him, he pursued work as a common laborer. Jim and Terence also demonstrate that not all urban fugitives covered a vast physical distance when they escaped. Some simply decided to break ties with their legal owners. When they escaped from their masters and stayed in the same city, they could make use of their existing networks and judge the labor market based on their own firsthand experiences. At the same time, there were considerable dangers involved, such as the risk of being recognized by someone who would report to one's owner.

Black people that worked for Whites in the cities often coordinated additional labor on their behalf, serving in effect as subcontractors for their owners. For example, enslaved artisans could hire other workers for legwork if needed, and enslaved house servants could hire artisans for repairs or other services around the house. White mechanics in Charleston complained about the power of enslaved domestic workers to hand jobs to mechanics and craftsmen on behalf of their owners: "Many of the most opulent Inhabitants of Charleston, when they have any work to be done, do not send it themselves, but leave it to their Domestics to employ what Workmen they please."[40] Through this system, enslaved city dwellers could hire runaways without the knowledge of slaveholders.

Not all free Black Americans, however, were willing to support urban fugitives in their search for work, especially when it pertained to economic positions that had taken years to achieve or were generations in the making. Free Black artisans, for one, particularly in a community as small as the one in Charleston, would have resented an intrusion by newcomers who would compete with their vested jobs. This does not mean that free Black Charlestonians refrained from hiring fugitive themselves, for they could profit from cheap labor. In 1854, a fugitive man with an unknown occupation was discovered together with a runaway carpenter (from a different owner), both employed by the same free Black man in Charleston. In the same year, a woman and her two children, who had escaped three years prior, were captured by two police officers "whilst in the yard + employment of a free Mulatto woman."[41] Just as White employers did, some members of the free Black population capitalized on the vulnerable situation of undocumented workers.

Gendered Spaces

Urban work spaces were gendered spaces. While a considerable level of work was open to Black women in cities, there was not much choice because options for women were finite and few.[42] In southern cities, Black women labored as laundresses, cooks, domestic servants, housekeepers, and peddlers.[43] In Charleston, they worked as market women, seamstresses, and to lesser extent bakers, pastry cooks, and midwives.[44] Significantly smaller numbers of female runaways appear in the official jail records of southern cities, which reflects the overall trend of more men fleeing slavery and fewer women being apprehended. In line with the general demographic trends of the runaway population, women gravitated to the cities in lower numbers because their chances to secure economic mobility were heavily curtailed by their race, their gender, and their unfree status.

Enslaved women were lower skilled than men but some possessed skills or found work that could yield an acceptable income, and despite the limited opportunities for women to make money, at times female runaways were able to work in a "good" sector. In Charleston, for instance, Amelia or Anne, twenty-four years of age, was a mantua maker (an overgown worn by women) by trade and her owner knew that she was engaged in that capacity after her escape: "She works for respectable families about the city, and says she is free," the ad informed. "She has been absent about two years, and was seen in King street last week."[45] King Street was one of the most affluent streets in the city, and the fact that Amelia frequented the upper classes of Charleston points to very high skills that no doubt attracted attention. The escape of Linda, "a tall thin mustee, well looking," was advertised in Charleston in 1859: "When last heard of she was acting as a stewardess on board of a steamer from this place. She has been out about three years, and passes herself for free."[46] Linda's example was very rare for female runaways; most waterworkers were men.

The aspiration to find a decent job also had a long-term component to it. Fugitive slaves were illegal city dwellers, yet it is likely that some hoped to legalize their status and to modestly improve their economic position. Life was strenuous in the cities but it also offered hope to Black people. Through hard work and saving it was possible for some to acquire modest forms of property, which was the foundation for upward mobility in the nineteenth century.[47]

Poverty rendered people vulnerable, while owning land, real estate, and commodities (or other human beings) partly relieved property holders from the negative effects of racial and gender discrimination.[48]

Escaped women had better chances than men to avoid detection. Not only did African American women outnumber men in most southern cities (with Richmond the exception), which increased their protection, men tended to work outside, on the streets and harbors, and in groups, which could jeopardize their cover. The lesser visibility of working women helps explain the much lower numbers of female runaways in local jails. Martha, originally from Richmond, was an enslaved washer, ironer, and cook when she fled her owners in Charleston in 1844. She was believed to "seek employment in that capacity,"[49] a capacity that implied that she would be working indoors or in backyards rather than being exposed on the streets. In fact, many refugee women tried to find work as domestic servants. It was not a profession tied to specific skills but it did require experience and references who would vouch for a runaway or an undocumented person, which furnished them with a degree of protection.[50] A cousin, friend, or more distant acquaintance who gave recommendations and put fugitives in touch with employers was fundamental. Women forged these ties in kitchens, back alleys, and markets.

The nature of domestic work was oppressive, with long hours, but the wages were usually constant and the work did not fluctuate seasonally.[51] Domestic work was one of the only options for women to earn a decent income. In Charleston, they made around $8 per week.[52] On the one hand, domestic servants were more exposed to the risk of being detected due to their physical closeness to their usually White employers. This happened to Milly, who was "supposed to be in Richmond," according to a newspaper, where she had been hired in the household of one Fleming Griffiths. She fled and was suspected of hiring herself to another employer as a free woman.[53] On the other hand, the private sphere they worked in also provided runaways with a certain degree of protection, since their work was performed mostly behind closed doors rather than out in public spaces and their employers were unlikely to turn them over to the authorities. In 1850, an editor of the *Charleston Courier* lamented the shortage of domestic slaves for families: "Nothing is more difficult than getting any servant, and nothing is more impossible than getting *a good one*."[54] Once a family found a trustworthy servant to work and live in their midst, they would not let her go if they suspected that she could not prove her free status. Besides, employing a runaway slave gave employers more power in an already uneven relation.

Like their male counterparts, female runaways matched their expectations and strategies to what met them at their destinations. They knew that most jobs were poorly remunerated except domestic and related services like cooking, and that they most likely would stay below subsistence level with what they earned. If they did not have acquaintances in strategic positions to vouch for them, laundry was a more plausible solution. Runaway slave ads conjecturing female escapees to be engaged as washerwomen are a case in point. Being one of the main occupations of Black women, it was unobtrusive, which is why it was an acceptable job for runaway slaves. Although physically arduous, it did not require special skills and could be performed by women and girls of all ages. The largest benefit was that they could work in their own homes (for piece rates), thereby being less exposed than market women and peddlers and less dependent than domestic servants who directly worked for their employers. Also, when women took to the streets to pick up or deliver clothes and linens, they were much more discreet than a group of dock or construction workers.

Laundry was particularly important for female runaways in Baltimore, where nearly all Black women were listed as washerwomen and where it was relatively easy to blend in with them.[55] When washing became increasingly commercialized in the late antebellum period, more women came to work in large-scale laundries for wage payment, which aggravated their situation.[56] Black women saw no option to work as seamstresses in Baltimore, even if they were very able workers, because there, this occupation was monopolized by White women. But they could do it in Charleston, which explains why seamstresses comprised a significant share of the runaways hiding in Charleston.[57]

Besides domestic service, laundry, and sewing, sex work was a tenable option for many Black women, including fugitives from slavery. In the nineteenth century, sex work was in a gray zone between illegality and tolerance. In Baltimore, it was also not a very commercialized field before the 1830s, from which time on more board-in brothels (where sex workers also resided) were established. Although urban prostitution was frowned upon, yet not explicitly illegal, it was not until the 1840s that authorities began to crack down on it, which also lowered the social standing of women and girls working in that occupation. In the 1850s, then, the numbers of Black and White women and men charged with keeping a brothel and of women involved in these services grew.[58] This was related to the broader context of reforms against "social ills."

Take, for instance, Catharine Murphy, Bridget Fagan, and Nancy Davis, the last one being of African descent, who were arrested in a brothel on Girod Street in 1852 in New Orleans "as lewd and abandoned women and vagrants."[59] The two White women "were required to furnish vouchers or go to the Work-House. Nancy [the Black woman] was sent to the Work-House for six months."[60] New Orleans and Charleston are places for which evidence suggests that mixed-race brothels were not uncommon. In 1849, a thirteen-year-old White girl named Mary Ann Warren was recovered "from a house of ill fame kept by a negro woman on Phillipa street" in New Orleans. In 1850, "Margaret Doherty, *f.w.c.* [free woman of color], and Margaret Gregg were last night locked up in the Second Municipality, being charged with keeping a brothel."[61] The last notice did not only reveal that Black and White women worked alongside each other as prostitutes but also that a White woman and a Black woman ran a business together.

Sex work could generate more income in a couple of hours than in several weeks of seaming shirts. Many women did not follow this work as a main occupation but rather as an on-and-off by-occupation or to get through a difficult period. Transient men who entered the port cities through the docks provided ample demand.[62] In this light, prostitution was a viable and effective work choice that followed the logics of a free market.[63] Consequently, the prostitution business grew with the cities and the traffic therein. Charleston authorities complained about the volume of this phenomenon in 1820 and acted against the expansion of "public Dancing Room[s]" within the limits of the city.[64] Strikingly, women were not actually taken up for *working* as prostitutes but for *being* "loose women," highlighting the aspect of social control.[65] Also, "public dancing," "disorderly houses," and "loose women" point to the vague legal definition of who qualified as prostitutes.[66]

Legal cases explicitly reveal that illegal residents were sex workers. Elizabeth Harris's hearing at the First District Court in 1850 (dealing with a dispute other than prostitution) included the testimony of a witness recounting that Harris "formerly lived in Natchez, and was then reputed to be a slave. Her son had been offered to witness for sale. Since that time, she has lived in a brothel in New Orleans." Her departure from Natchez seemed to be connected to the sale of Harris's son, and it is possible that she followed him to New Orleans.[67] Being mid-century, it was too late for Harris to be manumitted legally. Hence, she was either a fugitive slave or, if she managed to be released from slavery, an undocumented resident.

Another case involved Mary, who ran away from Robert Howren in Georgetown, South Carolina, in 1824. After two months, he advertised for her, describing her as having "yellow complexion, large black eyes, an un-common handsome set of white teeth, lips very red and speaks remarkably drawling—small statue." Howren had purchased Mary some years prior at auction in Charleston, where she apparently returned to because "she has been seen by a black woman in Charleston, within a few weeks. She has changed her name to JANE, and says she lives with a White woman who keeps a house of ill fame." A full year after Mary's escape, she was still advertised for in the newspaper.[68]

Regulatory Regimes

Although it was desirable for runaway slaves to integrate into the *free* Black population, race was not the only code that permeated the labor market; local regulations also had to be reckoned with. A great many of these restrictions were not only based on race but also on legal status, and very often, the two were related. In order to make good choices, fugitives had to read the local coding of labor and act accordingly. Peddlers in Baltimore were required to acquire licenses, vendors had to get permission to sell certain goods, and boatmen needed to register to operate their businesses on the Chesapeake Bay and the rivers.[69] Varying from location to location, the obligation for Black people to apply for special permits to carry out certain works meant additional obstacles for fugitives and other people without documents and registration.

From the mid-antebellum era onward, the legislative situation of free African Americans grew tighter. The provisions on prohibitions of assembly, for example, not only affected their social lives but also their economic lives. Since Black people still had to make money somehow and respond to human needs, they were driven into semi-clandestine or illegal economic and social activities at the margins of mainstream economy and society. Yet, being on the fringes did not mean being independent from the economy, and economic fluctuations always hit these people hard, including the crises of 1837 and 1857. Because Black people were reduced to the lowest-paying jobs, they had to work more to make ends meet.

Working longer hours could be risky for people of African descent, for there was a curfew whose violation could end with a night in the workhouse or a painful fine. These "disciplinary measures" compelled poor laborers to work even harder in order to make up for the lost money or time. Between September 1836 and September 1837, 573 slaves were convicted in Charleston for being on the streets after curfew without a pass.[70] When a Black person

TABLE 5.1 Urban enslaved populations, 1800–1860. Development of the urban enslaved populations per city, showing the overall decline of urban slavery.

	1800	*1810*	*1820*	*1830*	*1840*	*1850*	*1860*
Baltimore	2,800	4,700	4,400	4,100	3,200	2,900	2,200
Richmond	2,300	3,100	4,400	6,300	7,500	9,900	**11,700**
Charleston	9,800	11,700	12,700	15,400	14,700	19,500	**13,900**
New Orleans		6,000	7,400	9,400	23,400	17,000	**13,400**

Boldface entries highlight the three cities that had very similar enslaved populations by 1860.
   Source: See table 3.1.

was detected at night and no identification was produced because the person was a runaway, an illegally free person, or a legally free person without documents, they could be sold into slavery.

In Richmond, Curetta and her daughter Betty were charged with going at large and hiring themselves out. The two women, who belonged to Helen Briggs, lived on their own on 9th Street. Working as washerwomen, they would "sometimes be employed in carrying home clothes to or later an hour as 9 at night."[71] In Baltimore, Black people petitioned or had White people petition the mayor for passes that allowed them to be on the streets after curfew.[72]

Due to the overrepresentation of enslaved workers in certain areas, it was better for some runaways to pass as hired slaves. Depending on the context, this could work in the manufactories in Richmond, at the wharves in Charleston, and on the levee in New Orleans. In theory, this was exactly the same situation they had just escaped from, but in practice, the daily lives of self-hired slaves were much more akin to those of free Blacks than to those of most slaves. In Baltimore, where urban slavery was never abundant and where it had almost died out by the eve of the Civil War, this option would not have crossed the minds of many. In the other three cities, passing as a slave could be a promising strategy. In New Orleans, authorities were aware of this phenomenon from the earliest days of American rule onward. The Réglement de Police of 1804 evidenced that there was an interest "to prevent Negroes [. . .] from hiring themselves, when they are runaways."[73] In spite of the different developments of urban slavery in Richmond, Charleston, and New Orleans, by 1860 the absolute numbers of slaves were comparable (see table 5.1).

Richmond was an especially remarkable case. In 1860, 40 to 50 percent of urban slaves were in hired labor conditions. This comprised 4,700 to 5,900 people.[74] Black Americans held in bondage were an integral part of the city's industry, which was mostly centered on tobacco and flour. Although tobacco slaves—since the 1840s mostly men—found themselves under constant surveillance in the factories, they were only regulated by the official slave laws before and after working hours.[75] For runaways passing as self-hired slaves, the working conditions might have resembled slavery, but after the work was done they lived de facto free in the city.

Urban slavery had many faces. For runaways passing as slaves, it offered many possible scenarios. Bondswomen in cities cooked; cleaned; washed, made, and repaired clothes; cared for very young and very old people; and simply did everything their masters and mistresses demanded. Most worked from five o'clock in the morning until curfew. Men also worked as domestics, for example as valets, gardeners, or table servants, or took care of horses and carriages and ran errands. Even children, usually under the age of ten, were used as household servants, errand boys, and child-minders.[76] A New Orleans paper informed its readership that Catharine Rieley, a White woman, "who lives opposite to the Orleans theatre, was yesterday arrested on charge of harboring a runaway slave boy and claiming him as her property."[77] Passing a refugee off as one's property could both be a method to aid a fugitive or a strategy to obtain ownership of a slave by fraud.

Non-runaway illegals also disguised themselves as slaves, which demonstrates how precisely they monitored the reality around them and made choices accordingly. Free Black people came to Louisiana with forged passes describing them as slaves in order to circumvent the contravention laws that prohibited them entry as free Black persons. These activities were reported by the attorney general in 1857. Phoebe Black, a free Black sex worker, was charged with passing off as a slave a woman named Sarah Lucas who was originally from Louisville, Kentucky. In 1849, Black had, according to Lucas's testimony, lured her into New Orleans with the promise to procure her a job as a chambermaid.[78] Undocumented women were sometimes deceived to maneuver them into dependent work relations.

When fugitives or illegals hired themselves out to employers over a longer period of time, they could cross paths with census takers. It appears that some of them were even included in the records. Similar to the listings of the First African Baptist Church in which the status of certain people was left blank or where the space for the owners of enslaved members was filled in with a question mark,[79] census enumerators could at times not identify the owners of alleged slaves. In the space provided for the name of the slaveholder, census takers then wrote "hired," "owner Unknown," simply "unknown," "Owners names not known," or that the slave belonged to "an estate." Historian Loren Schweninger, who looked into these cases, concluded that the employers of these slaves did not know the actual owners of their hired workers.[80] Placing these people within a large illegal population, it is, however, very likely that employers either knew that they had runaways in their employ or that they simply did not look into the background of their employees.

Because self-hire was prohibited, those engaged in it were already familiar with an illegal activity before the escape. It took great boldness, determination, and—in the best case—the experience of having worked as a self-hired slave to successfully pretend to be a self-hired slave. Passing as such was for male runaways a way to engage in the skilled work they had been trained for in slavery. This way, they were able to make more money than they would if working below their skills. At the same time, there was scant hope of someday legally owning property or marrying.

The police, of course, assumed that self-hired slaves had owners and were therefore cautious to go too hard on them.[81] This was helpful. Even in those places where respective laws were passed, political will to enforce the codes was weak. Robert Lacy, for instance, an enslaved man who was tried in 1839 in Richmond for "going at large and hiring himself out," was discharged and his case dismissed.[82] A customary hands-off approach created valuable spaces for runaway slaves, and their willingness to pass as slaves underscores their awareness of the realities of the urban labor markets in a slaveholding society.

Badges and Tickets

Self-hire constituted as much a springboard to escape slavery as a strategy to make a living afterwards. The case of Charlotte is striking because it speaks to both scenarios. She "CAME to Charleston from Beaufort, some time since, by permission of her Mistress." Charlotte never returned to Beaufort "but hired herself out, and taken in washing, ever since, in Charleston." Because she was "from the windward coast of Africa [and] has her country marks on her face," Charlotte would not have stood a good chance of passing as a free woman. Yet, the subscriber found it relevant to add that "she has neither badge nor ticket to work out."[83] A similar account is the one of Jim, a tailor by trade. His owner Alexander England knew that "Jim has a ticket to work out, that he got from me, dated in February last" and suspected that "he may show that and hire himself to a Taylor." Jim absconded in June 1821. By June 1822, he was still not found. A couple of years prior, Jim had already passed himself off as a fisherman, revealing the flexibility and adaptability of many who seriously fought for breaking free from bondage.[84]

Comparable to slave passes, tickets were slips of paper written by slaveowners to give permission to their slaves to hire themselves out and were easily and frequently forged. Mary's Charleston owner knew in 1829 that she was passing herself off as a self-hired washerwoman. Calling herself Mary M'Lean, she ran away from 101 East Bay but stayed in Charleston. "She has been repeatedly seen on the Green, washing clothes—and not having a Badge, is supposed to have got some person to write a ticket for her."[85] Everybody who was able to write "a tolerable hand" could furnish slaves who sought to detach themselves from the control of their owners with such papers. These informal licenses were not only a way to control the enslaved population but also gave those who used them a certain protection, both from harassing watchmen and Whites who could be spoiling for a fight. Some slaveowners wrote tickets for a specific time range or occupational task, while others furnished their bondspeople with vaguely phrased papers.

Newspaper notices demonstrate the spaces these tickets opened for hired slaves. Richard had "a weekly working pass which is expired," to work on the wharves.[86] Dinah, "having a great many free relations," had with her a "nolimited ticket, to look for a master, which she has taken advantage of."[87] Police were aware that tickets could and were easily forged and sometimes apprehended slaves for having "no ticket," a "bad ticket," or a "doubtful ticket."[88] Because these apprehensions also happened late at night, slave tickets cannot be approached as something profoundly different from slave passes, and the boundaries were very blurry.

In theory, tickets for hired slaves were not a sufficient identification in Charleston. Municipal ordinances reveal that slaveowners were from 1800 onward required by law to purchase badges given out by the treasurer of the city, who kept a register of all the slaves who obtained them. Legislation was rather strict, stipulating that slaves had to wear these badges on visible parts of the body and employers had the duty to demand to see them. If an employer was caught hiring a slave who did not possess a badge, he had to pay a $5 fine plus the wages he had agreed upon with the slave's owner.[89] The feasibility of this ordinance was questionable from the very beginning and the impracticalities were plenty. To name just one, before the incorporation of Neck, both Charleston and Charleston Neck required separate badges for slaves. As a consequence, hired slaves who crossed Boundary Street for work had to have two badges. It is hard to imagine that this was carefully controlled.

Besides great inconvenience, procuring badges was a costly expenditure next to the taxes on slaves that had to be paid regardless.[90]

Intended to put a cap on the number of hired slaves in Charleston, obtaining a badge could also facilitate the endeavors of runaways in need of employment. Pompey was "a Painter by trade, and has constantly been employed working out, being furnished with a badge." When he absconded in 1812, he could easily find work by showing his badge.[91] In 1833, an ad informed that Delia, an eighteen-year-old wet nurse, carried a badge with the number 1234 with her and warned all persons against hiring her.[92] Clarinda, seventeen years old, "round face, good set of teeth," was described as "very talkative, and well known in the city." Having "many relatives here," the subscriber J. W. Schmidt assumed that she "resorts certain houses in the city and suburbs." He also added her badge number, 176, to the announcement.[93] Most ads, however, stated that runaways did not have badges and presumed that they would try to hire themselves out nevertheless: when March, "well known about the city," was advertised for, the announcement claimed that "he will, no doubt, say he has permission to work out, but has neither ticket nor badge."[94]

The production of slave badges gives insight into the number of hired slaves in Charleston. As calculated by Harlan Greene, in 1808 and 1809, between 300 and 400 badges were issued, and in 1860, more than 5,000 badges were distributed. This number covered around 25 to 30 percent of Charleston's urban bondspeople.[95] The actual volume of hired slaves was much higher, given that a great many slaveholders disregarded the ordinances, and slaveholders from outside Charleston sent their people into the city. Additionally, the tag counts did not include large numbers of self-hired slaves and nominally free African Americans who mingled with the enslaved hired population.

There are narratives that explicitly deal with the topic of passing as self-hired slaves. James Matthews, who found work by waiting at a stevedore's stand, was loading cotton bales onto a ship. Pretending to have a master to whom he answered, Matthews told his coworkers than he had to hand over his entire wages to his owner.[96] This was a necessary lie that corroborated his story and likely increased the solidarity of his coworkers, who often were in similar situations. John Andrew Johnson also testified to the slave tags and how this ordinance could keep people from working: "One morning, as I was going to join a gang of negroes working on board a vessel, one of them asked me if I had my badge? [. . .] When I heard that, I was so frightened that I hid myself [. . .]."[97] Johnson's ignorance regarding the local regulations for self-hired slaves nearly cost him his freedom. Others who were not as lucky were arrested and put in the workhouse.

Badges for hired-out slaves were also required in New Orleans, and controls occurred occasionally, as well as amendments in badge ordinances establishing the fines for people forging tags. Free persons "who shall have counterfeited one or more of such badges" were to be fined $50 "with expenses and costs, for every such offense." Slaves were to receive twenty-five lashes at the police jail, and "every slave wearing a badge not specially obtained for him from the Mayor of this city, shall receive fifteen lashes" unless their master redeemed them by paying $2.[98] Just like in Charleston, slave badge laws were regularly neglected, and employers did not ask for licenses or identification. In Richmond, no such badges existed and illegally free men and women could pass as self-hired slaves in large numbers. In Baltimore it was not necessary to pass as a slave.

The existence of the slave badge law and the fact that a great many slaveholders obeyed it was unique to Charleston. While badges there were forged, too, it was more complicated because they were made of copper. In other cities, including New Orleans, Mobile, Savannah, and Norfolk, tags were very likely made of paper or another impermanent material—although legal ordinances of New Orleans stipulated them to be of brass.[99] Whatever the reason, Charleston was the only place where these ordinances were executed, which shows the feasibility in the light of political will. Runaways often knew about the regulatory regimes in general while their distinct local implementations and executions were important information that could decide about freedom and enslavement. Rather than experiencing slave badges as a regulation of enslaved people's activities, fugitives used them to trick their employers into believing that they were hired slaves.

A Changing Demography

Both male and female fugitives depended on Black-coded jobs. The coding of labor, however, was not static, and there were lower-class Whites who were as desperate to make a living in the cities as Black people were. With significant effects on the racial landscape, the changing urban demography influenced where runaways worked in the cities. Two contradictory forces were at work in the antebellum era that had a lasting impact on the economic position of people of African descent. First, indentured servitude had, with a few exceptions, vanished from the United States and apprenticeships were sharply declining. These trends pulled White people out of unfree labor relations and underscored the opposition between slavery and freedom.[100] Second, following the theory of the second slavery, the institution managed to adapt to modern work relations, industrialization, and capitalist labor markets with an increasing flexibility of enslaved labor to the changing needs of the market. Calvin Schermerhorn has shown that free and unfree labor was not easily distinguishable anymore with hundreds of self-hired slaves in the cities. Therefore, occupations became segregated as a whole, as did workplaces.[101]

Although Whites always enjoyed a higher social status, on an economic level White workers competed on a daily basis with enslaved and free Black workers for jobs and wages. For some of them, economic advancement might have seemed as far away as for Blacks. The blurring of the free/unfree labor divide fed into capitalism, which was never meant to put an end to unfree labor. Nor was it intended to be within equal reach for all. Seth Rockman has neatly summarized that "historians must define capitalism through the power relations that channel the fruits of economic development towards those who coordinate capital to generate additional capital, who own property rather than rent it, and who compel labor rather than perform it." The control of other people's labor power, in other words, was key to socioeconomic mobility. People performing physical labor, however, had little say in their labor relations.[102] One of the few ways to improve things was for working-class Whites, consequently, to demarcate themselves from those at the very bottom of society.[103]

Although the numbers of African Americans in southern cities grew continuously, the numbers of White residents grew faster from the 1830s on. This was foremost related to the influx of Europeans, among which the Irish were the most numerous. Indian lands in the West that were confiscated by the federal government became, by then, too expensive for poor and lower-middle class Whites to purchase, and so the bulk of impoverished Irish immigrants, fleeing the potato blight, came to live in American cities. New Orleans constituted the second-largest entry port after New York during the middle of the century. Next to it, 130,000 immigrants arrived in Baltimore between 1820 and 1850. In Richmond, the Irish made up 46 percent of male unskilled laborers in 1860.[104]

White laborers visibly changed the faces of southern cities. Northern visitor John DeForest wrote in 1855 to his brother that "the crowd of porters & coachmen that met us on the dock [of Charleston] presented not above half a dozen black faces. Instead I saw the familiar Irish & German visages whom I could have met on a dock at Boston or New York."[105] These newcomers integrated into the lowest segments of the labor markets where they encountered unskilled African Americans, among whom were many runaway slaves. In particular, Irish newcomers were rivals because so many of them were unskilled, especially from the mid-antebellum era on.[106]

The phenomenon of sharpening color lines, which had a strong political and cultural side, translated into the economic sphere and affected the way in which White Americans saw Black labor. Slaves were destined to work for the benefit of White men, and Blacks and Whites working together was, for most Whites, unthinkable. To reserve the better-paying jobs for White Americans, Blacks were pushed out of certain skilled and semiskilled occupations and into more menial sorts of work. Urban occupations with the most promising future prospects were artisan trades, and although free Black men eagerly aspired to them, these were exactly the ones Black Americans were most likely to be barred from.[107] Opportunities for quality work further decayed relative to the respective place and African Americans found themselves ever more relegated to underclass work.

Labor exclusion of Black Americans worked in a variety of ways. Native Whites had come to refuse working with slaves and, in many places, with Black people in general. Frederick Law Olmsted saw in New Orleans that "employers could get no white men to work with their slaves, except from Irish and Germans."[108] In places where both Blacks and Whites worked, they often were still segregated by task. Olmsted noted, for instance, that in his hotel in Richmond, the chamber servants were all Black while the dining room servants were Irish.[109] On occasions when a White man accepted work alongside Black men, other White foreigners might turn against him and force him out.[110] Besides striking, White workers at times formed loose or more organized consolidations to push their competitors out, often using strong rhetoric or physical means to achieve their goals. In the mid-1850s, the *Daily Journal* of Indiana summarized these dynamics for three of the four places under analysis here. In New Orleans,

> rival white labor has driven or frightened black labor, a great measure, from its chief employment as draymen, long shore men and mechanics. [. . .] In the Carolinas the white mechanics recently formed a combination to drive the slaves from their branches of labor. In Baltimore, last week, the white caulkers formed a combination and resolved that no black man, free or slave should be allowed to work at their business. [. . .] Consequently every negro caulker was driven from the ship yard by force. It seems the white association had power to arrest all business [. . .].[111]

Black people, due to the prohibition of assembly, could not organize themselves in the same manner as White people. The participation of runaways in the labor forces of southern cities was high, and an organized labor movement was weakened through the presence of undocumented workers and the

general vulnerability of the Black population. Instead of complaining or rioting, they presented themselves as law abiding and respectable. Assaults by
Black workers on White workers were extremely rare and mostly no more
than impulsive bursts by individuals.

Another way to enforce segregation was by petitioning. This was the established tool of the lower-middle and new middle classes, and the purpose was
often in favor of White trades and skilled occupations.[112] Working-class Whites
also used petitions to achieve political goals, but more so toward the end of the
antebellum period. Combined with the power of customary law, persuasion,
intimidation, and violence, the heavy competition from Whites of the lower-
middle and working classes aggravated the precarious situation of free Blacks.
These animosities against Black workers were not only spontaneous acts by
White Americans (and later immigrants) but indeed a well-planned strategy
involving formal and informal organizations and associations.[113]

The legislative framework rendered Black Americans' status extremely
unfavorable, which left them with nearly no civil and legal rights. In any
confrontation with employers, coworkers, competitors, or even free Black
people who could prove their own freedom, the undocumented got the
short end of the stick. In fact, as historian Jim Cullen has argued, the first
five decades of the nineteenth century were the best time to be a White man
in terms of upward mobility.[114] They refused to work at eye level with Black
people while Black people ferociously tried to fight the idea of being equated
with slaves. It was an unequal struggle. Black laborers felt the pressure every
day and Black leaders loudly articulated their warnings from the 1830s onward.[115] Although the precariousness of Black Americans in the urban labor
markets grew, an ever-increasing number of runaway slaves joined them in
the cities. Their absorption was facilitated by the growing segregation of
workplaces.

The dynamics of expelling Black Americans increased through the competition of poor European newcomers, yet it did not affect all places in a similar manner. Newspaper announcements show job openings and reveal racial
preferences for certain occupations. In Baltimore in the first three decades of
the nineteenth century, almost all job ads for domestics referred to Black
women. After this time, White women pushed into the sector: wanted immediately "At the Baltimore Laundry, a few more WASHERWOMEN (white).
Colored women need not apply—Irish or German preferred," read a job ad
from 1853.[116] This was a huge problem because White American women had
already monopolized seamstress jobs in Baltimore, and when Europeans be-

gan to join the labor market, they competed with Black women in one of their very few occupations as laundresses.[117]

Charleston, by contrast, maintained a variety of jobs with and without preferences of skin color.[118] Some sectors, like domestic work, stayed Black-coded in a number of southern cities as a continuation of the White/ Black–master/slave relations explicit in slavery. It was less uncomfortable for employers to exploit people who looked different from themselves because they hardly identified with them.[119] And so, 4,500 enslaved women labored as domestics in Richmond by 1860.[120] Many Richmonders were perhaps also reluctant to let Irishwomen into their homes, who were of a new, suspicious group. Hence, blackness allowed fugitive slaves and undocumented residents to enter certain segments of the labor market while at the same time ensuring their exploitation in these segments.

Thomas Pinckney, South Carolina's former governor, confirmed the reluctance to hire White domestics: "The habits of our inhabitants render them averse to employing such [White] domestics; having seen these offices constantly occupied by slaves, they would, with reluctance, exact similar services from those whom nature, as well as the law, have made their equals."[121] Yet, the closer to the Civil War, the more accustomed White employers grew to the idea of employing White before Black workers. When the wage difference between Whites and Blacks was narrow, historian Michael Thompson has claimed, they often preferred Whites.[122]

And so, African Americans lost many professions but largely managed to maintain their presence in water-related work, for example, as oystermen and seamen, and as hucksters and brickmakers. Also, both men and women were still present in service jobs by the mid-century. These included barbers, cooks, waiters, laundresses, domestic servants, and porters.[123] While it is indisputable that Black people's positions in an increasingly competitive labor market became ever more tenuous, there were still job opportunities, but often not work that would feed a family or provide a steady income.

Accepted Exploitation

Over the course of the nineteenth century, the urban marketplace grew to be a central element of the national economic growth. Work became more specialized and reliant on the division of labor, and small shops gave way to factories and heavy machinery.[124] Industrialization and mechanization increasingly reduced skilled labor to unskilled. Laundering, seamstressing, day labor, cartering, and factory work—the occupations the majority of nominally free and enslaved Black Americans followed—offered no future.

The large numbers of refugees and undocumented Black people in southern cities certainly impacted the labor markets. Capitalist labor markets were supportive for runaways to integrate because they did not rely on personal acquaintance but rather on flexibility and adaptability. Because they were even more vulnerable than legally free African Americans, it is likely that their presence in the labor markets partly contributed to the low-wage situation. The heavy competition and the disadvantages for people of African descent that resulted from this became a tangible reality every time wages were paid.

Seth Rockman has shown that until the 1830s, hired slaves, free Blacks, and immigrant and native Whites received the same remuneration for the same work in Baltimore.[125] When in 1838 150 laborers were needed for the Baltimore & Ohio Canal, the subscriber offered $1.25 per day without mentioning a preference for race.[126] Yet, looking at the entire antebellum period and at all southern places, people of African descent were on average less remunerated for their work than Whites. Black people, to defend themselves against the dynamics of exclusion, were forced to offer their labor power cheaper and, hence, kept the overall wages low. George Teamoh, whose testimonials are extraordinarily rich for this topic, stated that wages for Black men at a Norfolk dry dock ranged from $1.50 to $1.62 per day in the 1840s. White workers received $2 or more.[127]

Importantly, companies were far from satisfied with the stability of the labor supply.[128] Especially in the 1850s, the constant complaints by employers about labor shortages made dissatisfaction visible. This did not necessarily mean that there were not sufficient workers but rather that the wages were considered to be too high, the term of service too short, or that employers could not afford to hire and fire people at will. In essence, it meant that employees retained limited power to bargain about working conditions.[129] The complaints about them show that workers in the sense of free capitalist markets were not desired at most times. Rather, employers had an intrinsic interest in commanding a workforce confined in power. Racism among the lower classes was a welcome tool to keep the competition going and even Irish and German laborers were at times pitted against each other. As a result, wages fell dramatically, from $1.25 to 87.5 cents a day at the Chesapeake & Ohio Canal in 1839.[130]

It was usually up to the employers to set the wages, but at times there were also attempts to formalize exploitation. The City Council of Charleston tried to freeze the daily wages of Black day laborers and porters at $1 in 1837: "For a full day's labor, which is to be from sun rise till twilight in the evening, (allowing one hour for breakfast and one hour for dinner) one dollar—and for less than a day's labor, at the rate of twelve and a half cents for an hour."[131] In New Orleans, enslaved day laborers were equally not permitted to earn more than $1 a day.[132] When wages or transport rates were fixed by municipal governments, Black people had to go under these rates.[133] Those paid by the day had to work harder to prove their worthiness and those being paid by piece, for instance seamstresses, had to produce more in order to make up for the pay gap.

Frederick Douglass received $1.50 in 1838 when he "was able to command the highest wages given to the most experienced calkers."[134] This was a relatively high wage, as day laborers earned $1 per day on average in the first decades of the antebellum era and $1.25 to $1.50 closer to the Civil War. Approaching mid-century, wages did not grow in parallel with other parts of the economy. As other historians have observed, the high supply in the labor markets, caused by the competition of Black Americans, lower-class White Americans, and European immigrants led to an anomaly in the 1850s when economic growth and declining wages for unskilled and semiskilled workers coincided.[135] When George Teamoh started working at a dockyard at the Richmond Basin in 1853, he earned $1.25 per day as a common laborer.[136] This was less than he had made as a hired slave a couple of years earlier and the same salary unskilled construction workers had received fifteen years prior.

As a contrast, the average yearly price to hire an enslaved woman in Richmond was $34 during the first four decades of the nineteenth century; for men it was $70.[137] Slaveholders who made a business out of training and hiring out their bondspeople, like one from South Carolina, continuously raised the hire rate of their slaves: in 1820, the monthly pay was between $2.50 and $3.50; by the 1820s and 1830s, it was between $5 and $7.[138] Knowing that remuneration for free and enslaved Black people did not really differ meant that free African Americans had to offer their labor to comparable conditions. Indeed, Brazilian historians Eulália Lobo and Eduardo Stotz have claimed that wages for those who were seen as "free" workers probably even derived from the hiring prices of slaves.[139]

Immigrant and native Whites in some segments of the labor market surely had the same or similar wages as Black people, but in theory had a greater variety of occupations to choose from. To name just one example, Philip Whitlock was a Polish-Jewish immigrant in the Butchertown neighborhood of Richmond. Although he started off with a very low income of $2.50 per week for his first job, he quickly rose up making $6 to $7 as a tailor. This was a job coded White and Whitlock was taken in by his own ethnic network.[140] Besides the actual lower wages Black people often received, White men benefitted from what W. E. B. DuBois has called "psychological wage" and David Roediger "wages of whiteness." These concepts refer to a compensation of low wages by the social and political privileges White men possessed.[141]

If times were hard for Black men, there were even harder for Black women, especially when they were single. Being in a relationship with a man did not mean for American women to live a life of ease, but being single almost always included drudgery and poverty. In all cities, Black women were confronted with major hardships just to make ends meet. The racial division of the labor market was for them further aggravated by gender hierarchies that placed them in a doubly disadvantaged situation. This was a time when White Richmonders and Baltimoreans expressed grave concerns about the working and living conditions of poor *White* women, many of whom could barely make a living as seamstresses or laundresses.[142] If White women had such a difficult time then one can only imagine the struggles that African American women—especially those who lived in the city illegally—faced. It was an arduous life. A mother without the financial support of a husband had to literally work round the clock for her family, and overwork took its toll on many women.

This is even more disturbing when considering that women strongly outnumbered men in the South and even more so in the cities. Since the income of a Black man rarely sufficed to feed a family, Black women who stayed at home were rare, which created serious problems when it came to raising children. Those who followed more stable occupations also faced disadvantages. Service professions and jobs that required customers were more lucrative if the clientele had means to spend. Even those occupations that looked good on paper usually did not pave the way for economic advancement. White customers, due to their greater purchasing power, were important to Black service providers but often the latter were stuck with a clientele belonging to the lowest classes themselves. Black people with a very dark skin had additional disadvantages since Whites preferred to do business with mulattos. In 1860, 94 percent of free Blacks in South Carolina lived in extreme poverty. At the most, they had some clothes, a number of things used in the household, maybe some tools, and even less often a mule or cow. Some had little amounts of money but they desperately depended on wages.[143]

At the same time, there were a great many things, real and imagined, material and ideological, that connected the lower classes of all races, nativities, and sexes. One could claim that the initial material situation of runaway slaves and European immigrants did not differ much when they arrived in the cities. To prep German immigrants, travel reports sold in Germany featured sections with recommendations on certain occupations and assessments of the competition with free Black Americans.[144] Widespread discussions about the rapid integration of Irish Catholic immigrants in the nineteenth century and the relative success story of their moving up and acquiring "whiteness" often focus on the racist climate in society. Less often they account for the actual and very real legal barriers that kept African Americans from advancing. For example, tax payments for Black people were higher than for Whites. Immigrants, by contrast, did often not pay taxes, as observed by a free Black inhabitant of Charleston. This was why they got rich soon, he claimed.[145] In short, no group was in such a long-lasting and precarious situation as people of African descent.

An undocumented status, which did not require tax payment, could be beneficial for a person or a family because they could either save the money if they did have it or escape the consequences of nonpayment if they did not have the money to pay taxes. This was also why White people did not pay poll taxes when they could not afford it. However, these requirements were much lower for White than for Black people, in most states significantly less than $1 per year. When a White person could not meet these expenses, they would be listed as insolvent.[146] In contrast, Black people could be jailed, and nonpayment of the jail fees could send them back to forced labor or slavery.

In general, over the course of the antebellum era, the property value of free Black Americans decreased, as did the proportion among them who owned property. In 1850, free Black property owners in Baltimore constituted a mere 0.06 percent of the city's inhabitants.[147] Remarkably, this was still too much for some White Marylanders. In 1860, the spokesman of the Baltimore convention asked to legally bar Black people from purchasing houses or leasing them for more than a year.[148]

Unequal taxes, discouragement to register one's residency, and risks of legal protest were different forms of vulnerability explicitly aimed at people of African descent. People passing themselves off as self-hired slaves had no voice at all. Robert Steinfeld and Stanley Engerman have argued that taxation and immigration can serve "to lower incomes and change the amount and/or nature of work free workers were 'willing' to do."[149] These strategies maneuvered Black people into conditions where they were forced to engage in qualitatively lower and quantitatively higher work. Consequently, extreme precariousness disproportionately hit Black people. In a society that self-identified as a White man's nation, the majority of policy makers, employers, and citizens saw no problem with this state of affairs: it was an "accepted exploitation."[150]

RUNAWAYS GRAVITATING to southern cities knew that employment opportunities were limited and economic shortcomings were ample, but nonetheless they preferred a life in poverty over a life in bondage. With racial slavery and whiteness marking not only the social realities of people but also their experiences in the labor markets, the racial, legal, and gender codes of work determined which jobs were open to Black people. African Americans found themselves increasingly enmeshed in exploitative labor relations, a precarious situation that was aggravated by the competition with urban White Americans and European immigrants.

Through legislative arrangements that degraded free Black people to the status of slaves, and political projects that excluded them from the idea of nationhood, they were essentially blocked from access to social and economic mobility, and it did not help that large numbers of runaway slaves and undocumented residents belonged to their group. With parts of the Black population being illegal, and slavery as a powerful tool to keep free Black people in their illegitimate limbo, people of African descent as a group were vulnerable and extremely exploited in the labor market.

This occurred at a time when labor demands in southern cities gradually moved away from enslaved labor and toward more flexible, malleable wage labor. This was in large part related to nascent capitalist developments which, with their reliance on flexibility and low labor costs, created conditions that tolerated the presence of the undocumented. Volatile, much less binding labor arrangements proved beneficial for fugitive slaves and other illegals who were reliant on a measure of distance from their White employers. And so, the changes in the urban economy created spaces where runaways could find work and secure their survival, depending on age, ability, skills, and sex. Ultimately, however, the jobs fugitive slaves found in the cities were not that different from those of other illegals, free Blacks, or impoverished immigrants. Like all poor people in the urban labor market, fugitives had precarious employment, suffered limited work opportunities tied to seasonal jobs, and struggled to make a living. Their economic integration was, together with their social integration, the most pivotal element in explaining how they navigated southern cities.

CHAPTER SIX

Urban Politics and Black Labor

Fugitive slaves and their allies in southern cities were in large numbers able to carve out spaces to live and work, yet not all managed to elude the long arms of their owners and the oppressive laws. Between February 1850 and December 1860, Louisiana's First District Court, which covered the Orleans Parish, handled twenty-seven cases of men and women accused of either harboring, stealing, or hiding runaway slaves. Between 1852 and 1860, the Records of Prisoners Committed to the Parish Prison document 4,602 entries of arrests, of which 11 were related to slave flight.[1] The most surprising thing about these numbers is how low they are, given the monetary value of men and women belonging to the highly mobile group of slaves who made up the majority of runaways, and the emotional involvement of many slaveholders in their escape. They are all the more surprising in comparison to earlier times, when arrests and convictions related to fugitive slaves in the South were significantly lower, revealing that the 1850s were a decade in which legislative measures against fugitive slaves and those who helped them were most strictly executed.

If slave fugitivity in southern cities was so common, why did the authorities not take more rigorous steps to apprehend runaways? For all the tumult about this issue in national politics, they did not seem to try very hard to confront the problem in the places where they had most control. This non-enforcement is telling in the light of the intricate political structure of the southern states: urban-rural animosities, diverging interests between state capitals and economic centers, competing political claims of different elite groups, class conflict between slaveholders and non-slaveholding Whites, and the fact that the presence of precarious low-wage laborers was advantageous to growing cities.

Slaveholders were traditionally responsible for legislation regarding racial control in the cities. Yet, nineteenth-century cities were places where political and economic interests were constantly negotiated. Growing increasingly complex, the interplay of different social groups, whose power and leeway evolved over time, impacted the political climate in Baltimore, Richmond, Charleston, and New Orleans. Economic development, expansion of suffrage, and foreign immigration brought about a restructuring of civic power and views about the labor of Black people. The diversification of political power, which had hitherto rested almost exclusively with the dominant plan-tocracy, entailed different responses toward the presence of fugitive slaves, undocumented residents, and free Black Americans in southern cities. Look-ing at these different political positions reveals how frictions and fissures between economic interests opened up spaces for fugitive slaves while also threatening their endeavors.

A Slaveholders' World

Southern cities were strongly influenced by the presence of slaveholders. This was most visible in Charleston, the place with the highest density of large-scale, wealthy planters. Unlike Virginia, where they often lived on the plantations and frequented the capital for pleasure and business, in South Carolina, they were mostly absentee masters who lived in massive town houses around the waterfront of Charleston, and ran their agricultural busi-ness and the management of their enslaved workforce remotely, with agents and overseers managing the day-to-day work on plantations.[2] Comparable to New Orleans, Charleston had a variety of light industries but the most es-sential work was performed on the waterfronts by enslaved workers. After around 1820, the importance of the port of Charleston declined, yet it was a relative downturn, and export output as well as the demand for labor in-creased in absolute terms. Many wharf owners were also plantation owners and often employed their own bondspeople in the city alongside additional hired workers.[3]

The concentration of wealth that characterized Charleston was not re-stricted to the planter class. The middle ranks of society were also often slave-holders. In 1830, 87 percent of White households in Charleston owned slaves.[4] This very high number reveals that large shares of lower-class Whites could not afford to live within the physically limited city, despite working there. Slaveholders, including those who were not wealthy planters, as well as hirers of slaves had an interest in a tight environment of social and racial con-trol. Their numbers grew in the antebellum period as did their representation in municipal politics. The core city was, hence, dominated by people with a stake in slavery—and its regulation was worth a great deal of money to them. In 1859, Charleston expected expenditures of $100,000 for the City Guard.[5] Due to its small size and geography, the city of Charleston was indeed one of the few places that could be successfully surveilled.

The dominance of slaveowners is clearly recognizable by the fact that Charleston's municipal laws had their interests at heart. One of them, for instance, stipulated that if a person gave a ticket to a slave excusing them from evening curfew—"after the beating of the tattoo [curfew] without the knowledge of the owner or employer"—the person who issued the ticket should pay $20 to the owner or employer. Those people actually benefitting from enslaved labor, namely the owner of the slave or the person hiring them, were acquitted from any responsibilities in the matter. Or, if a slave was arrested for violating evening curfew, the warden was either to fine the slave, or "at the request of the owner to order the said slave to be corrected, with no less than five or more than nineteen lashes in the Work House, without subjecting the owner of said slave to any expense or charge at the said Work House." In other words, the master of the workhouse was neither allowed to reject incoming slaves nor charge slaveowners for his "services."[6] In both cases, the costs of slave control were levied on third parties.

The slave badge laws that we saw in chapter 5, which visibly identified enslaved men and women working for other people than their owners, were very sophisticated in Charleston, as was the city's workhouse. Also called the sugar house, it was located on the corner of Magazine and Mazyck (now Logan) Streets. Before the incorporation of Charleston Neck in 1850, which enlarged the city to the north, the workhouse was right in the middle of the city. Providing services for slaveholders, workhouses functioned as centers of punishment and as "storages" for enslaved people. While detained at the workhouse, bondspeople were punished for disobedience so that they could afterward return to their owners with a restored or increased value.[7] In Charleston, the centrality of the workhouse worked both symbolically (as a reminder for Black people of their supervision by White authorities) and strategically. With an architecture that resembled a fortress, it was accessible from all parts of the city by foot, and slaveholders, hirers, and police could commit and retrieve their victims at any time.

Correction in the workhouse was not free of charge. Although the clerk of the workhouse was generally "subject to owner's order," as the police recorded, in many cases slaveholders had to pay fees for the accommodation and disciplining of their property.[8] In the 1830s, food and lodging cost $18^{3/4}$ cents per day per slave, and the same amount was charged for "confining" and "delivering" slaves. A "better diet," putting on and taking off irons cost extra.[9] Workhouses saw a high number of enslaved people passing through and spending days or weeks there. In Charleston, it also functioned as the first receiving station for runaway slaves throughout the entire antebellum period. In 1800, it was made known that "if any negro or other slave taken up as aforesaid [working out without ticket or badge], should prove to be a run-away from any person residing without the limits of this city, the master of the work-house shall, in such case, proceed as is directed by the law respecting runaway slaves."[10] This also reveals that runaways from within and outside of the city were approached differently. When a person was suspected of having escaped from an owner in Charleston, no advertisement was placed in the paper, an additional measure that saved slaveholders expenses.

White abolitionist Angelina Grimké reported that a wealthy female slave-owner regularly brought her slaves to the workhouse to have them chastised: "One poor girl, whom she sent there to be flogged, and who was accordingly stripped *naked* and whipped, showed me the deep gashes on her back—I might have laid my whole finger in them—*large pieces of flesh had actually been cut out by the torturing lash*."[11] Perhaps the slaveholder herself was mentally or physically not able to carry out the sentencing of those whom she regarded as deserving of punishment. Or, she preferred to create an artificial distance between the suffering of her slaves and her own persona.

Grimké also mentioned the treadmill, an installation to exhaust and torture enslaved men and women. It was a cylinder-shaped stepped wooden wheel that was moved by stepping from one step to the next. She reported that "she [the same slaveholder] sent another female slave there, to be imprisoned and worked on the tread-mill. This girl was confined several days, and forced to work the mill while in a state of suffering from another cause. For ten days or two weeks after her return, she was lame, from the violent exertion necessary to enable her to keep the step on the machine."[12] It was a Sisyphean work. While indeed used to grind corn, productivity was not its main purpose: it was to mete out punishment to enslaved inmates who often were forced to work the mill several days in a row.[13]

Invented in Great Britain, the treadmill was initially seen as a progressive development within the nineteenth-century penal system. According to Diana Paton, it brought the element of labor into discussions of efficient modes of punishment before it became rather quickly relegated to a barbaric instrument.[14] It was introduced in Charleston in the 1820s and there is evidence pointing to its continued operation into the late 1840s.[15] The language of the time emphasizes the function of the treadmill as punishment. Corporal punishment could be turned into "work at the Tread Mill," read the ordinance of the City Council, as if the physical pain that the treadmill inflicted was not a corporal punishment. This applied to "all negroes and persons of color committed to the Work House as vagrants, fugitive slaves, or otherwise," and it was the duty of the Commissioner to make sure "that a due degree of individual labor may at all times be steadily maintained." To this end, everyone who was not "committed for punishment on the Tread-Mill" was to be kept "at labor in cracking stones, for grading and Macadamizing the streets," for which the city was to provide "all requisite instruments and materials."[16]

Unlike Grimké, James Matthews did not visit the workhouse as an observer. He was incarcerated there for three months as a penalty for running away. He described the cells as "little narrow rooms about five feet wide, with a little hole up high to let in air." After a most brutal initial whipping, Matthews

> was kept in the cell till next day, when they put me on the tread mill, and kept me there three days, and then back in the cell for three days. And then I was whipped and put on the tread mill again, and they did so with me for a fortnight, just as Cohen [his master] had directed. He told them to whip me twice a week till they had given me two hundred lashes. My back, when they went to whip me, would be full of scabs, and they whipped them off till I bled so that my clothes were all wet. Many a night I have laid up there in the Sugar House and scratched them off by the handful.[17]

These accounts expose the naked cruelty of what it took to keep enslaved people under control in the urban environment.

While slaveowners were the main people who sent slaves to the workhouse, the police also committed Black people every month, but those numbers were never high enough to constitute the majority of the inmates. For the eighteen months for which information is available in 1859 and 1860, Charleston law enforcement transferred between zero and 118 people to the workhouse, including apprehended runaways.[18] The total number of inmates was on average 211. As chart 6.1 shows, this number peaked in January months. The structure of the labor market for slave hire and the more numerous slave flights around Christmastime suggest that many slaveholders committed their bondspeople to the workhouse for safekeeping during that period, showing that slaveholders were aware of possible escape attempts and took intentional actions to try to prevent flight.

According to historian Larry Koger, runaways usually were penned up in the workhouse between five and thirty days.[19] During this time, they were in contact with slaves who were committed by their owners, either for having run away or for entirely different reasons. Keeping slaves to be corrected for wrongs alongside slaves who visibly expressed their desire to escape in the same place was ironic because it brought them into close contact with each other—both literally and figuratively. Due to the large numbers of runaway slaves who mingled at any time with the enslaved, the workhouse was a place that contradicted the interests and intentions of slaveowners and local

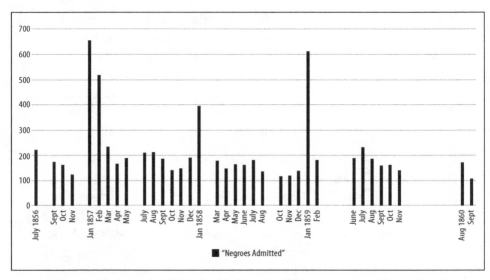

CHART 6.1 Black people jailed in the Charleston workhouse, 1856–1860. The number of inmates in the Charleston workhouse peaked annually in January. Proceedings of the City Council of Charleston, S.C., 1859 I; and Charleston (S.C.) City Council, Proceedings of Council, POC-002 M: 1859-1870, CCPL.

authorities. Since free African Americans were sent there too, it was essentially a place where both groups of Black people met. For example, when Julia, a free Black woman, was arrested for not having a ticket half an hour after curfew hit Charleston, she was lodged in the workhouse for a day.[20]

Authorities were aware that free people and local slaves alike were often committed as runaways. The numbers were high because owners of slaves were neglectful in procuring badges or furnishing them with passes and tickets. In 1821, the city council of Charleston, in a move to distinguish enslaved from free inmates, "resolved that a Committee be appointed to enquire what Persons of Color are now confined in the Work House as Fugitives, and whether any Certificate or Evidence to the contrary can be produced [...] so as to authorize their discharge."[21] This resolution was intended to ensure that free African Americans suspected of being runaway slaves were not jailed for too long a time, which would mean that they were often unable to pay the jail fees. In these cases, the workhouse clerk would be left alone with the costs of accommodation.

In other southern cities, similar but not identical race-based methods of discipline and punishment were meted out to both enslaved and free Black people, and reflected the particular economic and cultural contexts of each specific urban space. New Orleans' jail for Black people, the so-called calaboose, resembled the workhouse in Charleston and was called "hell on earth" by autobiographer William Anderson.[22] Yet, it was just one of several places where White people exercised domination over lower-class people of African descent. New Orleans' geography of control also included the whipping house (which corresponded to the police jail), located behind the administrative buildings at Jackson Square on Chartres and St. Peter's Streets. Black people were sent there after curfew, where they had to prove their free status. Black people were also detained in the parish prison, the police jail of the Third Municipality, and the workhouses of the First and Third Municipalities.[23] In one of these prisons, Swedish traveler, feminist, and novelist Fredrika Bremer encountered two enslaved women imprisoned there by their owner for two years.[24] This was exceptional, and must have either been an extreme case of punishment or a conflict of ownership.

In these places, free and enslaved people were routinely disciplined by law enforcement to ensure that social and racial order were maintained in the cities. Slaveholders and authorities tended to collaborate rather than conflict with one another over the punishment of the enslaved, with jailers often thoroughly examining and inspecting people suspected of having escaped from slavery on the behalf of slaveholders.[25] John Brown, for one, escaped slavery in Georgia and went to New Orleans, where he was warned by Black cotton drivers at the port who immediately recognized him as a runaway that he "should be certain to be taken up before night, and put into the calaboose or prison; and that I should be flogged every morning until I told the name of my master."[26]

Cities of Capitalists

Despite this clear infrastructure of racial control and the fact that municipal leaders in New Orleans were highly invested in slavery, the city's diverse social composition had room for a much more dynamic picture than in Charleston. Nineteenth-century cities were centers of commerce, transport, administration, some industry, and a number of other services.[27] Together, these sectors united a very diverse crowd of people with different business interests and different ideas about how to make use of the urban space. Being strongly geared towards investing in a lucrative future, American investors put New Orleans through an intense and rapid phase of modernization in the first half of the antebellum era. The city had no major industrial center, but merchants and others developed smaller industries, including sawmills, cotton mills, sugar refineries, and distilleries. In the 1820s, modern technologies introduced a steam-powered cotton mill, yet the principal economic sectors in New Orleans were trade and exchange. At the same time that Charleston slumped toward decline, New Orleans became the second most important American port after New York, and this port was the second largest employer after the government. The merchants who ran the port were tied to the planters of the hinterland because they were responsible for shipping their cotton and sugar abroad; they also invested heavily in land and slaves. While merchants sometimes saw planters as antagonists rather than allies,[28] their shared business endeavors meant that New Orleans' economic diversity lagged far behind its demographic diversity.

If slaveholders in other southern cities wielded as much power as their counterparts in Charleston, fugitive slaves seeking refuge in urban enclaves would find little there. Yet, Louisiana planters lived in New Orleans in much lower numbers than South Carolina planters in Charleston, and legislation, debates in the vernacular press, and the physical environment indicate that they were less concerned with racial control in the city. Cultural differences within New Orleans' ruling circles split the city into three municipalities, each with different systems of local law enforcement and social order. Planters, who made state politics in the capital of Baton Rouge and mostly gravitated to New Orleans for business and amusement, took urban social control much less seriously than elsewhere. This opened up niches for fugitive slaves to stay.

In general, urban slavery never had the scale that agricultural slavery did, and after experiencing slight growth between roughly 1830 and 1850, it decreased in almost all places. This was most visible in Baltimore, which was an important trading hub, milling center, and place of production. During the second slavery, Maryland slaveholders were less powerful than their neighbors in Virginia. Those whose businesses still revolved around plantations with a large enslaved workforce partook in the state politics in the capital Annapolis, where they clung to their conservative, slavocratic worldviews.[29] Baltimore, meanwhile, offered an opening space for progressive, daring, and modern business endeavors similar to those taking place in Philadelphia and New York.[30] These metropolitan entrepreneurs were more inclined to follow the economic restructurings around wage labor they saw happening in the North.

The growth and success of Baltimore, which had been a small town at the turn of the nineteenth century, was related to the wheat business—not to tobacco and, with it, enslaved labor. In the city itself, the merchant community had little overlap with the slaveholding elite and its members were often newcomers themselves (migrants from Pennsylvania and immigrants from Germany and Ireland). Equally important was the commercial nature of Baltimore's industrial sector. Many capitalist leaders considered production as a means to improve the infrastructure of their mercantile businesses. In New Orleans, by sharp contrast, merchants pushed against investments in railroads and ports because they feared the introduction of superior goods from the western part of the country.[31] Therefore, Baltimore, unlike other places, saw a political unity between commerce and production relatively early, which rendered the institution of slavery less important to the city's growth. Heavy industry concentrated capital, which had the power to execute considerable control over the government and to command large labor forces.[32]

Industry in Baltimore was able to grow at a rapid pace because slaveholders had never been a dominant force in the city. Their absence influenced labor relations. With commerce being the main driver of the economy and the textile industry being the main employer in the city, market relations came to replace relations of household paternalism. In other words, market relations worked better for the nature of Baltimore's economy than slavery. Because urban employers had a high demand for seasonal and casual workers, the market for labor power was more dominant than the market for owning laborers.[33]

Richmond was likewise an important industrial center; at the same time, it differed from Baltimore in its heavy reliance on enslaved labor. Virginia counted the highest number of enslaved people at any time during the antebellum period, despite the expanding Cotton Empire and the high prices Virginia slaveholders charged when selling their slaves south. By 1860, Virginia had nearly half a million bondspeople, turning the eastern part of the state into the place with the highest concentration of enslaved workers, slaveholders, and planters in the entire South. Although the importance of tobacco production was dramatically dissipating elsewhere in the South, in Virginia it increased in the late antebellum period and the Piedmont remained the country's largest tobacco region. In addition to tobacco, which was very labor intensive, Virginia produced wheat, which only demanded seasonal attention. Enslaved workers from the Tidewater wheat plantations turned into a "labor reserve" for commercial and industrial demands (as well as laborers for urban households) when planters hired plantation hands out to urban industries during the off-season.[34] By using their enslaved laborers flexibly and seasonally, Tidewater planters were able to counteract the replacement of slave with wage labor in Richmond as the city became an industrial power.

A characteristic feature of the period of the second slavery was its relationship with wage labor, coerced labor, subsistence labor, and industrial production.[35] For employers, it was effective to create a workforce as diverse as possible and to combine laborers who were in different conditions, a strategy that prevented laborers from allying with one another and kept them replaceable. The creation of an undocumented working population was an additional benefit for the economy of growing cities. This was, in fact, a double advantage for runaways and others who tried not to raise attention in the cities: a weakened slave system meant that slaveholders had less power over the urban space, and demand for diverse labor facilitated a growth of illegal workers among whom runaways could become invisible.

Despite all these open spaces for fugitives from slavery, municipal authorities felt increasing pressure from the state and surrounding counties to tackle the runaway slave "problem." The fact that little happened in this regard testifies to the rural-urban antagonisms that characterized so many southern states. New Orleans, Charleston, and Baltimore were not only the most populous places in their respective states, they were also the most economically powerful. The relation between Baltimore and Annapolis is telling: the city of Baltimore and Baltimore County accounted for three-fourths of the manufacturing product of Maryland in 1850, and it was an important market for agricultural products from the state. Maryland had long experienced sectionalist strife, which was in earlier times most pronounced between the Western and Eastern Shores of the Chesapeake Bay. But this animosity was eventually overshadowed by an ever more powerful Baltimore (and, with it, northern Maryland).[36]

As Barbara Fields has observed, the "predominant form of sectionalism" was the continuous struggle of the slave counties in eastern and southern Maryland to prevail over the northern regions and, in turn, the struggle of the northern counties to "release themselves from political subordination." And Baltimoreans and northern Marylanders had good reasons for resentment: Baltimore City's representation in the House of Delegates was limited to four delegates, a stipulation grossly disproportionate to its inhabitants; Maryland's enslaved population reinforced the political representation of the slave counties with full numbers (not at a ratio of three-fifths as on the federal level); and a new law introduced heavy tax privileges for slave property.[37] Why, then, should Baltimore's leadership be concerned with spending resources on catching runaway slaves? The motivation was small as Baltimore, like other southern cities, was a weak link in the slave system. In Virginia, by contrast, these fractures of state politics were much less pronounced because Richmond was the capital.

Political tensions between state capitals and the largest cities were exacerbated by the fact that planters needed the ports to export their slave-grown products and claimed jurisdiction over them through the legislature. The Seamen Acts were the most blatant example of how the law was used to control port labor. First introduced in 1822 in South Carolina and followed by various states of mainly the Lower South, the Seamen Acts authorized the incarceration of sailors and seamen of African descent during the time a ship was anchored in a port.[38] The act not only harmed merchandising, but sailors usually spent a great deal of time in the cities and money on the local economies during the days and weeks they were on shore. State legislators appeared to place the well-being of the institution of slavery over the well-being of the economy.[39]

Economic players in the cities savaged one another. While state authorities and White laborers demanded the incarceration of foreign seamen, local merchants, ship captains, and free African Americans pressed against it.[40] Proprietors in New Orleans warned the authorities that they would redirect the steamers to Lafayette, which was not part of New Orleans before 1852 and did not partake in the Seamen Act. Merchants in each district of the city—whose business culture was still divided along ethnic lines in the 1850s—approached the police to convince them to ignore the law that required prosecution of free Black people from outside the state, who were not legally allowed to be in Louisiana. It must have (partially) worked because in 1851, a justice of the peace publicly defended the inactivity of police.[41] Less control of free Blacks meant a safer environment for fugitive slaves, and explicit non-enforcement of an act against sailors meant that runaway men especially benefitted from this leniency.

While the planter elite maintained a firm hold on most of the slaveholding states, a few places developed a business elite with decreasing stakes in slavery. Industrialists, merchants, and financiers formulated demands on their employees that deviated from those of slaveholders, which made life easier for undocumented and illegal people. And time was on their side. Throughout the antebellum period, those players grew stronger and more important to urban economies. Although never as dominant as in the North, the new southern middle and upper classes came to play significant roles in their arenas. As owners of capital, these men shaped economic change and the transformation of society.[42]

Apart from the benefits of cheap, powerless labor, however, it would be a mistake to interpret the interests of industrialists as hostile to those of planters and to make clear-cut distinction between the two groups. Plantation owners had a stake in transporting their cotton to ports and selling tobacco, wheat, and sugar to the manufactories and refineries. To cement their

interests in important urban centers, they cultivated relations with merchants, slave traders, powerful relatives, and policy makers in the cities.[43]
Moreover, merchants and industrialists often owned or employed enslaved
workers themselves. In 1850, 80 percent of Richmond's leaders were slaveholders, even though the city's political class increasingly diverged from
Virginia's planter class. And it seems that slaveownership came to be concentrated in the hands of the powerful: by 1860, 80 percent of Richmond's adult
male slaves were either owned or hired by municipal officials[44]

By using enslaved labor in industry and production, Richmond was the
most obvious example of a strong planter class that was flexible enough to
accommodate its own interests of slaveholding alongside the progressive economic promises of capitalist production.[45] On the one hand, this revealed the
compatibility of slavery and industrial production. On the other hand,
the profitability of industrial slavery was tied to wages, board money, and self-
accommodation, which effectively turned slaves into semi-wage workers.[46]

The combination of a relatively flexible slave system with progressive
business sectors rendered Richmond the great exception with regard to urban slavery, which continually expanded until its abolition. As the shining
star of the second slavery, Richmond became more and more integrated in a
net of improving infrastructure, logistics, transportation, production, and
services. On the eve of the Civil War, the James River, the Kanawha Canal,
and five railroads connected the city to its hinterland, the northern states, and
the deeper South, and affirmed Richmond's position as a buzzing hub in the
Atlantic-world economy.[47]

In order to secure their business endeavors in cities, capitalists assumed
positions in local politics. Between 1840 and 1860, professionals, merchants,
lawyers, and other businessmen made up roughly three-quarters of Richmond's city council, controlling the city's civic affairs as well as the policies
concerning city building. They were also able to direct tax money into private
industries. Some of them were invested in internal improvement works and
were in constant need of cheap, disposable workers to dig canals and lay railroads in the state, and to pave city streets.[48] As such, they provided the infrastructure for the growth of their own sectors. Yet, infrastructure demanded
high investments, maintenance, and constant improvement of the city as a
magnet for investors and businessmen. Public debt grew.[49] Money for public
works, such as gasworks, waterworks, and street building, was never sufficient and the tax revenue was too scarce to finance important innovations. As
the changing attitudes toward Black people reveal, cheap labor, which could

be recruited from the private sector, including that performed by fugitive slaves and other illegals, became more and more relevant in southern cities.

Illegal but Efficient

The advantages of an illegal part of the population were obvious to city and state authorities. They willingly executed menial jobs at a very low cost, and did not claim poor relief when not working. In some places, Black men and women were accepted into poorhouses but always in much lower numbers than White residents.[50] Mostly, African Americans organized themselves independently to provide for the needy and to guarantee mutual benefit.[51] The downside for cities was that they did not receive taxes from these undocumented, unregistered people.

The advantages of a vulnerable workforce for employers were even clearer. During a time when flexibility was one of the most highly demanded qualities of unskilled labor, owning enslaved workers impeded versatile and short-term employment. Additionally, bondspeople had to be clothed, fed, housed, and cared for in old age. The great difference between free and enslaved labor was that free laborers could partially bargain about the conditions of their employment (although this was even minimally the case within slavery). The less access a worker had to legal protection, the more employers were able to benefit economically.[52] A diverse workforce that was partly undocumented was a boon for capitalists, as was the lack of regulatory measures from policy makers. Black people who hung in the balance between slave and free status allowed employers to avoid the external costs inherent to cheap labor.

The attitudes toward tackling the issue of illegal and undocumented people in the cities were as incomprehensible and complex as the general position toward Black people, and were constantly changing. Despite fugitive slave laws on the state level, the execution of legislation on the local level remained lax at best. In 1854, petitioners in South Carolina claimed that slaveholders found their runaway slaves hired by free Black people in Charleston. Being from rural St. Paul's Parish, they stressed that employing runaways in the city was "antagonistic to the Agricultural interests of the State." The judge, however, declared that it could not be proven "that the person hiring was aware that his [hired] slaves were runaway."[53] In southern cities, there was never any discussion about enacting a law that would have forbidden the employment of somebody else's slave without the owner's consent.[54]

Another example for such a case is from Missouri, where in 1852 Henke & Henke, a company engaged in railroad construction, was indicted for hiring a slave "to maul rails" without the consent of his master, owner, or overseer. Henke & Henke was not found guilty because the law only prohibited the dealing or trading of somebody else's slaves, not their employment. The Supreme Court found that the law "does not include the manual labor of the slave, however wrong it may be to hire or induce a slave to work or labor for a person without the master or owner's knowledge and permission."[55] The courts were seemingly in a situation in which they tried to balance the demands of slaveholders and to protect the economic performances of progressive business.

In Virginia, the power of the industrialists became very apparent in 1850, when the General Assembly ordered that it was henceforth the duty of the owner, not the hirer, to pay for the recovery costs of runaway slaves.[56] Connected to this, it would have been impossible and undesirable to round up all illegal Black residents in the cities. Not only were their numbers too large but, more importantly, the urban economy profited from Black labor, and if Black people who resided illegally in the cities were to be eliminated then the industries would have suffered a great deal. The 1850s were the decade when these developments became most visible. In Richmond, the business elite was by that time clearly dominating the municipal government.[57]

In other places, too, legislation suggests that running away was somewhat tolerated if the labor power was not lost to the state's economy. In Maryland, a new law of 1831 prohibited the hire, employment, or harboring of illegal free Black immigrants to the state, but no mention was made of runaway slaves *from* Maryland. And although a reward of $6 for persons apprehending runaway slaves was made mandatory in 1806 and increased to $30 in 1832, by 1860 the reward was retracted if the runaways did not remove themselves a sufficient distance: "No reward shall be paid under this section for taking up any slave in the county in which said slave is hired, or in which his owner resides." Additionally, from 1860 on, the commitment of an assumed runaway slave to jail was only to be announced in the Baltimore city paper instead of the surrounding areas and in Washington, D.C., as was earlier practice.[58] Slave flight from the city of Baltimore or Baltimore County did not entail a mandatory bounty that would have encouraged bystanders to be on the lookout for absconders.

This is remarkable because it is likely that during this same time, escapes of slaves from Maryland increased generally.[59] Already in 1849, slaveholders from Maryland's Eastern Shore complained that their bondspeople were fleeing in large numbers: "If something is not done, and that speedily too, there will be but few slaves remaining on the Eastern Shore of Maryland in a few years. They are running off almost daily." In 1856 alone, sixty slaves allegedly absconded; another wave of flights took place in 1858.[60] Many of them went to the northern states, while a great many others went to Baltimore.

Given that businessmen were increasingly involved in municipal politics and had largely taken over local governments in some places, they also got a foothold in the police force and from here could enforce or ignore laws. The ineffectiveness of and lack of commitment by police helped to create spaces for all illegals to navigate. Law enforcement, to be clear, was not an autonomously operating entity. The extension of public authority and public law went hand in hand with the centralization and management of the production process. The emergence of the modern police force in the nineteenth century was connected to the economic interests of the rising commercial elite class, which prioritized fighting disorderly conduct over combatting crime. In this manner, the police contributed to ensuring "a stable and orderly work force [and] a stable and orderly environment for the conduct of business." Policemen were foremost instructed to keep the working class in line rather than aggressively pursue and eliminate crime or criminal behavior. By financing the police, who essentially acted on their behalves, through tax money, elites also reverted the costs of protecting their businesses to the public.[61]

In this light, the view that slaveholding interests' domination of the antebellum social order was universal becomes complicated. In places other than Charleston, supervision and patrolling was not as strict and it was less challenging for fugitive slaves to walk the streets, find employment, and live unmolested. Moreover, police answered to local politicians temporarily in charge rather than having a self-maintaining system of quality assurance. They were blatantly brutal and corrupt. Many drank while on duty.[62]

Corruption and lack of regulation could benefit undocumented people. In 1858, when New Orleans was in its sixth year of a modernized police force, the local press reprinted a story about runaway slaves who were "becoming a source of very considerable trouble now." The police, however, did not regard fugitive slaves as part of the official tasks they were paid to perform and stated: "The police authorities contend that it is not part of their regular duty to hunt after runaway negroes." Not entirely wanting to let this source of extra income slip by, however, they added that "if they [the watchmen] do ferret them out, it must be done outside of their regular business, and with a view of liberal consideration."[63]

Since a bounty could motivate watchmen to find runaways, slaveholders constantly sought them out to be on the lookout for their missing slaves. And although some were apprehended, this happened on a much smaller scale than one might expect. Official complaints by slaveholders were rare. Occasionally, however, a master would lose his patience, like A. B. Shelton, whose runaway slave Armstead Meckins was not taken up in Richmond although "he has been seen every day since" he ran off in February 1844. To incentivize the police, Shelton offered a reward of ten dollars only if Meckins would be brought back within the remaining two weeks of the month. Otherwise, he would only pay the legal fees.[64] Policemen, who were often non-slaveholding White men and, in the later antebellum period, increasingly Irishmen, did not feel any commitment to catching other people's slaves.[65] This could have been different if policy makers had identified runaway slaves in southern cities as a major concern and if they had incentivized police accordingly.

Through corruption, disregard, and laxness, the police contributed to the toleration of runaway slaves in southern cities, depending on who was in charge of giving the orders. They generally failed to effectively enforce laws passed at the state level designed to keep free Blacks and slaves separate, and to make slaves more visible to the authorities by enforcing the laws that required all Black people to carry passes or free papers at all times. In this context, non-enforcement went hand in hand with ignoring the issue, and urban authorities essentially tolerated the presence of runaway slaves in their cities.

From Private to Public Slavery

Despite the successful maneuvers of a great many runaways to become invisible in the urban disorder, smaller numbers did not make it and were apprehended by slave patrols, civilians, or watchmen. While fugitives and Black people without documentation, whose presence in the cities was overlooked, helped to diversify the workforce, those caught were used to feed the labor regime in a different way. The rise of industries and the increasing dominance of capitalist employers changed the ways in which labor was recruited. When prices for slaves increased significantly, the individual worker became more valuable—and this had an impact on runaway slaves as well as on the Black population as a whole.

Over time, the perception of the profit of workers changed. One way to read this is in the sentencing of enslaved offenders. While executions of slaves were generally rare in Virginia, from around the turn of the nineteenth century, bondspeople who were convicted offenders saw their death penalties carried out in lower numbers than in later times.[66] In the 1830s, many enslaved men and women found guilty of a severe crime and condemned to be executed had their sentence commuted by the governor to sale and transportation out of the United States.[67] Traders often sold them in the British Caribbean (and prior to 1821, in Spanish Florida).[68] With this, policymakers aimed at getting rid of slaves deemed dangerous to the public safety without forfeiting the investment in them. Exceptions were made for slaves who committed especially severe crimes, like infanticide.[69]

By the late 1830s, enslaved offenders who committed murder could also be reprieved for sale and transportation. This even applied to a convicted murderer of a White man. These developments mirrored the rising prices for enslaved workers after the crisis of 1837. Since the Commonwealth of Virginia officially purchased sentenced criminals from their owners, large financial loss was avoided by reselling or forcibly employing them. In the early 1840s, for example, George Mosby was not an exception when his death sentence for stealing money from his owner was reprieved for twelve months in prison and he was moved to the penitentiary.[70] The governor realized that the labor force was something on which the state could capitalize, and he was certainly also influenced by dominant slaveholders who lobbied for compensation.

In the 1850s, finally, the death penalty was nearly obsolete and slaves were directly sentenced to sale and transportation which, in turn, was often commuted to lifelong labor on the public works. Slaves were by that time so valuable that the state often had to dig deep into its pockets to reimburse the owners. For instance, Pompey, sentenced to sale and transportation for killing the free Black woman Elisha, received a commutation by the governor to "labour on the Public works" in the Virginia penitentiary. His price was fixed at $1,060.[71] The placement of slaves and free Blacks in work camps both reflects the changing ideology behind punishments and the growing value of Black bodies as a source of labor, especially the bodies of men.

Due to difficulties to procure enough financing for public works, "internal improvement" and chain gangs were one of the main sectors in which apprehended runaway slaves were coerced to labor.[72] The chain gang was one of increasingly few integrated work sites in Richmond, unlike New Orleans, where it was all-Black beginning in 1829. Discussions about the management of convict institutions reveal that racially segregated facilities were preferred, yet this standard was only fulfilled when it did not render the work of the captives less efficient. In the 1850s, the Louisiana Penitentiary was for efficiency reasons leased out to a private company. Black and White convicts were officially required to work separately from one another "but the Lessees deem it impracticable by the present arrangement of work shops and yards," reported the Board of Directors. And so, this practice was condoned.[73]

FIGURE 6.1 Runaways committed to the state depot. From 1858 on, Louisiana sought to administer its runaway slaves in centralized form through the Runaway Slave Depot in Baton Rouge. Daily newspapers give an impression of the dimension. *Daily Advocate*, April 18, 1959.

Runaway slaves, who were caught but not reclaimed, and men and women suspected to be of that group, were especially singled out by the growing numbers of penitentiaries and workhouses and put to work for the benefit of the state. Jail ledgers and "Committed"-advertisements give an approximate impression of this dimension (see figure 6.1). Those who were not delivered back to their owners were forced to power the economic system created by political, economic, and business leaders.

Historian Aaron Hall has claimed that White citizens were in favor of employing Black people as public slaves because "being a slave-master state was a collective, democratic project for Louisiana's enfranchised white public, who exercised their political power to sustain the program and receive its benefits."[74] Louisiana owned about 100 men between 1834 and 1860 who labored mostly, but not exclusively, outside the cities and towns to maintain water routes; other states also leased slaves. The Louisiana state engineer constantly requested to purchase more slaves, in a process that was essentially labor recruitment within the system of slavery. Detained runaway slaves (usually men) were equally victims of what Hall has called "indirect public slavery."[75]

Even when considering the fact that fewer enslaved women fled slavery in the first place, we can perhaps detect a correlation between the significantly higher share of male runaways that were taken up and the work requirements of this indirect public slavery, which was foremost geared toward hard labor on construction sites.

Testifying to the presence of fugitive slaves in the New Orleans chain gang, Alfred Wilkinson from New York stated:

> I stayed in New Orleans three weeks: during that time there used to pass
> by where I stayed a number of slaves, each with an iron band around his
> ankle, a chain attached to it, and an eighteen pound ball at the end. They
> were employed in wheeling dirt with a wheelbarrow; they would put
> the ball into the barrow when they moved.—I recollect one day, that I
> counted nineteen of them, sometimes there were not as many; they were
> driven by a slave, with a long lash, as if they were beasts. These, I learned,
> were runaway slaves from the plantations above New Orleans.[76]

The public display of a chain gang of runaway slaves in the center of New Orleans was a way for White New Orleanians to demonstrate that the government was in firm control of the dangerous elements of the slave system. It sent an incisive message to enslaved and illegal people that they could perhaps escape the control of an individual slaveholder but never the control of slaveholding society. Racial control might also be, alongside economic considerations, a factor in the deployment of runaways. Besides cleaning the streets and repairing the dikes, race-based chain gangs displayed a racial and gendered violence that disguised itself as legal punishment.[77] The lawful dimension worked towards creating a sense of criminalization of people of African descent and, vice versa, exacerbated the feeling of superiority of White people.

Louisiana was the state that capitalized most visibly on the capture of fugitive slaves. In 1857, a runaway slave depot was opened in the capital of Baton Rouge with the purpose of storing them all in a centralized spot.[78] Prior to 1857, the police jail of Baton Rouge had functioned as a primary prison for runaways. All runaway slaves detained in county jails throughout the state were to be delivered to Baton Rouge if not claimed by their owners after two months.[79] The official rhetoric advocated through the legislature was that it would make life easier for slaveholders who now did not have to scan all county jails separately in search of their property. Yet behind this stood a massive apparatus of distributing extremely cheap labor to state-sponsored and state-owned projects. In fact, the runaway depot was explicitly established for the Internal Improvement Department to access laborers.[80] If unclaimed, runaway slaves caught up in this machinery became property of the state after twelve months.[81]

Already in 1817, the city council of New Orleans had issued an ordinance stating that "all such male slaves as have been brought to the police jail, and have not been claimed within three days" were to be put in the chain gang. Indeed, all runaways were expected to labor on the public works unless indicated otherwise. In 1840, the ordinance was amended to include female runaways who were not claimed within five days, and "who are capable to work, shall be employed at the works of the city."[82] Historian Rashauna Johnson has, in a similar fashion, stated that the New Orleans penal system served "to remove from the urban landscape those persons who threatened the interests of the local planter and merchant elite and to use their labor to build local infrastructure."[83] These measures clearly demonstrate the relationship between slavery and the criminal justice system.

Likewise, the city government of Richmond employed slaves to pave the streets, clean and maintain the capitol grounds, remove trash, and to work as sanitarian laborers (especially during epidemics).[84] These tasks were the lowest, dirtiest, and most dangerous. Besides municipal authorities, the federal government also made use of this form of labor. Testifying to the involvement of the U.S. government in southern slavery, formerly enslaved George Teamoh stated that "above hundred, if not thousands of slaves [were] employed on the government works" in and around Norfolk in the 1840s.[85]

The availability of runaways, however, was not as easily predictable as the purchase or hiring of slaves. But the initial investment costs involved were also much lower. While the considerable employment of fugitive slaves in public works might appear to support a case for authorities to catch as many escapees from slavery as they could, the system was far from being optimized and they faced a number of obstacles in exploiting the labor of Black people.

Resistance was a reality and active. Because runaways, the enslaved, and free Black people met in urban places of confinement, these places were hubs of information exchange. Henry Bibbs, for example, while detained in Bedford jail, Kentucky, instructed two enslaved inmates about how to get to Canada, and countless slaves fled from jails and prisons, with or without the help of others.[86] Public works projects, during which workers were only incarcerated before and after work, were another site of flight. In New Orleans, this must have happened so frequently that in 1838, the First Municipality decided to guard itself against possible legal claims of slaveowners whose property absconded while working for the city: "When slaves detained in the police jail, are employed in any of the works of the Municipality," resolved the legislators, "the owner or owners of said slaves, shall not in any instance have the right to complaint against this Municipality on account of running away."[87] This ordinance mirrored the resentment that many slaveholders harbored toward the chain gang and public works, where working conditions were miserable and many slaves died.[88]

Multitudes of runaway slave ads in cities asked that runaway slaves be delivered at a certain home address, indicating that slaveholders wanted to avoid their bondspeople ending up in prisons, as Kelly Birch and Thomas Buchanan have suggested.[89] Charleston issued clear, official instructions about how to deal with runaways, and virtually all other southern cities advised on what to do with Black people on the streets after curfew. Actions like these marked a shift from slaveholders to municipal authorities as the key agents in controlling and punishing Black people in the public space, thereby ensuring that the maintenance of slavery was a collective undertaking.[90] Evidently, the cooperation between slaveholders and authorities was not seamless, as they often clashed about ideas of how to handle Black labor.

Authorities confronted major administrative challenges in dealing with runaways. They had to be careful not to infringe on the legal ownership of slaveholders because the legal system was liable to protect private ownership. The involvement of jailers and sheriffs had to be administered; jails and penitentiaries regularly struggled with financial issues, which raised doubts about their effectiveness and efficiency; and the responsibility to pay the jail fees was a constant nuisance between private slaveholders, jailers, and authorities. Especially in the worldview of larger slaveholders, it was they who had established this infrastructure of slave control and discipline.

Often, runaway slaves were apprehended and advertised but not claimed by anyone. In a number of cases, they stayed in jail so long that the costs for their confinement exceeded the sum for which they were eventually sold. In the 1820s, after a 402-day detention in the county jail of Caroline County, Virginia, the fees for Sam amounted to $124. Since Sam was, according to the jailer, "infirm & crippled," he was sold for $78.40.[91] The jailer of Abbeville District, South Carolina, was in 1856 "bound to receive" a senior enslaved woman called Daphney who was committed as a runaway. After being jailed for twelve months, advertised, and offered for sale, nobody took an interest in purchasing Daphney since she was described as "very old + utterly worthless." The expenses of the jailer piled up to $131.62, including $10 for the year-long "Committed" ad in the paper, which he was legally obligated to place.[92] It also happened frequently that the owners of detained runaways could not be located. When in 1818 fugitive Jim died in jail after 170 days, the jailer of

Kershaw Parish, South Carolina, sought reimbursement for the expenditures for lodging, medicine, and the burial.[93]

Other times, slaveholders were aware that their bondspeople were in jail but, mostly out of economic considerations, refused to claim them. In the 1840s, Benjamin Bryan faced the problem that "five runaway slaves belonging to five different individuals whose names are given and who reside in the State, died in the jail [of Baton Rouge] of which he is the keeper, without having been claimed by their owners." Since the respective slaveowners did not pay "any part of their expense," he petitioned the House of Representatives "to remunerate him for the outlay to which he has been subjected on account of the said negroes: wherefore the petitioner claims from the state the sum of $544 85 cts., as per account, for keeping, feeding, clothing and burying said negroes, as well as for the Doctor's bill."[94]

Slaveholders who eschewed the support of their old or incapacitated slaves—and thereby once again refuted the myth of slavery as a paternalistic social system—appeared to be no exception, and a committee was convened to look into the matter. Citing the sum of $869.19, which had been paid in the past four years in the context of similar claims, the committee recommended the House not to comply with Bryan's or future requests: "If the State indulged in the liberality of paying" for the accommodation of slaves in jails, "merely because the owners of the slaves are unknown, or, if known, refuse to acknowledge the claims presented to them, your committee are of [the] opinion that such a system of appropriation and remunerations would require all the resources of an inexhaustible treasury."[95] Jailers like Bryan had to defray the costs on behalf of much wealthier southerners. As with those slaveholders who received financial compensation from Virginia for the slaves who were expelled or deployed on the public works, they shifted the costs of maintaining unwanted workers to the public.

The treasuries of Maryland confronted additional expenditures. Unlike in other states, if Black persons were jailed as runaways but later believed to be free, they were from 1817 onward to be released and the expenses were levied on the county. Unsurprisingly, some years later the General Assembly complained "that Baltimore county is subjected to great annual expense on account of negroes being committed to the jail of that county, on suspicion of being runaway slaves."[96] The law, however, remained unchanged until the Civil War. The logical consequence was that Baltimore police reduced the frequency of the apprehension of people they assumed to have escaped from slavery. Here, the inefficient coordination within the criminal justice apparatus worked partly in favor of Black Americans.

Views on Black Labor

The decline of slavery in Maryland did not catch those in power by surprise. When the attitudes toward Black work began to shift, employers found their own ways to secure cheap labor. In Baltimore, legislation stipulated that Black people who did not work in the service of White economic interests could be apprehended and forced to work and their children could be bound out as apprentices. Moreover, the Maryland penitentiary stipulated strict minimum terms for free African Americans. In 1817, it was one year, in 1825, two, and in 1839, eighteen months.[97]

Penitentiaries opened in 1800 in Richmond, in 1811 in Baltimore, and in 1835 in Baton Rouge. South Carolina did not have one before the Civil War. In Maryland, the inmates engaged in the manufacture of cotton and woolen goods, boot and shoemaking, carpet weaving, and stone cutting. They also lent their labor to commercial manufacturers.[98] In Baton Rouge, women washed and mended in the prison laundry while men had a series of occupations, including the making of bricks, shoes, cabinets, saddles and harnesses, and cigars, along with spinning, weaving, blacksmithing, corn grinding, cooking, and baking. From 1842 onward, they came to labor on internal improvement projects, the same year that Louisiana started to commute death sentences into lifelong labor on the public works.[99] Business reports show that the efficiency of these punitive institutions varied from place to place. With an average return of $53.48 per inmate beyond the expenses of maintenance in 1842, the Maryland penitentiary yielded substantial profits.[100] By contrast, policy makers in Louisiana struggled over decades to render the state's prison cost-efficient, a project that continued to fail even after the privatization of the institution.[101]

Although penitentiaries were originally envisioned to reform White men, they were systematic attempts to extract labor from people who were considered exploitable and unproductive. Contemporary politicians noticed that Black people ended up there disproportionally.[102] This included runaways, who essentially were slaves without owners, as well as free Black people whom some White southerners likewise considered slaves without owners. Consequently, those who were found without papers, or apprehended for committing a crime, were held and forcedly put to work. Their targeting was legally and politically less complicated because authorities did not need to clash with slaveholders over the use of their bondspeople's physical labor. The control of the free Black population equaled the control of the workforce, as Barbara Fields has claimed,[103] and comprehensive legal restrictions rendered people without documentation particularly vulnerable. The extreme criminalization of free African Americans and the discriminatory social and economic conditions they faced facilitated their imprisonment.

At times, White citizens articulated their understanding of the penitentiaries' labor as for the "common good." In 1825, "The Memorial of the Richmond & Manchester auxilliary Society for Colonizing in Africa," a branch of the American Colonization Society, suggested to the Virginia General Assembly "to furnish the emigrants with a few articles of coarse clothing, with farming utensils, and with such other articles manufactured in the State Penitentiary."[104] The petitioners' position was largely in line with that of employers who regarded the labor power of poor people as the property of society as a whole, another ideology that disadvantaged Black people.[105] The pendulum could, however, also swing in the opposite direction. In Baton Rouge, White mechanics petitioned for years against the competition of products that came out of the penitentiary.[106]

With a more general view, mechanics in Charleston, "suffering under the distress incident to the situation of those who have to live by their labor," petitioned to be relieved from the "competition of Negro and Colored Workmen, whether Bond or Free." Claiming that their situation had become dire in the previous years and that they struggled to provide for their families, these men asked to more forcefully execute the laws prohibiting the self-hiring of slaves. This was not the first time they asked, and they reminded the state senate that they already had been "disappointed in their hopes."[107]

Approaching mid-century, non-slaveholding Whites grew more assertive in their resistance toward Black competition in the labor markets. White mechanics wrote countless petitions to state and city authorities to ask that actions be taken against the competition by enslaved and free Black Americans. The Maryland legislature was swamped with them, yet none of the petitions with an aim at driving Black people out of certain occupations was granted. But one from 1827, which demanded to exclude people of African descent from the transportation sector, was of special interest, because it provoked Baltimore merchants to file a counterpetition.[108] Very obviously, employers insisted on their right to choose their workers based on their own calculations.

In the 1820s, former South Carolina governor Thomas Pinckney supported free White workers in their fight against enslaved competitors. This was surprising given that Pinckney was a planter and slaveholder himself. Yet, he spoke out against the omnipresence of enslaved labor in Charleston. It was 1822 after all, and Denmark Vesey's failed rebellion still was in front of mind.

Framing his concerns in an economic manner, Pinckney reasoned that if employers hired White labor instead, they "would not have to maintain the superannuated, the infirm, or the indolent, who are now so heavy a tax on the proprietor." Rather, they would "contract for efficient service" and pick a specific worker with the specific skills he needed on a specific day. And, "if the person employed, should be incapable or unwilling to perform, he would be discharged, and a more suitable subject engaged."[109]

In a nutshell, Pinckney's argument was that wage work was more efficient than slavery because hirers did not have to pay for the externalities of labor. He did not manage to convince a sufficient number of supporters,[110] which is hardly surprising given the relationship between South Carolina and slavery. South Carolina planters crafted the most antidemocratic society of all American states and fiercely insisted on slavery as a way of life. Immigrants and free African Americans posed a threat, an "internal free-labor challenge to slavery," as historian Manisha Sinha has put it.[111] They defended the institution of slavery rigorously and unrelentingly and did not shy away from acting destructively to their own economy. This defense and protection of urban slavery conflicted with the introduction of efficient innovations and underlined the power of slaveholders over merchants. Due to the backward technology at Charleston's wharves, enslaved labor power was in higher demand than it would have been otherwise.[112] But the planters also thought that by employing slaves in the city rather than White workers, they had the city firmly under their command. And although this was certainly truer in Charleston than in other cities of the South, the successful camouflaging of so many runaway slaves among the enslaved population contradicts the image of White control over the Black population. Strikingly, Pinckney's idea to restrict slave labor to rural areas showed his realistic assessment of the urban environment, which did not have to depend on slavery.

Pickney's pioneering thoughts were taken up again later when southern cities became more populated with White residents and the share of slaveholders among the southern population fell. In the 1850s, the national economy grew more complex and local politics had to correspond more to regional and national concerns. At the same time, cities became more powerful and local leaders formed associations to present their interests at the state level.[113] There are, however, numerous examples pointing to reverse developments to White replacing Black labor. Tobacco manufacturers in Richmond employed free Black men, White women, enslaved women and men, and children during the first half of the antebellum period. By 1840, enslaved men composed the majority of tobacco factory workers; in some places they constituted the entire workforce. At the same time, Joseph Anderson, owner of the Tredegar Iron Works, experienced difficulties in controlling a White labor force.[114] Accounts like these show that society's attitude towards the laboring classes was neither linear nor uniform.

Political speeches reveal that the question of who was to form the laboring classes in southern cities was complicated by the fact that throughout the South, different voices spoke in favor of and against Black and White labor at different times. Colonel C. W. Jacobs, member of the House of Delegates in Maryland, who strongly opposed "free negroism" and evoked the "terrors of Haiti," claimed in 1859 that there were "in all our large cities and towns, enough poor and needy whites to perform the little handy jobs that free negroes monopolise." Jacobs's view of Black people was that *"some of them* are industrious, but the vast majority are so much dead weight upon the State and her resources."[115]

In the same year, the Convention of Maryland Slaveholders "came to the conclusion that it was highly inexpedient to undertake any measure for the general removal of our free Black population from the State. [...] Their removal from the State would deduct nearly 50 per cent from the household and agricultural labor furnished by people of this color, [...] would produce great discomfort and inconvenience to the great body of householders, would break up the business and destroy the property of large numbers of landowners and land-renters." Showing no interest in expelling free African Americans from the state anymore, the committee concluded that it would be better to "make these people orderly, industrious and productive."[116] Thomas H. Hicks, governor of Maryland from 1858 to 1862, also made clear that free Blacks who worked were not the problem, especially not "in her populous city [Baltimore], and in the more thickly settled portions of the State."[117]

Ideas of who should constitute the laboring classes fluctuated throughout the South. The situation was complex and regionally and locally diverse. As long as measures like compelling hired-out slaves to wear badges were not enforced; slave patrols, police guards, and night watches were understaffed and underpaid; and the majority of Whites' petitions against Black competition remained fruitless, runaway slaves and other undocumented African Americans were beneficiaries of the illegal labor market. It secured their employment, and hence survival, and safeguarded their anonymity. However, the changing attitudes toward Black labor culminated in the late 1850s in a situation that for the first time negatively impacted southern cities of refuge.

The Power of Democracy

The 1850s were a period in which lower-class Whites were politically very active, especially in cities. Even recently arrived immigrants were mobilized by political parties. Counting thousands of wage laborers, immigrants often came to constitute the majority of White adult men. Parallel to the dominance of capitalist interests, lower-class Whites discovered the political power of the masses and did their best to influence politics to their own advantage. In Charleston, for example, stevedores first became increasingly White and then increasingly active in political, economic, and labor debates. Other White workingmen, too, gained access to local and, later, state institutions.[118]

Politically, European immigrants grew relatively strong because they knew how and were allowed to organize themselves. On a social level, they relied heavily on their intra-ethnic networks and established forums for political discussion aimed at benefitting their own kind. As newcomers in society, it was important to position themselves on the right side of the racial divide. Independent of whether they ever came to endorse slavery on a personal level, the political priority for immigrants was to broadcast their potential to be good American citizens.[119] Their political awareness was channeled through participation in voting. Visitors like Alexis de Tocqueville were struck by the "equality of conditions" they observed in the United States.[120] Nevertheless, democratization of the political and civil spheres did not improve the material conditions of the lower classes, and the 1850s were a period in which White poverty was increasing in a great many southern cities.

Seen in this light, it is not surprising that from the point of view of traditional pro-slavery nationalists, the largest cities in the South hosted their political enemies.[121] Lower-class Whites were left behind in socioeconomic terms, and cities like New Orleans and Baltimore posed a threat to White unity precisely because the conditions of White wage earners in a society dominated by slavery were unique. The contradictions between democracy and the hierarchies produced by racial slavery loomed especially large. The strategy of training slaves, which increased their monetary value both in regard to hiring rates and sales prices, had left White people behind and the new republic essentially failed to produce an independent class of White mechanics.[122] This backward position clashed with the promises of capitalism, which claimed that in theory every individual free laborer could escape their fate by means of upward mobility. When suffrage rights were extended to non-property-holding White men, the opposition of the White working classes to the competition from slaves and free African Americas became more strongly politicized.[123]

Nineteenth-century democracy entailed, according to Eric Hobsbawm, "the growing role of the common man in the affairs of state." Yet "from the point of view of ruling classes the important thing was not what 'the masses' believed, but that their beliefs now counted in politics." As a consequence, while White society became more heterogeneous, every group within it had to be given the impression that their political voice was taken into account. Especially the middle classes, who insisted on representative governments, and the lower classes, whose mobilization promised vast numbers, had to be accommodated.[124] Fugitive slaves appeared as an obvious target because they presented an economic threat to large parts of the voting population.

But fugitives were hard to locate because they often successfully camouflaged among the urban Black populations. For those in power in the cities, it was more practical to go after undocumented residents in general. Their numbers were much larger and they legally did not belong to individual Whites. In 1853, Joseph Mayo became the first popularly elected mayor of Richmond. Under his administration, illegal free Black residents were systematically arrested, imprisoned, and forced to work. In a revealing study, Carey Latimore has analyzed how legally manumitted but illegally in the state residing free Black Americans and their offspring in Richmond were systematically tracked in times of labor shortage, jailed, and hired out for exceptionally low wages in order to pay off their jail fees.[125]

In Mayo's logic, this was only consistent. On taking office, he promised to intensify control over Black Richmonders and to "make Negroes and mulattos know their places and obey the law."[126] Besides providing cheap labor for private employers, these moves also demonstrated to the public that the mayor was acting against the large illegal free Black population that constituted an economic threat to practically every social group that had the right to vote—except for the industrialists, who dominated the city's political elite.

In earlier decades, people without documentation were also arrested. The records of the Richmond city sergeant show that Black people were apprehended for "going at large and want of free papers." Most managed to pay off the jail fees for the time they were being held captive. John Tale, for example, jailed on April 6, 1841, was able to prove his free status, and was released on April 14 after paying $3.79. Anderson Freeman had to pay $10.17 because he was incarcerated longer. In an extreme case, Sarah Ann Farro remained captive for 226 days. In the end she (or somebody else) paid the costs of $85.39.[127]

Others defaulted. Lucy Briggs, apprehended on November 22, 1841, proved her free status on April 19 of the following year. Six days later she was nevertheless hired out at the Old Market at public auction, probably because her jail fees were not paid. Ellen Banister was hired out for two years and eight months, and Jim Finney for the period of ten years.[128] The reason these durations of forced labor were so long was that the Richmond's Hustings Court accepted daily hiring rates of as little as ten cents. Black people unable to prove their freedom were sold.[129] In these events, refugees from slavery could end up in the police's net as "by-catch."

The criminalization of African Americans rendered their subsequent incarceration and forced labor easier and more acceptable. The Society of Friends observed these procedures in 1844. Stressing that the punishment was disproportionate to the offence committed, they warned that free Black Richmonders without papers were regularly apprehended, jailed, and sold, and their children held in perpetual service.[130] These political measures benefitted the social groups of small-scale slaveholders, small merchants, and middle-class craftsmen who could either not afford to buy or hire slaves, or who were disproportionally affected by slave flight, as well as other employers who sought to decrease their labor costs.

Carey Latimore, counting about 600 such cases between 1850 and 1860 in Richmond, has identified tobacco processors (partly from wealthy families) and artisans among those hiring discount workers. He has emphasized that this kind of labor relation reduced the willingness of the nominal masters to assume any responsibilities for the hirelings' well-being. Not being White, they could not sue against abuse; not being enslaved, they did not present a long-term investment. Conversely, the startling truth was that those borrowing criminalized, illegalized workers from the municipality, "had every incentive to push [them] to the limit to extract as much labour as possible."[131]

During strong economic cycles, which created a high demand for unskilled labor, the arrest and forced hiring-out of undocumented Black Richmonders was frequent. Inversely, after the Panic of 1857, which negatively affected the manufacturing business, police arrested fewer African Americans for lack of identification. In 1858, twenty-nine criminalized Blacks were hired out; a year later, it was only twenty-two, and in 1860, eleven. While such measures may have constituted a legal assault on the free Black population of Richmond in theory, in practice, from the 1840s on, efforts by the city authorities to genuinely try to keep Black people out of Richmond proved half-hearted at best, as Latimore has noted.[132] For fugitives, who were by definition illegal, this condition had visible consequences only when the law was enforced. When it was not, those in power could make use of the threat to enforce it as a mode of labor control.

Throughout the South, hitherto loose and sporadic measures against the undocumented became somewhat more systemic in the last decade before the Civil War. The spike in arrests from 1857 to 1860 corresponded with acute fear and frustration among White residents due to economic crises and overcrowded labor markets. Mayors, even if not affiliated with the Democratic Party, saw themselves responsible for pleasing their nontraditional base. Municipal authorities in various cities likewise undertook steps that served the double purpose of alarming the Black communities and signaling to lower middle- and lower-class Whites that something was being done to target the people whom they saw as their rivals in the job market.

For example, for all the slaveholders who purchased slave badges and filled the trove of Charleston's treasurer, significant numbers did not. In 1859, after decades of White tradesmen and laborers complaining about the issue, the mayor decided to set an example. Lamenting that "the procuring of badges for slaves is a matter very much neglected by parties having servants to hire," the city authorities started to fill the dead letter with life and instructed the police "to rigidly enforce the ordinance."[133] The instructions resulted in higher numbers of arrests of people who worked without badges in November and December, which underlined the—surely unexpected—commitment to enforce the law (see table 6.1). This enforcement affected bondspeople, slaveowners, and those without official documentation. A local paper informed in December that "scarcely a day passes that some owner has not to pay the penalty incurred for this neglect." The penalty referred to was indeed delicate as "the fine imposed for one omission would pay for a badge for five or ten years."[134]

These two months of stricter enforcement at the end of the year 1859 probably came right in time to have slaveowners invest money in the tags for the following year, and afterwards the arrests paused for three entire months. After beginning anew around April 1860, the seizures of Black people for "working without badge" soared again in the following summer months, when more enslaved people than ever before were taken up. This period represented the only time in which slave badge laws were *actually* enforced. Slaveholders gravitated to the city treasurer in large numbers to prevent even higher financial cuts. In the summer of that year, the *Charleston Courier* testified to the new situation: "It is estimated that in the last two or three days as many as three or four hundred badges have been sold by the City Treasurer. Some sixty or seventy negros have been brought up by the Police before the Mayor for working out without a badge. Most of them were those who were

TABLE 6.1 Selected arrests in Charleston, 1858–1860. Arrest patterns show the stricter enforcement of laws targeting Black people in the late 1850s.

	Runaways		Slaves without pass		Improper ticket		Working without badge		Nonpayment capitation tax	
	M	F	M	F	M	F	M	F	M	F
Dec. 1858	9	2	10		4		1			
Feb. 1859	12	1	16	2	3	1				
March	6		16	3	2	1	13	3	2	1
April	14	2			5		7	8	1	3
June	15	2	8	1	4	1	5	1	4	7
July	10	5	14	3	12				2	
August	13	6			10	1		3		
September	15	2	10		2	1				
October	13	3	11		7	2				
November	10		**20**		11	2	11	3	4	3
December	5	3	**21**	8	8		8	2	**12**	**20**
Jan. 1860	*		**15**	6	*				*	
February	11	2	**19**	1	5	1			°	
March	9	2	**21**	2	10	2				
April	9	3	**20**	8	13	2	**14**	**13**	3	
May	~	4	**23**	3	7		**17**	**28**	8	17
June	16	4	**18**	5			**12**	**20**	9	16
July	17	4	7	4	7		**9**	**31**	6	14
August	9	3	12	4	4		**39**	**54**	5	10
September	9	1	**19**	5				2		
October	7	5	**20**	4	9	1	6			

Boldface font highlights entries of special interest that are discussed in the text.

  *Illegible one-digit number

  °Illegible

  ~Illegible two-digit number

  Source: Proceedings of the City Council of Charleston, S.C., 1859 I; Charleston (S.C.) City Council, Proceedings of Council, POC-002 M: 1859–1870, CCPL.

under the mistaken notion that they were free and did not require it." The mayor then announced that these people were not free.[135]

    Women were overrepresented among these arrests, which seemed to be an exception as earlier patterns, prior to the summer of 1860, show that women were for all selected offenses (being a runaway slave, having no pass [usually after curfew], working without a badge, and nonpayment of annual capitation taxes) less often arrested than men. Although Black women outnumbered Black men three to two in 1860,[136] they were usually less exposed than men because they tended to work indoors and attract less attention. It stands to reason that in 1860, the enforcement of the slave badge law occurred through crackdowns at specific work sites. The high arrest rates of women indicate that in the four months from May to August, the police targeted marketplaces, where women were overrepresented, and spared the wharves and manufactories. This had the effect of causing maximum publicity while avoiding the resentment of merchants and manufacturers, who more directly depended on male workers. Gender, then, not only shaped slave flight but also the politics of retrieval.[137]

The crackdowns were not only directed at slaves working without badges. In late 1859 and throughout the year 1860, racial control after curfew was also tightened, as the arrests of enslaved men without passes show. December 1859 furthermore denoted the absolute highest persecutions for nonpayment of capitation taxes (see also table 6.1). The generally precarious economic conditions of the lower classes in the 1850s, the ideology of White supremacy, and the expansion of suffrage led people to demand more concessions. It is therefore no surprise that lower-class Whites, who had mostly refrained from petitions as a political tool, discovered this channel.

Accordingly, Charleston's stevedores asked for the complete exclusion of enslaved coworkers from their business in 1859. The men signing this petition were from diverse origins, including English, Spanish, northern, southern, and Canadian men, but all felt united in their cause as free White workers. Decision makers, however, were cautious. Stevedores did not own slaves, Michael Thompson has argued, a circumstance which made them suspicious. Because those in power did not want to lose their slaves working on the wharves nor forfeit the strength of slavery in all possible branches, the petition was rejected. The stevedores then joined the White artisans and redirected their efforts at a less effective but more easily winnable fight: they started to attack free Black workers.[138]

Democratic mayor Charles Macbeth gave in to the pressure. It was easier for him to grant White workingmen this smaller concession and curtail their attacks on enslaved competitors. In August 1860, the newspapers announced that the manumission laws of 1820 and 1822 would be executed without mercy, which would have meant enslavement for a significant number of people. For many Black people, this went too far. About 1,000 free African Americans, many with high professional skills, fled Charleston in late 1860 and early 1861. Most of them went to northern cities.[139]

The crackdowns spread through the South. In Richmond, an order threatened to have the sheriff arrest "delinquent free negroes" who did not pay their taxes for the year 1857.[140] Some of those who lived there illegally came under pressure to petition for an official permit. Whereas in the entire decade of the 1830s, only six petitions were handed in (of which all were permitted to stay in Richmond); in the year 1860 alone, there were forty-one cases—nineteen were allowed to stay, seventeen had to leave.[141] This was still not a large amount, and in all of Virginia, there were only 124 cases of free African Americans residing illegally in the state between 1830 and 1860.[142] This could have gone differently if the political will to remove these people had been stronger.

In New Orleans, 913 runaway slaves were arrested during fifteen months in 1858 and 1859.[143] Additionally, authorities announced rewards of $10 for policemen and civilians who arrested Black people who were in the state in contravention of the law.[144] Of those people who were committed to the parish prison for being in Louisiana illegally, none were women.[145] Contrary to Charleston, it is likely that the controls occurred mostly on the docks where men worked.

Prior to this, the offense of being in Louisiana illegally was only problematic when people committed other crimes for which they were arrested. Now, the accompanying news coverage was massive and people stormed the mayor's office, calling for his registration. Most people accused of contravention were handled by the recorder, who gave them a warning. If they did not leave and were taken up again, their cases could end at the First District Court. Unsurprisingly, many people did not appear at the hearings[146] and disappeared in the crowd, just like they had done before. Only in Baltimore were runaway slaves and other undocumented people spared from systematic roundups. The negligible presence of slavery in the city and the sheer numbers of legally free people protected the masses.

To complete the picture, in the last years before the Civil War, laws that foresaw the punishment of those who abetted slave flight were reintroduced, strengthened and, for the first time, executed with visible effects. The mayor of New Orleans tightened the sentence for passing as free and for aiding fugitive slaves.[147] Virginia released a code "to more effectually prevent the escape of slaves" in 1856. In the aftermath, several White men received delicate prison sentences, mostly five or six years.[148] Men and women who were caught forging papers for prospective fugitives likewise ran higher risk of being prosecuted and found guilty.[149] Although the sudden execution of these ordinances provoked panic among the urban Black populations,[150] these attacks should foremost be seen as an assertion of control by White society over Black people. Without downplaying the troublesome effects that the raids must have had on the free Black, undocumented, and refugee populations in southern cities, these measures were essentially of a short-term, sporadic nature.

It was clear that these actions were not adequate to accommodate the desire of most White Americans in the Upper South, which was to get rid of the entire free Black population. The brief revival of the American Colonization Society in the 1850s (after a gradual decline in the 1830s) reflected this. Suddenly, deporting all Black people in the country turned into a solution that seemed desirable to many Whites. The way they saw the world, slavery could not be abolished because Black people remained inferior, and when free, posed a severe threat to the racial order, and only worked under coercion.[151] The most visible and literal exclusion of Black people from American society was the infamous *Dred Scott v. Sandford* case of 1857, in which the Supreme Court ruled that no person of African descent could claim citizenship in the United States.[152] Nevertheless, it was not possible to force Black people out and it was likewise not possible to incarcerate them all. What municipal governments could do, however, was to aggravate their lives, spread fear among the urban communities, and simultaneously reassure and empower White residents by making them feel supported and protected.

THE ATTITUDES TOWARD fugitive slaves in urban spaces depended on the constant negotiation and division of political power between different groups. These groups had partly converging, and, more importantly, partly diverging understandings of and interests in Black labor. Slaveholders constituted the highest political authorities in the southern states, yet merely ruling in their own favor became increasingly challenging as industrial capitalism began to encroach on agricultural economies. Far from claiming that urban slavery was not relevant to the South anymore, urban-rural rivalries in state politics emerged as a clear weak spot in the slave system.

As new classes of financiers, merchants, and industrialists grew stronger, they filled important local political positions. Their businesses depended on a plentiful and cheap labor force, and the more powerful this capitalist middle class became, the more absorptive the respective city grew vis-à-vis fugitive slaves and other undocumented people who could be easily exploited as wage workers. At the end of the day, urban employers benefitted most from the tolerance by political leaders and law enforcement of undocumented Black residents and the presence of runaway slaves. In no event was the labor power of a slave refugee lost to White society. When they succeeded at blending in with the urban Black populations, they deliberately integrated in the lower sectors of the labor markets. In the fewer cases that they were caught, they were either sent back to labor for their owners or forcefully employed by the state or local governments. The collaborative relations between authorities and slaveowners never eliminated the tensions between them, which became very visible in the treatment of runaway slaves.

Toward the end of the antebellum era, the lower and the lower-middle classes achieved a stronger political voice. Primarily driven by resistance to economic competition by Black people, they demanded what White supremacy had promised them. Political leadership, now increasingly divided between planters and industrialists, tried to stall action for as long as possible. Yet, in the last years of the 1850s, democracy had provided lower-class Whites with enough power and legislators began to go after free people of African descent, especially the undocumented. This had a devastating impact on illegal spaces of refuge and increased the discovery of fugitive slaves.

The Ambiguities of Illegality

Hardly discernable yet vitally important, thousands of enslaved people found illegal refuge in antebellum southern cities. The prototypical urban fugitive slave was a fit man in his twenties who had had several owners, witnessed close family members get sold away, and worked in a profession that provided him with mobility. His horizon was broader than that of the majority of enslaved Americans. He had a network of acquaintances in the city to where he escaped, had been there before, and integrated into the Black community of a lower-class neighborhood. In the city, he worked as a day laborer on the docks, tirelessly trying to make a living. He attempted to behave and act like a free man in order to avoid attention, frequented underground spaces for socialization, dodged the watchmen, steered away from crime, and was eventually buried in an all-Black cemetery.

This fugitive and the thousands of men and women whose experiences resembled his were able to find spaces in southern cities where they could live unmolested through the interplay of different actors: fugitives, their allies, and their receiving societies crafted these spaces deliberately; slaveholders were unable to prevent flight; state legislators—wittingly or unwittingly—produced a large population of illegal people that camouflaged fugitives; local authorities did not attribute sufficient importance to the issue; and urban employers benefited from it. And the growing White urban middle classes, driven by a desire to distinguish themselves from poor people, constructed physical places that supported the invisibility of people who should not be there. These aspects combined to create de facto beacons of refuge in the midst of slavery.

Studying runaway slaves in the antebellum South has produced an account full of ambiguities. In the era of the second slavery, expansion and intensification rendered the institution tighter. The number of those caught in bondage grew, and the possibilities to exit slavery decreased. A gigantic domestic slave trade and the curtailing of manumission practices turned the lives of enslaved men and women in the American South into an impasse. Things looked dire for millions. At the same time, the changing nature of slavery produced scenarios that turned out to be beneficial for a small group. The slave hiring system was of particular importance because it created an enslaved population that experienced a significant degree of autonomy. Enslaved people who became the "new fugitive slaves" used this opportunity to broaden their horizons, enlarge their networks, forge new contacts, and try their best to pass as free or as self-hired slaves. Ironically, slave hiring also contributed to keeping slavery alive in cities and led to job competition for the free lower classes.

In the early of portion of the period between 1810 and 1860, New Orleans absorbed most fugitive slaves. The restructuring of the administrative apparatus after Louisiana's inclusion into the American republic, the disunity of city authorities along ethnic lines, and the cultural variety of the population created a constellation in which runaways did not attract attention. In the second half of the antebellum era, Baltimore, the city with the highest growth rates and where urban slavery had the least relevance, surpassed New Orleans and became the dominant city to which enslaved people escaped. Charleston must have received more runaways than Richmond in the first decades of the era, but due to Richmond's development into an industrial center as the nineteenth century progressed, it came to absorb men and women who both passed as free and as self-hired slaves. In Charleston, fugitives faced more challenges as the greater presence of slaveholders produced the tightest geography of control of all four cities.

Each of the cities housed thousands of Black Americans. The growth of this population was the most relevant cause behind the increase in slave flight. For individual free Black men and women, the legal and social situation deteriorated because White Americans culturally and economically resented Black people and pushed them closer to enslaved people, and legislation grew increasingly tight around them. This hardening exclusion produced disadvantageous structures for Black people but at the same time provided unique spaces where free, enslaved, and runaway people of African descent lived beyond the constant control of dominant society.

Economically thriving and demographically expanding urban centers formed the most promising spaces of refuge. Urban labor markets, increasingly obsessed with a diverse, cheap, and flexible workforce, offered anonymity and non-apprehension in return, and became attractive places of escape for people who constantly had to be on the watch for anything that might send them back into enslavement. While in the short run, this worked to the advantage of fugitives and other undocumented people, in the long run, it harmed the socioeconomic position of all Black workers.

Changing demands for labor also affected fugitive slaves who were caught. Although plantation slavery was a most brutal work regime, it would be too simple to claim that enslaved people had little to lose and that, if caught, the labor on the public works, in the chain gangs, or in penitentiaries and workhouses was not much worse than working in bondage. As has been shown, most fugitive slaves in southern cities were not plantation hands; they were carriage drivers, hucksters, washerwomen, tradesmen, or caulkers. In the cities, the majority must have worked under the never-ending pressure of making enough money to make ends meet, and the highly repressive, physically dangerous, and isolated work regime of the correction houses was at least as unbearable as the most violent plantations.

Importantly, political discussions about the presence of fugitive slaves in southern cities were extremely limited. This topic was complex and conflict-laden, and southern city leaders were cautious in adding it to their regular political agendas. Consequently, countermeasures were sporadic and symbolic, and urban fugitives remained an integral part of southern cities. Indeed, White people of the lower and lower middle classes were the ones whose economic and cultural resentment of Black people eventually caused the only recorded measures that were taken with noticeable impact. At the end of the antebellum era, Whites were politically strong enough to demand concessions from the authorities to act against Black city dwellers. For reasons of practicality and political expediency, executive actions were directed at the undocumented Black population and dozens of men and women of African descent were arrested.

The Question of Resistance

Family separation was often the trigger to flee, yet by becoming short-distance migrants, fugitives could stay close to home, networks, kin, and loved ones. Conversely, the lack of social contacts in more remote places impeded long-distance flight of runaways. After all, only a small share of all fugitives to the northern states were aided by informal organizations like the Underground Railroad. Although true freedom in the South remained far away and runaway slaves could not expect to ever be legally free, the consequences were not that drastic when remembering that their lives did not differ much from the lives of other free African Americans. The fact that there was work did not imply that they could get out of poverty. Racism, economic discrimination, social exclusion, and the negation of political rights were realities Black Americans in the northern states likewise experienced every day. "Full freedom," as Frederick Douglass conceptualized it, was not achievable.

Nevertheless, the abolition of slavery in Maryland and Louisiana in 1864, and in Virginia and South Carolina through the Thirteenth Amendment to the U.S. Constitution in 1865, was a victory for all those who had fought against the immoral system of slavery. Historian Manisha Sinha, having shown the variety of different actors and methods involved in the movements that eventually led to the abolition of slavery, concluded that "slave resistance, not bourgeois liberalism, laid at the heart of the abolition movement."[1] This contestation occurred in the case of men and women who escaped to southern cities in a much more clandestine manner, which has led historians to underestimate their numbers and vigor. In the North and abroad, an impressive number of formerly enslaved people who had escaped enslavement were fundamental in the fight for abolition, including Frederick Douglass, Sojourner Truth, and Ellen and William Craft. Those who stayed in the South, despite silently disappearing from plantation ledgers and reappearing in reward announcements, resisted slavery in a different, yet no less important way. And the runaway slave advertisements that were issued the next day, and the day thereafter, and sometimes months and years after that, likewise lay proof to their speaking with a very loud and public voice that refused to accept their enslavement.

In southern cities, it was fugitive slaves and their helpers who stood at the forefront of defying slavery. Black southerners took on considerable risks to aid runaways. They helped them access papers, provided information, connected different dots within their networks, supplied shelter, and supported them in finding work. Absorption into the urban Black communities, paired with seemingly rare instances of betrayal, speaks to a high degree of collaboration and solidarity. Seen in this light, southern fugitivity emerges as collective action and once more attests to resistance to slavery as lying at the heart of the Black experience before the Civil War.

One is left to wonder how things would have evolved had the Civil War not steered American history into new directions. Were the increased arrests in 1859 and 1860 a singular warning or an indication of an imminent escalation in the relation between southern city authorities and Black city residents? Could the situation have possibly derailed so dramatically that the executive would have systematically persecuted all illegal and undocumented people of African descent and either enslaved or deported them? Given the stakes industrialists, large merchants, and other employers in the cities had in labor at discount prices, it is unlikely. Yet, given the growing political strength of the White lower classes, it is not impossible. Fortunately, we will never find out.

The Anticipation of Undocumented Migration

Should we think of people who had escaped slavery and lived in southern cities as free or unfree? This book has attempted to argue that this line cannot be easily drawn. Rather, it has argued that the Black population was much more heterogenous than historians have hitherto assumed. Analogous to fugitive slaves in the South, parts of their receiving society likewise had an illegal status because they violated state or municipal legislation. These people were either manumitted illegally or lived in a place against the law. Like fugitives, they had no documentation to prove their free status or legal residence.

This process of illegalization as a by-product of racialized legislation went in two directions. First, undocumented people struggled with similar scenarios as runaways, including tax payments, registration of property, asserting themselves against employers and contractors, hiding from watchmen, and, most importantly, living in very fragile conditions, which could at any time be questioned and contested. This brought them closer together. Secondly, the fact that an illegal Black population existed in the American urban South made them relatively easy targets of police surveillance and repressive executive measures. Runaway slaves could fall victim to these measures even if they were not explicitly targeted, and the occasional arrests of undocumented people aggravated the risks for fugitive slaves. Criminalization and suspicion were a strong force in all Black Americans' lives, a circumstance that corresponded with those who fled enslavement. After all, slavery continued to haunt all Black people in the United States, regardless of their status.

This new perspective allows us to pause, for the time being, the discussions on "degrees of freedom" and instead turn our attention to the everyday struggles of runaway slaves in southern cities and their relation to the broader economic and political framework. Indeed, analyzing fugitive slaves together with their host societies in southern cities connects their experiences to those of other precarious social groups in history that have lived in conditions of vulnerability and undocumentedness, subject to discretionary policing and susceptible to coercive labor regimes. However, we never discuss whether undocumented day laborers in present-day Los Angeles are "free" but rather emphasize their legal and economic insecurity. Following this thread, *Escape to the City* has attempted to think about fugitive slaves in ways similar to how the experiences of present-day undocumented people have been approached by historians and social scientists.

Applying concepts more commonly associated with contemporary debates on migration, such as "illegality" and "undocumentedness," raises new questions that, it is hoped, help steer the discussions of the lived realities of Black Americans in nineteenth-century labor markets in new directions. The perspective of illegal workers is important to account for their contribution to the urban economies as well as for a reduction of their professional skills. Then and now, being active in the labor markets is both a fundamental element to securing one's survival and at the same time an additional risk that increases one's visibility, and, hence, the odds of apprehension. Male runaways in particular, who were more often trained in skilled and semiskilled occupations than women, integrated into the economy below their professional capacities, a common phenomenon for migrants.[2]

Strikingly, capitalist development, which relies on flexibility and low labor costs, created conditions beneficial to the undocumented. Because undocumented Black Americans were willing to offer very cheap labor, they contributed to the economic success of their cities. In turn, growing industries—and all other sectors that developed alongside them—demanded more labor, which was again met by the pliant group of powerless workers. The absorptive labor markets created spaces for more fugitive slaves and other undocumented people, and the number of illegal and undocumented workers in southern cities grew correspondingly.

The parallels with today are also visible in the concept of American sanctuary cities. Whereas in the nineteenth century, southern cities did not intentionally turn into spaces of refuge, it can be argued that *by outcome* they functioned similarly in the sense that large numbers of escaped slaves could live there *relatively* undisturbed. This observation matches the definition of current-day American sanctuary cities that "don't fully cooperate with federal efforts to find and deport unauthorized immigrants." They are often driven by the idea of refraining from reporting undocumented residents. In a way, their champions hope to render the city a safer space for their heterogeneous population.[3] For the antebellum U.S. South, it was not the case that any hospitality for the undocumented was driven by comparable humanitarian concerns. Slavery was universally accepted by southern policy makers as the foundation of the social order. If a city decided to not actively tackle the problem of fugitive slaves, it was almost always due to the economic interests of White leaders, and to a lesser degree, a desire to avoid the expenses that came with the regulation of runaways.

When slavery was abolished in the United States in 1865, slave fugitivity disappeared with it. However, many of the other phenomena that have played a part in this narrative did not. Societal exclusion of Black Americans and spatial segregation persisted and expanded. Criminalization of Black people became normalized and the forced labor of convicts institutionalized. People of African descent were not readily accepted into society despite becoming full citizens in the years following the war. And while nobody Black could henceforth be illegalized and (mis)taken for a slave due to a lack of documentation, less than two decades later the Chinese Exclusion Act of 1882 kicked off a new era of undocumentedness, this time targeting people migrating across international borders. It would come to full flower in the twentieth century and continue to produce vulnerable and exploited men, women, and children—people who "should not be here"—in the twenty-first. In a way, the de facto illegal status of fugitive slaves in the antebellum era anticipated illegal migration in today's world, which shows little signs of abating.

Notes

Abbreviations

BCA   Baltimore City Archives, Baltimore, MD
CCPL   Charleston County Public Library, Charleston, SC
EKL   Earl K. Long Library, University of New Orleans, New Orleans, LA
HML   Hill Memorial Library, Louisiana State University, Baton Rouge, LA
JFK   Library of the John F. Kennedy Institute, Free University Berlin
LaRC   Louisiana Research Collection, Tulane University, New Orleans, LA
LOC   Library of Congress, Washington, DC
LVA   Library of Virginia, Richmond, VA
MHS   Maryland Historical Society, Baltimore, MD
MSA   Maryland State Archives, Annapolis, MD
NOPL   New Orleans Public Library, New Orleans, LA
SCDAH   South Carolina Department of Archives and History, Columbia, SC
SCHS   South Carolina Historical Society, Charleston, SC
SCLC   South Caroliniana Library, Columbia, SC
VHS   Virginia Historical Society, Richmond, VA
VSA   Virginia State Archives, Richmond, VA

Introduction

1. Buchanan reacted to a memorial by the Society for the Abolition of Slavery in Pennsylvania, which had originally been presented to Congress in 1790. Buchanan, "Speech on the Slavery Question," 317–19.

2. The literature is vast. A very short selection includes Franklin, *From Slavery to Freedom*; Foner, *Story of American Freedom*; Blight, *Frederick Douglass*. For a more pessimistic account, see Meier and Rudwick, *From Plantation to Ghetto*.

3. *Historians against Slavery*, "HAS Definition of Slavery."

4. Nicholson, Dang, and Trodd, "Full Freedom," 700; Foner, "Tribune of His People," 25.

5. Miller, *Problem of Slavery as History*, 10.

6. "Freedom against the law" follows Christopher Hill's observation of seventeenth-century English law not as an instrument of justice but of oppression. Hill, *Liberty Against the Law.*

7. Bloch and McKay, *Living on the Margins*, 5.

8. This is the nineteenth-century equivalent to the classification of illegal migration into four common forms: entry without authorization, entry on the basis of fraud, visa overstaying, and violation of the conditions of a stay. Papademetriou, "Global Struggle with Illegal Migration."

9. Heisler, "Sociology of Immigration," 77.

10. For a critique of rigid separations between different categorizations of migrants, for example, refugee, labor, and family migration, see Schrover, "Labour Migration."

11. Kok, "Family Factor," 215–16; Bacci, *Short History of Migration*, 55.

12. Kok, "Family Factor," 216.

13. There are a number of topics that are not included or not put to the forefront, such as the experiences of fugitive slaves during wartime, because the aim of this book is to draw a representative account of the processes that made slave flight possible in everyday conditions.

14. Tomich, *Prism of Slavery*, 57–61; Tomich, "Second Slavery and World Capitalism," 481–82.

15. Northup, *Twelve Years a Slave*, 93.

16. Contemporary testimonies like slave narratives and interviews express clearly the view of enslaved people that slavery was morally wrong. See, for example, Douglass, *Narrative of the Life*; Jacobs, *Life of a Slave Girl*, 55; Drew, *North-Side View of Slavery*. Abolitionist organizations also declared publicly that slaves had "a right to flee from bondage." Foner, *Gateway to Freedom*, 83.

17. Sweeney, "Market Marronage," 205.

18. The Upper South encompasses Maryland, Delaware, Virginia, North Carolina, Kentucky, Tennessee, and Missouri. The Lower South encompasses South Carolina, Georgia, Florida, Alabama, Mississippi, Arkansas, Louisiana, and Texas. References to the Deep South include Georgia, Alabama, Mississippi, and Louisiana.

19. Jones, *Birthright Citizens*.

20. Being "undocumented" was not an official status in the antebellum era, yet it reveals a political agenda and social dynamics that maneuvered people into a de facto illegal status long before the process of illegalization of migration took place.

21. Franklin and Schweninger, *Runaway Slaves*, 86–89.

22. For a short selection, see Litwack, *North of Slavery*; Hill, *Freedom Seekers*; Gara, *Liberty Line*; Foner, *Gateway to Freedom*.

23. Studies on urban slavery include Wade, *Slavery in the Cities*; Kimball, *American City, Southern Place*; Takagi, *Rearing Wolves*; Dantas, *Black Townsmen*.

24. Tilly, "Cities and Migration," 1; Kenny and Madgin, "Every Time I Describe a City," 4.

25. Wade, *Slavery in the Cities*, 21–22; Takagi, *Rearing Wolves*; Goldin, *Urban Slavery*; Lewis, "Slavery in the Chesapeake Iron Industry."

26. Kimball, *American City*, xviii.

27. Ginsburg, "Escaping through a Black Landscape," 52, 54, 63; McKittrick, *Demonic Grounds*, xxii–xxiii; Camp, *Closer to Freedom*.

28. Rockman, *Scraping By*, 11.

29. Newman, "Rethinking Runaways," 50.

30. On temporary runaways and maroons, see Franklin and Schweninger, *Runaway Slaves*; Camp, *Closer to Freedom*; Aptheker, "Maroons within the Present Limits," 151–52; Diouf, *Slavery's Exiles*.

31. Olmsted, *Our Slave States*, 476.

32. *American and Commercial Daily Advertiser*, October 31, 1816; *Daily National Intelligencer*, 1832; *Federal Gazette and Baltimore Daily Advertiser*, June 9, 1794; *Charleston Daily*

Courier, December 15, 1859. For more examples, see *Federal Gazette and Baltimore Daily Advertiser*, September 4, 9, 1817; *Baltimore American*, September 27, 1804; *City Gazette and Commercial Daily Advertiser*, January 6, 1823; Howard District Register of Wills (Petitions), Petition of Charles G. Haslap, February 9, 1847, Schweninger Collection, MSA.

33. Mullin, *Flight and Rebellion*, 39–40.

34. New Orleans (LA) Police Jail of the Third Municipality, Daily Reports, 1838–1840 (February 1, 1838–April 30, 1839), TX205, 1838–1840, NOPL.

35. Baltimore City Jail (Runaway Docket), 1836–1850, MSA; Proceedings of the City Council of Charleston, SC, 1859 I; Charleston (SC) City Council, Proceedings of Council, POC-002 M: 1859–1870, CCPL; Daybook of the Richmond Police Guard, 1834–1844, Alderman Library, Special Collections, UVA, transcribed in Sorensen, "Absconded"; Richmond (VA), City Sergeant, Mss 3R415661, Section 1, Register 1841–1846, VHS; Stith, *Message of the Mayor to the Common Council*, October 11, 1859, in Wade, *Slavery in the Cities*, 219; Powers, "Black Charleston," 27.

36. *Charleston Mercury*, May 11, 1838.

37. *Annual Report of the State Engineer to the Legislature of the State of Louisiana*, 24.

38. Zeuske, "Nicht-Geschichte," 79.

39. Together with a few interviews conducted by the Federal Writers' Project in the 1930s under the auspices of the Works Progress Administration, these are the most important sources in which the voices of the runaway slaves themselves can be heard. See the digitized collection "Born in Slavery." For a discussion of the authenticity of slaves' autobiographies and interviews see Ernest, "Introduction," 4, 8–9. A critique by John Blassingame is concerned with slave narratives' representability. With the bulk of accounts stemming from the Upper South and more than one-third written by runaways, the average slave had no voice in them. Blassingame, "Using the Testimony of Ex-Slaves," 80–84. Since this study does not claim to present an account of the institution of slavery, or of the average slave on the plantation, but precisely runaway slaves who are disproportionately represented as authors of narratives, their autobiographies offer a justified and helpful tool.

40. Camp, *Closer to Freedom*, 2.

41. Zeuske, "Nicht-Geschichte," 76, 79.

Chapter One

1. Hughes, *Thirty Years a Slave*, 78–79.

2. Lane, *Narrative*, 7–8.

3. Berlin, *Many Thousands Gone*, 13, 29.

4. Davis, *Problem of Slavery*, 41–48.

5. Kolchin, *American Slavery*, 65–66.

6. Melish, *Disowning Slavery*.

7. Helo, *Thomas Jefferson's Ethics*, 43.

8. Berlin, *Many Thousands Gone*, 219–24.

9. Sinha, *Slave's Cause*, 66, 85–86.

10. Blackburn, "Introduction," 3–5.

11. Ryden, "Manumission."

12. Berlin, *Generations of Captivity*, 43, 93, 95, 119, 135.

13. Wolf, *Race and Liberty*, 6, 72; Sinha, *Slave's Cause*, 92.

14. *Nashville Union and American*, November 19, 1860, in Berlin, "Free Negro Caste," 307.

15. Geggus, *Impact of the Haitian Revolution*.

16. Vesey and thirty-four others were executed before a revolt happened. Spady, "Power and Confession," 287. Together with Gabriel Prosser's attempt to march enslaved coconspirators into Richmond in 1800, and Nat Turner's rebellion in 1831 in Virginia, Vesey symbolizes the most important insurrection by enslaved people in the United States. During Turner's rebellion, slaves killed close to sixty Whites. Local authorities apprehended or killed most of the rebels, and White mobs and militias additionally killed more than one hundred enslaved and free Black people in the aftermath of the rebellion. Turner himself was hanged. "Nat Turner's Rebellion, 1831," Gilder Lehrman Institute of American History.

17. "An Act for the Better Regulation and Government of Free Negroes and Persons of Color," 462.

18. Landers, *Black Society in Spanish Florida*, 252–53.

19. General Assembly, "An ACT to amend the several laws concerning slaves"; Wolf, *Race and Liberty*, 125.

20. Kotlikoff and Rupert, "Manumission of Slaves in New Orleans," 173–74; Taylor, "Free People of Color in Louisiana."

21. And only in these places were manumittees allowed to remain in the state. Berlin, *Slaves Without Masters*, 138.

22. Whitman, *Price of Freedom*, 93–94, 96, 101; Whitman, "Diverse Good Causes."

23. When term slaves were apprehended, the court often prolonged the duration of servitude. See, for example, John Miller v. Negro Richard, August 3, 1847, Anne Arundel County Register of Will, Orders and Petitions 1840–1851, 201–2, MSA; Howard District Register of Wills (Petitions), Petition of Charles G. Haslap, February 9, 1847, Schweninger Collection, MSA.

24. Cole, "Capitalism and Freedom," 1021–23.

25. Grandy, *Narrative*, iv, 17–18, 21–22, 34, 40.

26. Tomich, *Prism of Slavery*, 57–61; Tomich, "Second Slavery and World Capitalism," 481–82.

27. Adams, *Great Britain and the American Civil War*, 13.

28. Tomich, *Prism of Slavery*, 57–61.

29. Baptist, *Half Has Never Been Told*, 25, 44–45.

30. Beckert, *Empire of Cotton*, 105, 110.

31. Mullin, *Africa in America*, 88; Kolchin, *American Slavery*, 96, 243.

32. Sugar plantations, foremost located in southern Louisiana, had the lowest birthrates and extraordinarily high death rates. Follett, *Sugar Masters*, 50, 95.

33. Pargas, *Slavery and Forced Migration*, 22.

34. Baptist, *Half has Never Been Told*, 69, 270, 286; Olmstead and Rhode, "Biological Innovation," 1123, 1165.

35. Kolchin, *American Slavery*, 192–93.

36. Jefferson, "Notes on the State of Virginia," 13.

37. Kolchin, *American Slavery*, 60, 94; Ford, *Deliver Us from Evil*, 526.

38. Morgan, "Three Planters and Their Slaves," 40–41.

39. McCurry, *Masters of Small Worlds*, 177–78.

40. Kenneth Stampp has claimed that by 1860, three-quarters of White southerners were neither directly (through ownership) nor indirectly (through family members' ownership) linked to slavery. In earlier decades, at least one-third of White families owned slaves. Stampp, *Peculiar Institution*, 28–30. These numbers forfeit part of their power when considering that a great many Whites aspired to slaveownership, both as an economic advantage and as cultural prestige.

41. Selfa, *Democrats*, 43.

42. Taylor, *Internal Enemy*, 6.

43. Fields, "Slavery, Race, and Ideology," 111.

44. Pargas, *Slavery and Forced Migration*, 26.

45. James Steer to John Minor, February 23, 1818, William J. Minor and Family Papers, HML, in Owens, *Species of Property*, 16.

46. Beckert, *Empire of Cotton*, 111.

47. Baptist, "Toxic Debts, Liar Loans," 78.

48. The Three-Fifths Compromise of 1787 established the American states' numbers of seats in the House of Representatives. Whereas every free person counted as one person, enslaved people counted as three-fifths of a person. This gave slaveholding states significant influence in federal politics. "What was the Three-Fifth-Compromise?" *Laws*.

49. Kolchin, *American Slavery*, 96.

50. Pargas, *Slavery and Forced Migration*, 2.

51. Kolchin, *American Slavery*, 139; Stevenson, *Life in Black and White*.

52. Tadman, *Speculators and Slaves*, 70–72. The term "Second Middle Passage" was coined by Ira Berlin to stress the similarities to the first Middle Passage, the transatlantic slave trade, including death rates, physical and psychological suffering, and separation of families. Berlin, *Generations of Captivity*, 173.

53. Pargas, *Slavery and Forced Migration*, 57–59.

54. Samuel G. Lipey [?] to Jonathan Jordan, June 18, 1842, Jordan and Twiggs Family Papers, SCLC.

55. Brown, *Slave Life in Georgia*, 17.

56. Carol Anna Randall (b. ca. 1855), Newport News, VA, Interviewer unknown (n.d.), in Virginia Writers' Program, *Negro in Virginia*, 171, in *Weevils in the Wheat*, 236.

57. Matilda Carter (b. 1959), Hampton, Va., Interviewer Claude W. Anderson (January 4, 1937), Virginia State Library, in *Weevils in the Wheat*, 68.

58. Berlin, *Generations of Captivity*, 169, ch. 4.

59. Stuart, "Three Years in North America," 347.

60. Dunn, *Tale of Two Plantations*, ch. 7.

61. Grimes, *Life of William Grimes*, 70.

62. Schermerhorn, *Money over Mastery*, 20.

63. *Charleston Mercury*, February 15, 1856.

64. Douglass, *Narrative of the Life*, 106.

Chapter Two

1. The headline of the ad, presumably to attract more attention, stated "$500 REWARD." *Charleston Mercury*, November 3, 1857; January 12, 1859.

2. Franklin and Schweninger, *Runaway Slaves*, 210–12.

3. Sorensen, "Absconded," 15.

4. Schafer, "New Orleans Slavery in 1850," 43.

5. Motte Plantation Record Book, Record Book, July–December 1854; Motte Plantation Record Book, Plantation Exeter, Work Book, January 1856, Dr. J. B. Motte, SCLC.

6. Delbanco, *War Before the War*, 107; Mareite, "Conditional Freedom," 58. The picture of men as the only protagonists of slave flight was further engraved in historians' minds due to the fact that almost nine out of ten slave narratives were written by men. Doddington, *Contesting Slave Masculinity*, 26, FN 22.

7. Women were furthermore in other ways essentially involved in flights, namely by supporting the ones escaping as well as aiding them after arrival.

8. White, *Ar'n't I a Woman?*, 70–71; Franklin and Schweninger, *Runaway Slaves*, 210–12; Parker, *Running for Freedom*, 71; Blassingame, *Slave Community*, 198.

9. Marshall, "Enslaved Women Runaways," 87, 97.

10. Accounts of rape of and sexual encroachment on women are plentiful in the narratives of African American women and men. See Jacobs, *Life of a Slave Girl*, 55; Keckley, *Behind the Scenes*, 38–39; Brown, *Slave Life in Georgia*, 17–19; Boney, Hume, and Zafar, *Autobiography of George Teamoh*, 94–95.

11. Schermerhorn, *Money over Mastery*; West, *Chains of Love*; West, *Family or Freedom*; Doddington, *Contesting Slave Masculinity*.

12. Ball, *Slavery in the United States*, 36, 287.

13. O'Donovan, *Becoming Free in the Cotton South*, 2.

14. Diouf, "Borderland Maroons," 184.

15. Malcom X, "Message to the Grass Roots," 10–11.

16. This also applies to other times and regions. See Meaders, "South Carolina Fugitives," 292; Johnson, "Runaway Slaves and the Slave Communities," 418.

17. Redpath, *Roving Editor*, 40–41.

18. *Daily Picayune*, December 16, 1853; Daybook of the Richmond Police Guard, October 17, 1836; November 8, 1840, UVA. The Richmond Daybook, moreover, features a number of entries on children and young adults from ages eleven to nineteen.

19. *City Gazette and Commercial Daily Advertiser*, September 3, 1821.

20. Marshall, "Enslaved Women," 103.

21. Berlin, *Slaves Without Masters*, 160.

22. Finch, *An Englishwoman's Experience in America*, 144.

23. *Federal Gazette and Baltimore Daily Advertiser*, November 4, 1817.

24. *Daily National Intelligencer*, October 1836.

25. *American and Commercial Daily Advertiser*, October 29, 1816; *Enquirer*, August 1, 1806; October 4, 1808.

26. *Augusta Chronicle*, May 20, 1826.

27. The problem of the categorization of skilled and unskilled labor is that it derives from work certified by craft guilds that could vouch for high quality. It therefore excludes the work of women who often learned at home or elsewhere where training was not linked to a certificate. Hoerder, "Transcultural Approaches to Gendered Labour Migration," 25.

28. *Federal Gazette and Baltimore Daily Advertiser*, September 4, 1817.

29. *Baltimore Gazette*, April 3, 1800.

30. Daybook of the Richmond Police Guard, February 2, 1837; January 11, 1838, UVA.

31. Cairns, *Youth Transitions*, 43.

32. Johnson, *Slavery's Metropolis*, 1–2, ch. 2.

33. Marshall, "Endeavor to Pass for Free," 166.

34. Douglass, *Narrative of the Life*, 31.

35. Zaborney, *Slaves for Hire*, 11–14; Morris, *Southern Slavery and the Law*, 132; Schermerhorn, *Money over Mastery*, 136; Goldfield, "Black Life," 130.

36. Corrected for bondspeople who were too young or too old to work, this corresponded to 71 percent of the actual enslaved male and 46 percent of the female labor force. Goldin, *Urban Slavery*, 36.

37. Takagi, *Rearing Wolves*, 35, 43, 94.

38. Johnson, *Experience of a Slave*, 24.

39. *Enquirer*, February 4, 1806; *Charleston Mercury*, February 15, 1856; January 12, 1859.

40. *Richmond Enquirer*, August 19, 1831.

41. Daybook of the Richmond Police Guard, April 22, 1839, UVA.

42. County Court Chancery Papers, February 19, 1855, LVA, in Race and Slavery Petitions Project, Series 2, County Court Petitions, University of North Carolina at Greensboro.

43. Schweninger, "Underside of Slavery."

44. Virginia forbade the self-hire of slaves in 1782 and again in 1819, Maryland in 1787, and Louisiana in 1806. South Carolina passed such laws in 1712, 1740, and 1783. Martin, *Divided Mastery*, 165.

45. *Charleston Courier*, September 12, 1850.

46. Schermerhorn, *Money over Mastery*, 107, 165.

47. "Harriet 'Rit' Ross, Caroline County," Biographical Series, MSA.

48. William R. Cox to William Cobbs, January 27, 1830, William Cobbs Letters, LVA.

49. Mary C. Spence Petition, Baltimore County, Maryland, November 15, 1826, Race and Slavery Petitions Project, Series 2, County Court Petitions, University of North Carolina at Greensboro, Schweninger Collection, MSA.

50. Russell, *North America*, 151.

51. *Charleston Courier*, May 9, 1825.

52. *Charleston Courier*, October 8, 1830.

53. *Charleston Courier*, September 12, 1850.

54. David Yates to Mother, July 30, 1824, Yates Family Papers, SCHS.

55. Martin, *Divided Mastery*, 4.

56. Douglass, *Life and Times*, 190.

57. Ball, *Slavery in the United States*, 368.

58. *Richmond Enquirer*, February 16, 1837.

59. Buchanan, *Black Life on the Mississippi*, 10.

60. *Richmond Enquirer*, February 16, 1837; *Daily Picayune*, April 24, 1853; August 27, 1852.

61. Cecelski, *Waterman's Song*, xiii, 31.

62. Bolster, *Black Jacks*.

63. McMaster v. Beckwith, April 1831, Docket #2017, Historical Archives of the Supreme Court of Louisiana, EKL.

64. Cecelski, *Waterman's Song*, xvi.

65. Enslaved coastal seamen were not only pilots but also captains. Thousands of black seamen emigrated sailing to Haiti between 1790 and 1830. Bolster, *Black Jacks*, 139–45.

66. Lusk v. Swon, June 1854, Docket #2852, Historical Archives of the Supreme Court of Louisiana, EKL.

67. Marciaq v. H. M. Wright, May 1857, January 1858, Docket #4645, Historical Archives of the Supreme Court of Louisiana, EKL.

68. *Daily Picayune*, October 22, 1859.

69. *Enquirer*, February 6, 1807.

70. *Charleston Mercury*, November 26, 1833.

71. Daybook of the Richmond Police Guard, UVA.

72. Richmond (VA), City Sergeant, Mss 3R415661, Section 1, Register 1841–1846, VHS.

73. Diverse runaway slave advertisements, mostly *Sun*.

74. Gutman, *Black Family in Slavery and Freedom*, 265–66.

75. *Charleston Courier*, December 9, 1835.

76. For example, *Augusta Chronicle*, date unknown, 1826.

77. Libby, *Slavery and Frontier Mississippi*, 52; Kimball, *American City*, 39.

78. Kolchin, *American Slavery*, 82, 99–100.

79. Forret, "Slaves, Poor Whites, and the Underground Economy."

80. Daybook of the Richmond Police Guard, January 11, 1838, UVA.

81. Ginsburg, "Black Landscape," 53.

82. Andrews, *Slavery and the Domestic Slave-Trade*, 142–43; Brown, *Slave Life in Georgia*, 16.

83. Pargas, *Slavery and Forced Migration*, 119–22.

84. Bayley, *Narrative of Some Remarkable Incidents*, 4.

85. Ball, *Fifty Years in Chains*, 36.

86. Schermerhorn, *Money over Mastery*, 135.

87. Robinson, *From Log Cabin to the Pulpit*, 46.

88. *Charleston Mercury*, February 14, 1844.

89. Stevenson, *Life in Black and White*, 209–10; Kulikoff, *Tobacco and Slaves*, 357; McMichael, *Atlantic Loyalties*, 51.

90. "Baltimore City and County Jail Runaway and Accommodations Dockets, 1831–1864"; "Committed" ads in various newspapers.

91. *City Gazette and Commercial Daily Advertiser*, December 21, 1821.

92. *National Intelligencer and Washington Advertiser*, July 21, 1809.

93. *Lexington Intelligencer*, July 7, 1838, in Pargas, "Seeking Freedom in the Midst of Slavery," 123.

94. Brown, *Slave Life in Georgia*, 17–19.

95. Ball, *Slavery in the United States*, 399.

96. Ainsworth, "Advertising Maranda," 207.

97. Libby, *Slavery and Frontier Mississippi*, 64.

98. *Daily Picayune*, March 13, 1849.

99. David Gavin Diary, March 24, 1858, SCHS. Gavin also noted that now, a trip from Charleston to Mississippi took two to three days by train; twenty-five years earlier it was about twenty days.

100. Anonymous, *Recollections of Slavery*, October 21, 1838. Originally published as a series with five installments, *Recollections of Slavery* appeared in *Emancipator*, the newspaper of the American Anti-Slavery Society, from August to October 1838. Hutchins, "No Author, Recollections of Slavery by a Runaway Slave." New evidence from the twenty-first century points to James Matthews as the author. Ashton, "Re-collecting Jim."

101. Frank Bell (b. 1834), Vienna, Va., Interviewer Claude W. Anderson (n.d.), Virginia State Library, in *Weevils in the Wheat*, 26–27.

102. Fifty percent of slaveholders held fewer than five people in bondage; American families who owned more than 100 slaves numbered no more than 3,000 by 1860. In total, 400,000 southerners claimed legal ownership of almost four million people. Most strikingly, less than 4 percent of adult White men owned the majority of all slaves. Stampp, *Peculiar Institution*, 28–31; Oakes, *Ruling Race*, xv, 38, 40.

103. For instance, *Sun*, August 31; October 15; November 24, 1852. Rewards roughly reflected the fluctuation of slave prices in the republic, which peaked in the 1830s and 1850s. Historians have made calculations about the value of antebellum slaves. In the mid-1850s, "prime field hands" cost upward of $1,200. Prices peaked for male slaves in their mid- to late twenties because then their productivity was highest. Men were on average more valuable, (women of twenty-seven years of age were priced at 80 percent of men of the same age) and professional skills likewise drove the price up. Hummel, *Emancipating Slaves*, 38–39; Fogel, *Without Consent or Contract*, 68, 70.

104. *Sun*, September 17, 1852. Based on a perusal of sixty-three newspaper notices between 1840 and 1860, Jeremiah Dittmar and Suresh Naidu have pointed to remarkable differences in reward money. The lowest amount was found for Mississippi, where bounties on runaway slaves averaged at $32. The highest median amount was $125, offered in Maryland; Virginia followed with $110. South Carolina slaveholders placed on average $47 and Louisianans $37. Dittmar and Naidu, "Contested Property," 6–7.

105. *Daily Advocate*, September 24, 1857.

106. Journal of Dugald McCall, 918 Box 1, Cross Keys Plantation, April 29, May 1, 1854, LaRC.

107. Journal of Dugald McCall, 918 Box 1, Cross Keys Plantation, May 11, June 5, 6, 7, 8, 1854, LaRC.

108. Petition by Edward R. Ware, Physician, Resident of Athens, Clark County, GA, November 28, 1855, SCDAH.

109. Besides newspaper announcements, slaveholders also had handbills written or printed to be distributed in courthouses, taverns, and post offices. Franklin and Schweninger, *Runaway Slaves*, 170, 238–39, 282; Ainsworth, "Advertising Maranda," 201–2.

110. Fehrenbacher, *Slaveholding Republic*, 205.

111. Wyatt-Brown, *Southern Honor*, 370–71.

112. Hadden, *Slave Patrols*, 74, 105–6, 139–40.

113. *Enquirer*, January 11, 1806.

114. *Charleston Courier*, May 15, 1826.

115. Petition by Edward Brailsford, November 26, 1816, Legislative Petitions, SCDAH.

116. Lewis L. Stiff to William Gray, May 25, 1842, Gray Papers, VHS.

117. For example, *City Gazette and Commercial Daily Advertiser*, July 18, 1822.

118. Scott, *Hidden Transcripts*, 2.

119. Anonymous [Matthews], *Recollections of Slavery*, October 11, 1838.

120. North Carolina Runaway Slave Advertisements, UNCG Digital Collections, University of North Carolina at Greensboro.

121. *Daily Picayune*, October 16, 1855. For slaves absconding from Richmond with diverse clothes, see *Richmond Enquirer*, August 19, 1831; September 26, 1837.

122. White and White, "Slave Clothing," 160.

123. White and White, "Slave Clothing," 174.

124. *Daily Picayune*, December 7, 1848.

125. It is questionable whether this description was helpful to recover him since the announcement was published three months after his departure and no information was provided about Andrew himself. *City Gazette and Commercial Daily Advertiser*, March 10, 1820.

126. *Charleston Courier*, September 12, 1850.

127. Ingraham, *South-West*, 56.

128. *Daily Picayune*, April 11, 1839.

129. White Americans often felt uncomfortable when seeing enslaved people who looked like them. John Simmons's master, for instance, had difficulty in finding a buyer for him because he had blue eyes and "a complexion so fair as to pass for white." *Charleston Mercury*, February 15, 1856.

130. *Charleston Mercury*, November 6, 1833.

131. Spalding v. Taylor et al., June 1846, in *Louisiana Annual Reports, Reports of Cases Argued and Determined in the Supreme Court of* Louisiana, I:195–97.

132. Grimes, *Life of William Grimes*, 71.

133. See chapter 5.

134. "Sarah Savage. Slave Pass, 1843," *Lowcountry Digital Library*.

135. Boney, Hume, and Zafar, *Autobiography of George Teamoh*, 74.

136. *Daily National Intelligencer*, 1832.

137. Takagi, *Rearing Wolves*, 119; Wade, *Slavery in the Cities*, 150–51.

138. Douglass, *Narrative of the Life*, 44.

139. Thompson, *Life of John Thompson*, 78.

140. Hughes, *Thirty Years a Slave*, 104–5.

141. William I. Johnson, Jr. (b. 1840), Richmond, VA, Interviewer Milton L. Randolph (May 28, 1937), Virginia State Library, in *Weevils in the Wheat*, 166–67.

142. *Daily National Intelligencer*, July 4, 1825. Thanks to Damian Pargas for sharing this source with me.

143. To the Virginia General Assembly, 1848, Petition by Ely Ball and Henry Satterwhite, Petition 11684607, Race and Slavery Petitions Project, University of North Carolina at Greensboro.

144. The State v. Wm Jackson F.P.C. Offence Aiding & Abetting Negro Stealing, Enticing a Slave to Run Away, Simons & Simons, SCHS.

145. *Richmond Dispatch*, January 16, 1861.

146. Unknown newspaper, February 1840.

147. *Daily Picayune*, August 27, 1852.

148. Laws of Maryland, 1796, ch. 67, XVIII, in Proceedings and Acts of the General Assembly, 1796, Vol. 105, 253; Laws of Maryland, 1818, ch. 157, 615; Session Laws, 1849, ch. 296, 373–74.

149. Camp, *Closer to Freedom*, 12.

Chapter Three

1. Sprague, *Anna Murray Douglass.*

2. Berlin, *Slaves Without Masters*, 41.

3. William Prentis, William Moore, Robert Bolling, Jack Hammon, and Nathaniell Harris to the Honble The Genl. Assembly of Virginia, December 1805, Accession #11680507, Legislative Petitions, VSA, Race and Slavery Petitions Project, Series 1, Legislative Petitions, LOC.

4. Berlin, "Free Negro Caste," 305, 311.

5. Curry, *Free Black*, 2–3.

6. William Walden, John Peyton, Churchill Berry, John R. Tanesly, and Charles E. Dodge to the General Assembly of Virginia, December 9, 1831, Culpeper County, Virginia, Legislative Petitions, VSA, Race and Slavery Petitions Project, Series 1, Legislative Petitions, LOC.

7. Berlin, *Generations of Captivity*, 164.

8. The number of free Black people in the state of Maryland increased from 8,000 in 1790 to 84,000 in 1860, rendering Maryland the state with the highest absolute number of free African Americans. They were only slightly outstripped by the enslaved (87,000).

9. Ayers et al., *American Passages*, 148; Whitman, *Price of Freedom.*

10. With slavery much more important in rural Maryland, the Maryland Constitution of 1851 prohibited the abolishment of slavery. Fields, *Middle Ground*, 20–21, 47.

11. Ashworth, *Slavery, Capitalism, and Politics*, 108.

12. Bromme, *Gemälde von Nord-Amerika*, 243.

13. Benson, Bremer, and Catt, *Letters of Fredrika Bremer*, 96–97.

14. Olmsted, *Seaboard Slave States*, 51.

15. Wade, *Slavery in the Cities*, 16–17; Vlach, "Without Recourse to Owners," 151.

16. The surge in the numbers of free Black people in the first decade of the nineteenth century can be explained by high manumission rates, with stronger repercussions in the two cities of the Upper South, Baltimore and Richmond, than in Charleston and New Orleans. Increasingly restrictive laws and rising slave prices provided further incentive not to manumit slaves and help explain the low variations in the 1850s. The percent trends from 1850 to 1860, however, should not be overestimated since there is considerable doubt about the accuracy of the 1850 census. Still, it remains remarkable that the growth rates of the free Black populations decelerated (and even turned negative) in the last decade before the Civil War before skyrocketing after the abolition of slavery.

17. Berlin, *Slaves Without Masters*, 177; Sheldon, "Black-White Relations in Richmond," 28.

18. Rodriguez, "Ripe for Revolt," 47–48.

19. Foner, "Free People of Color," 408, 411; King, *Essence of Liberty*, 27.

20. Olwell, "Becoming Free," 1.

21. *Charleston Daily Courier*, December 15, 1859.

22. Alfred Huger to Henry D. Lesesne, December 8, 1858, Alfred Huger Letterpress Books, 1853–1863, William R. Perkins Library, Special Collections, Duke University, Durham, in Johnson and Roark, *Black Masters*, 192–93.

23. Schweninger, "Prosperous Blacks in the South," 36–38; Woodson, *Free Negro Owners of Slaves*, 27–31.

24. Berlin, *Slaves Without Masters*, 34, 97.

25. *Richmond Enquirer*, November 6, 1840.

26. Sio, "Interpretations of Slavery," 103.

27. Jones, *Birthright Citizens*, 4–5, 19, 24.

28. Davis, "American Colonization Society," 14.

29. Hening, *Statutes at Large*, 128; American Colonization Society, *African Repository*, 99.

30. Baltimore, Ordinances, in Wade, *Slavery in the Cities*, 249; Fields, *Middle Ground*, 79.

31. Johnson and Roark, *Black Masters*, 43, 45.

32. Johnson and Roark, *Black Masters*, 45.

33. Higginbotham, *In the Matter of Color*, 206; Kolchin, *American Slavery*, 17, 82–84.

34. Morris, *Southern Slavery and the Law*; Campbell, *Slavery on Trial*, 45.

35. Flournoy, *House of Delegates, Senate & Virginia State Papers*, IX:162, LVA.

36. Berlin, *Slaves without Masters*, 93–94; Stampp, *Peculiar Institution*, 153.

37. These laws remained in force except in Maryland and Delaware. Berlin, *Slaves Without Masters*, 158.

38. Laws of Maryland, 1817, ch. 112, Early State Records Online, MSA; Legacy of Slavery in Maryland, "History of Runaways," MSA.

39. Foner, "African Americans," 16–19; Foner, *Story of American Freedom*, 33–34.

40. On Sunday schools, see Cornelius, *Slave Missions*, 132–34.

41. Executive Communications, The Speaker of the House of Delegates, December 4, 1820, LVA.

42. Carter, *Territorial Papers of the United* States, IX:34, HML.

43. In two months of the summer 1809 alone, thirty-four ships brought almost 2,000 free Black people and the same number of slaves from Cuba to New Orleans. Everett, "Emigres and Militiamen," 384.

44. John Watkins to Secretary Graham, September 6, 1805, in *Territorial Papers of the United States*, IX:503, HML.

45. General Assembly, "An ACT to amend the several laws concerning slaves."

46. Some, however, did leave. Leonard Curry has shown that in 1850, Virginia-born men and women had a share of around 40 percent of all out-of-state-born Black residents in Baltimore, Buffalo, Cincinnati, New Orleans, Pittsburgh, and St. Louis. Curry, *Free Black*, 5.

47. Besides dark figures emanating from the illegalization of certain groups of persons of African descent, there is an awareness among many historians that the U.S. censuses and city directories have to be used with care because Black and non-White people were structurally underrepresented. Wright, *Life Behind a Veil*, 44, FN 1.

48. Laws of Maryland, 1824, ch. 85, Vol. 141, 807, in *Absconders, Runaways and Other Fugitives*, 59.

49. Laws of Maryland, 1831, ch. 281, in Fields, *Middle Ground*, 36–37.

50. Landsford, "Manumission," 357.

51. Koger, *Black Slaveowners*, 77–78.

52. *Daily Picayune*, December 24, 1858.

53. Petition by Citizens from Berkeley County, January 16, 1838, Legislative Petitions, LVA.

54. Wright, *Free Negro in Maryland*, 114; Berlin, *Slaves Without Masters*, 92.

55. *Daily Picayune*, September 4, 1859.

56. Walker, *History of Black Business*, 60; Myers, *Forging Freedom*, 61.

57. Powers, "Black Charleston," 42.

58. William Ellison to Henry Ellison, March 26, 1857, Ellison Family Papers, SCLC; Copp, "O'Neall, John Belton," *South Carolina Encyclopedia*.

59. The city of Charleston earned around $10,000 with this legislation in 1859. Statement of the Finances of Charleston for Fiscal Year Ending August 31, 1859, in *Charleston Courier*, October 4, 1859.

60. Myers, *Forging Freedom*, 80.

61. "City Tax Returns," in *Charleston Courier*, October 4, 1859.

62. Brown, *Slave Life in Georgia*, 123.

63. See Legislative Petitions, LVA.

64. Lane, *Narrative*, 21, 24–25, 32.

65. Hustings Court Minutes, September 17, 1852, LVA.

66. Hustings Court Minutes, September 14, 17, 1852, LVA.

67. How exactly Harris was involved in Jones's finances or personal life is unknown. Elvira Jones to the Honorable the Speakers and Members of both Houses of the Legislature of the Commonwealth of Virginia, December 5, 1823, Richmond City, Virginia, Accession #11682304, Legislative Petitions, VSA, Race and Slavery Petitions Project, Series 1, Legislative Petitions, LOC.

68. Johnson and Roark, *Black Masters*, 44.

69. Koger, *Black Slaveowners*, 69–71.

70. Koger, *Black Slaveowners*, 69–71.

71. Daybook of the Richmond Police Guard, May 22, 1838, UVA.

72. Rockman, *Scraping By*, 27.

73. Extract from the Negro Register, Chesterfield County Court, January 8, 1855, Gray Papers; Richard West Flournoy to William Gray, October 10, 1855, Gray Papers, VHS.

Chapter Four

1. *Daily Picayune*, October 22, 1859.

2. Norman, *New Orleans and Environs*, 74–76.

3. Ingraham, *South-West*, 54–55.

4. *Charleston Mercury*, February 26, 1835.

5. Kimball, *American City*, 38–39; Takagi, *Rearing Wolves*, 101.

6. Wade, *Slavery in the Cities*, 85, 158; Din, *Spaniards, Planters, and Slaves*, 20.

7. Latrobe, *Journal of Latrobe*, 162–63.

8. Anonymous [Matthews], *Recollections of Slavery*, October 21, 1838.

9. *Enquirer*, June 7, 1805.

10. *Charleston Mercury*, May 8, 1832.

11. *Sun*, August 6, 1840.

12. Tilly, "Migration in Early Modern European History," 5–6, 8; Wilson, "Where Transnational Labor Migrants Go," 269–78.

13. Patterson, *Slavery and Social Death*.

14. Kolchin, *American Slavery*, 22–23.

15. Schermerhorn, *Money over Mastery*, 10.

16. This is the reverse interpretation of Sidney Chalhoub's claim that slavery in nineteenth-century Brazil allowed for some degrees of social advancement through competition, which had negative effects on the horizontal solidarity among the enslaved. Chalhoub, "Precariousness of Freedom," 409.

17. Ball, *Slavery in the United States*, 130–31.

18. Hodge, "Autobiography of Willis Augustus Hodge," referring to Gatewood, *Autobiography of Willis Augustus Hodge*.

19. Hall, "Slave Resistance in Baltimore," 306.

20. *Baltimore Patriot*, September 12, 1816.

21. Ginsburg, "Black Landscape," 51–66; Ginsburg, "Freedom and the Slave Landscape," 37.

22. William Read to Jacob Read, February 14, 1800, Read Family Papers, SCHS.

23. *Richmond Enquirer*, August 1, 1806.

24. Norman, *New Orleans and Environs*, 182.

25. Congo Square was also known as Circus Square and was renamed Place d'Armes in 1851. Donaldson, "Window on Slave Culture," 63–64. Consult the account of Benjamin Latrobe as one of the most insightful contemporary accounts of African and African American cultural expressions in the nineteenth century. Latrobe, *Journal of Latrobe*, 180–82.

26. *Daily Picayune*, March 22, ca. 1846.

27. McKittrick, *Demonic Grounds*, 92.

28. Franklin and Schweninger, *Runaway Slaves*, 170, 238–39, 282.

29. Wade, *Slavery in the Cities*, 150–51.

30. Hemphill, *Bawdy City*, 7, 38–39.

31. Daybook of the Richmond Police Guard, November 10, 1843, UVA.

32. Petition by Ruben Burton, Henrico County, December 21, 1825, Legislative Petitions, LVA.

33. *Charleston Mercury*, February 9, 1844.

34. *Charleston Courier*, April 9, 1860.

35. Fields, *Middle Ground*, 35.

36. Kantrowitz, *More than Freedom*, 124; Berlin, *Slaves Without Masters*, 76; Myers, *Forging Freedom*, 4; Kimball, *American City*, 69.

37. Anderson, *Life and Narrative*, 20.

38. Caroline Hammond (A Fugitive), Interview, 1938, in *Federal Writers' Project*. Vol. 8, Manuscript/Mixed Material, LOC.

39. Buckler, *History of Epidemic Cholera*, 31.

40. Ginsburg, "Black Landscape," 54.

41. Quoted in Berlin, *Slaves Without Masters*, 242.

42. *Charleston Courier*, September 23, 1845.

43. Olmsted, *Seaboard Slave States*, 52.

44. Transcriptions of Parish Records of Louisiana, No. 26 Jefferson Parish (Gretna), Series I, Police Jury Minutes, Vol. I: 1834–1843), HML.

45. McKittrick, *Demonic Grounds*, 18.

46. Brown and Kimball, "Mapping the Terrain," 302; Rabinowitz, *Race Relations in the Urban South*, ch. 5; Wright, *Life Behind a Veil*, ch. 4.

47. Goldfield, "Black Life," 124, 140.

48. Olson, *Baltimore*.

49. Olson, *Baltimore*; "Sanitary Report of Baltimore," *Ordinances of the Mayor and City Council of Baltimore*, 208–9, in Berlin, *Slaves Without Masters*, 258.

50. *Sun*, January 18, 1842.

51. Sorensen, "Absconded," 20; Brown and Kimball, "Mapping the Terrain," 297.

52. Takagi, *Rearing Wolves*, 97.

53. Kimball, *American City*, 74–75; Tyler-McGraw and Kimball, exhibit catalogue *In Bondage and Freedom*, 12.

54. Hanchett, *Sorting Out the New South City*, 9–10; Hodges, *Taxi!*, 12.

55. "Where Free Blacks Lived," *SCIWAY*.

56. Powers, "Black Charleston," 22.

57. Mayor's Court Docket Book, March 30, 1837; March 13, 1838, Valentine Museum, Richmond, in Campbell, *Slavery on Trial*, 31.

58. Campbell, *Slavery on Trial*, 65.

59. *Daily Picayune*, May 25, 1853; August 4, 1855. In 1854, Emilie Leon, a White girl of fourteen years, was, according to a New Orleans newspaper, abducted by Ben T. Haughton "who secreted her in a brothel in Gravier street, kept by a colored woman named Davis." *Daily Picayune*, April 29, 1854.

60. *Daily Picayune*, August 4, 1855.

61. Eckhard, *Digest of the Ordinances*, "Disorderly Houses," CCPL.

62. Hemphill, *Bawdy City*, 36.

63. *Charleston Mercury*, July 9, 1840.

64. Vlach, "Without Recourse to Owners," 151.

65. John Francis Delorme Petition, 1801, Petitions to the General Assembly, S165015, SCDAH.

66. Vlach, "Without Recourse to Owners," 153.

67. *Daily Picayune*, October 4, 1853.

68. *Charleston Courier*, January 16, [?].

69. *Daily Picayune*, October 22, 1859.

70. *Daily Picayune*, August 27, 1857.

71. Vlach, "Without Recourse to Owners," 158.

72. Vlach, "Without Recourse to Owners," 158–59.

73. Wade, *Slavery in the Cities*, 114.

74. Presentment of Grant Jury of Charleston District, March 1856, Legislative Petitions, SCDAH.

75. Wade, *Slavery in the Cities*, 266–67.

76. Schultz and McShane, "Engineer the Metropolis," 83.

77. Cain and Hong, "Survival in 19th Century Cities."

78. Takagi, *Rearing Wolves*, 45, 97.

79. Olmsted, *Cotton Kingdom*, 32–33.

80. Berlin and Gutman, "Natives and Immigrants," 1178; Mohl, "Industrial Town and City," 9.

81. *Charleston Mercury*, October 9, 1844. A similar ordinance is reported from New Orleans prohibiting the construction of wooden buildings "within what are denominated the fire limits." Norman, *New Orleans and Environs*, 69.

82. *Charleston Mercury*, August 24, 1857.

83. Buckler, *Epidemic Cholera*, 5; Olmsted, *Cotton Kingdom*, 42, 48.

84. Schultz and McShane, "Engineer the Metropolis," 82; Spain, "Race Relations and Residential Segregation," 87; Curry, *Free Black*, 11–12.

85. Olmsted, *Cotton Kingdom*, 39.

86. Records of the Charleston Police Department, Arrest Records and Morning Reports, Lower Ward 1855–1856, January 19, 1856, CCPL.

87. Douglass, *Narrative of the Life*, 38–39, 42.

88. *City Gazette and Commercial Daily Advertiser*, July 29, 1822.

89. Bromme, *Reisen durch die Vereinigten Staaten*, 156.

90. *Charleston Mercury*, June 25, 1860.

91. *Daily Picayune*, December 20, 1852.

92. *Daily Picayune*, January 19, 1855, in Schafer, *Becoming Free, Remaining Free*, 106–7.

93. The slaveholder was so committed to getting George back that he also placed the ad in the New York *Journal of Commerce*, the *Augusta Chronicle*, the Mobile *Mercantile Advertiser*, and the Boston *Commercial Gazette*. *Charleston Mercury*, June 23, 1835.

94. *Charleston Mercury*, August 21, 1832.

95. *Charleston Mercury*, May 8, 1832.

96. *City Gazette and Commercial Daily Advertiser*, March 30, 1813.

97. Phillips, *Freedom's Port*, 133, 140–42.

98. Raboteau, *Slave Religion*, 204.

99. Sinha, *Slave's Cause*, 130, 134–36.

100. Powers, "Black Charleston," 15–16.

101. Kantrowitz, *More than Freedom*, 21, 29; Walker, *Walker's Appeal*.

102. Kennedy and Parker, *Official Report of the Trials of Sundry Negroes*, 22–23, LOC.

103. Payne, *History of the African Methodist Episcopal Church*, 45, HML.

104. Kimball, *American City*, 143.

105. Gilbert Hunt, William B. Ballandine, Isham Ellis, Harison Dendridge, and James Greenhow to the Honorable the Legislature of Virginia, December 1834, Richmond City, Virginia, Accession #11683411, Legislative Petitions, VSA, Race and Slavery Petitions Project, Series 1, Legislative Petitions, LOC.

106. Olmsted, *Seaboard Slave States*, 24.

107. Kimball, *American City*, 8, 28, 45, 126; Raboteau, *Slave Religion*, 197; Takagi, *Rearing Wolves*, 547. Despite its remarkable autonomy, it was not until 1866 that the FABC was led by a Black pastor.

108. Takagi, *Rearing Wolves*, 58.

109. Raboteau, *Slave Religion*, 197.

110. First African Baptist Church (Richmond, VA), Minute Books, 1841–1930, June 6, 1852, LVA.

111. In the row behind the name, the church clerk would note whether a member was a free or, when a member was enslaved, write the name of the owner. In surprisingly many cases, the row behind the name was either left blank or doubts were made visible by a question mark. First African Baptist Church (Richmond, VA), Minute Books, 1841–1930, July 2, 1848; May 12, 1849, LVA.

112. Daybook of the Richmond Police Guard, February 15, 1844, UVA.

113. Potter, "History of Policing."

114. Olmsted, *Our Slave States*, 444.

115. Wade, *Slavery in the Cities*, 40.

116. Campanella, "Culture Wars."

117. *Journal of the First Municipality of the City of New Orleans*, October 19, 1836, LaRC. The three municipalities were divided into wards that elected a number of aldermen who, in turn, formed three Councils of Aldermen together constituting the General Council and answering to a single mayor. Campanella, "Culture Wars."

118. Rousey, *Policing the Southern City*, 4–6; Spitzer, "Rationalization of Crime Control," 200.

119. *Journal of the First Municipality of New Orleans*, July 27, 1840, LaRC. Note that the original source speaks of Robinson rather than Robertson Street. Although there existed a Robinson Street in New Orleans at that time, the location does not fit any possible patrolling scenario. The author therefore believes that the reference concerns Robertson Street.

120. This happened so often that watchmen had to pay a fine of $1 when found in that state. *Journal of the First Municipality of New Orleans*, July 27, 1840, LaRC.

121. Rousey, "Hibernian Leatherheads," 63–69.

122. *Picayune*, 1855, in Schafer, *Brothels, Depravity, and Abandoned Women*.

123. With the consolidation came name changes. The First Municipality became the Second Municipal District, and the Second Municipality became the First Municipal District. Campanella, "Turbulent History."

124. *Daily Picayune*, December 2, 1852.

125. Harring, *Policing in a Class Society*; "History of the Richmond Police Department," Richmond, Virginia.

126. Lundman, *Police and Policing*, 31; Potter, "History of Policing."

127. Records of the Charleston Police Department, 1855–1991, CCPL.

128. *City Gazette or the Daily Advertiser*, June 13, 1788.

129. *City Gazette and Commercial Daily Advertiser*, December 16, 1822.

130. *Charleston Courier*, September 20; September 23, 1845; *Southern Patriot*, November 2, 1840.

131. *Daily Picayune*, June 13; July 23, 1845.

132. Fields, *Middle Ground*, 53; Mohl, "Industrial Town and City," 8.

133. Din, *Spaniards, Planters, and Slaves*, 34, 195.

134. *Picayune*, July 19, 1837; Diouf, *Slavery's Exiles*, 108–9.

135. Mayor's Court Docket Book, May 21, 1838, Valentine Museum, Richmond, in Campbell, *Slavery on Trial*, 30.

136. *Daily Picayune*, September 8, 1850.

137. Ball, *Slavery in the United States*, 480–82.

138. Daybook of the Richmond Police Guard, April 30, 1840, UVA.

139. Paton, "Punishment, Crime, and the Bodies of Slaves," 923.

140. Laws of Maryland Vol. 141, 1068; Fields, *Middle Ground*, 79; Flanigan, "Criminal Procedure in Slave Trials," 543; Berlin, *Slaves Without Masters*, 320.

141. Olmsted, *Cotton Kingdom*, 37.

142. Lundman, *Police and Policing*, 28–30.

143. *Journal of the First Municipality of the City of New Orleans*, December 31, 1838, LaRC.

144. *Southern Recorder*, August 6, 1822, in Wade, *Slavery in the Cities*, 150.

145. For instance, Records of Prisoners Committed to the Parish Prison, 1852–1862, June 18, 1852–May 10, 1862, TX420, NOPL.

146. Records of the Charleston Police Department, Arrest Records and Morning Reports, Lower Ward 1855–1856, CCPL.

147. Breaking Charleston's curfew could lead to severe penalties. Eckhard, *Digest of the Ordinances*, "Disorderly Houses," CCPL.

148. Records of the Charleston Police Department, Arrest Records and Morning Reports, Lower Ward 1855–1856, January 7, 13, 1856, CCPL.

149. Kaye, "Neighborhoods and Solidarity," 12.

150. *Charleston Courier*, August 30, 1824; May 9, 1825. Mary's case will reappear in the section on sex workers in chapter 5.

151. *Charleston Courier*, January 16, [?].

152. French Statements of Alexis Bougny and Celestín Villemont, April 23, 1810, General Manuscripts, January 18, 1808–December 21, 1811, John Minor Wisdom Collection, LaRC.

153. First African Baptist Church (Richmond, VA), Minute Books, 1841–1930, May 6; December 28, 1848; December 1857, LVA.

154. This corresponds to research on other times and places, which has confirmed that undocumented immigrants have lower levels of criminal involvement. Rumbaut, Dingeman, and Robles, "Immigration and Crime," 473.

155. Campbell, *Slavery on Trial*, 22.

156. Governor and Council (Pardon Papers), s1061, 1826 26–73, MSA. I would like to thank Seth Rockman for sharing these sources with me.

157. Governor and Council (Pardon Papers), s1061, 1826 7–63, MSA.

158. Governor and Council (Pardon Papers), s1061, 1824 24–44, MSA.

159. Norman, *New Orleans and Environs*, 182.

160. *Daily Picayune*, June 24, 1845.

161. Donaldson, "Window on Slave Culture," 67.

162. First African Baptist Church (Richmond, VA), Minute Books, 1841–1930, January 1859, LVA.

Chapter Five

1. Curry, *Free Black*, 30.

2. Goldfield, "Black Life," 134–35.

3. Berlin, "Free Negro Caste," 311; Harris, *Making of the American South*, 104.

4. Johnson and Roark, *Black Masters*, 185.

5. Curry, *Free Black*, 29.

6. *Matchett's Baltimore Director*, MSA.

7. Goldfield, "Black Life," 133.

8. Berlin, *Slaves Without Masters*, 238.

9. Daybook of the Richmond Police Guard, August 16, 1836, UVA.

10. Schermerhorn, *Money over Mastery*, 147, 166; Takagi, *Rearing Wolves*, 3, 10–11, 24, 71.

11. Bradford, "Negro Ironworker," 139.

12. Daybook of the Richmond Police Guard, January 28, 1835, UVA.

13. Rood, *Reinvention of Atlantic Slavery*, 95–96; Kimball, *American City*, 29–30, 165.

14. Olwell, "Becoming Free," 1.

15. *Daily Advocate*, December 7, 1848; November 3, 1852.

16. Boney, Hume, and Zafar, *Autobiography of George Teamoh*, 87.

17. See chapter 2.

18. Gordon, Edwards, and Reich, *Segmented Work, Divided Workers*, 55–56.

19. *City Gazette and Commercial Daily Advertiser*, December 15, 1820.

20. Olson, *Baltimore*, 103.

21. Kerr-Ritchie, *Freedpeople in the Tobacco South*, 18–19.

22. Johnson and Roark, *Black Masters*, 177, 179; Rodriguez, "Ripe for Revolt," 44.

23. Rockman, *Scraping By*, 45–46, 73.

24. Schermerhorn, *Money over Mastery*, 168.

25. Anonymous [Matthews], *Recollections of Slavery*, October 11, 1838.

26. Boles, *Black Southerners*, 118–19, 121; Starobin, "Economics of Industrial Slavery," 132.

27. *Daily Dispatch*, November 28, 1860.

28. Rockman, *Scraping By*, 45–46.

29. Russell, *North America*, 151.

30. In Charleston, the "fixed proper stands," where porters were to offer their hired work, were announced in 1803. All of them were located near the waterfront where the wharves were. *Charleston Times*, November 11, 1803, in Thompson, *Working on the Dock of the Bay*, 44.

31. Wade, *Slavery in the Cities*, 41–42.

32. Anonymous [Matthews], *Recollections of Slavery*, October 21, 1838.

33. Schermerhorn, *Money over Mastery*, 23.

34. Johnson, *Experience of a Slave*, 25.

35. To the Honb Senate & Representatives of the State of South Carolina, Colleton Parish/District, South Carolina, Petition by I. Raven Mathews Sr. et al., December 7, 1854, Accession #11385404, Race and Slavery Petitions Project, Series 1, Legislative Petitions.

36. Boney, Hume, and Zafar, *Autobiography of George Teamoh*, 90–91.

37. *Daily Picayune*, October 25, 1855.

38. Johnson, *River of Dark Dreams*, 143.

39. *Daily Picayune*, May 12, 1850; *Cohen's New Orleans & Lafayette Directory for 1851*, Louisiana Division, NOPL.

40. To the Honorable the President and Members of the Senate of S. Carolina, Petition of Sundry Mechanics of the City of Charleston, n.d., S165015, Petitions to the General Assembly, SCDAH.

41. They had escaped from St. Paul's Parish in South Carolina. To the Honb Senate & Representatives of the State of South Carolina, Colleton Parish/District, South Carolina, Petition by I. Raven Mathews Sr. et al., December 7, 1854, Accession #11385404, Race and Slavery Petitions Project, Series 1, Legislative Petitions.

42. Myers, *Forging Freedom*, 90.

43. Berlin, *Slaves Without Masters*, 221; Myers, *Forging Freedom*, 43

44. Myers, *Forging Freedom*, 92; Rockman, *Scraping By*, 127.

45. *Charleston Mercury*, February 16, 1860.

46. *Charleston Mercury*, April 12, 1859.

47. On the attempt to legalize one's status, see chapter 3.

48. Myers, *Forging Freedom*, 114, 118–19.

49. *Charleston Mercury*, February 9, 1844.

50. Complicating the employment of runaways in domestic service was the arrangement in which domestic servants were placed by a slave-hire agent who functioned as a mediator between rural slaveholders and urban employers. This was frequent in Richmond. Weis, "Negotiating Freedom," 133.

51. Rockman, *Scraping By*, 140.

52. Children, however, were an obstacle to taking on such work. Murray, "Poor Mothers, Stepmothers, and Foster Mothers," 483–84. Therefore, mothers engaged in this occupation had to make arrangements like hiring a nanny to be able to keep their jobs. For an enslaved boy called George working for an enslaved woman as a nanny, which cost her a fourth of her income, see Ford Family Papers, 1809–1968, Manuscripts P, SCLC.

53. *Charleston Courier*, January 4, 1830.

54. *Charleston Courier*, September 12, 1850.

55. *Matchett's Baltimore Director*, MSA.

56. In a Philadelphia hospital, laundresses earned $3 per week in 1817, which was reduced to $2 in 1822. United States Department of Labor and Bureau of Labor Statistics, "History of Wages in the United States," 135.

57. Marshall, "Endeavor to Pass For Free," 170.

58. Cohen, *Murder of Helen Jewett*, 85; Hemphill, *Bawdy City*, 4, 6; Campbell, *Slavery on Trial*, 65.

59. *Daily Picayune*, August 27, 1852.

60. *Daily Picayune*, August 27, 1852.

61. *Daily Picayune*, April 9, 1849; August 17, 1850.

62. Rockman, *Scraping By*, 129.

63. Pluskota, "We Use Our Bodies," 653; van der Veen, "Rethinking Commodification and Prostitution."

64. Presentment of Grant Jury of Charleston District, October 1820, SCDAH; Eckhard, *Digest of the Ordinances*, "Disorderly Houses," CCPL.

65. Pluskota, "We Use Our Bodies," 655–56.

66. Blanchette and Schettini, "Sex Work in Rio de Janeiro," 492.

67. *Daily Picayune*, March 15, 1850.

68. *Charleston Courier*, August 30, 1824; May 9, 1825.

69. Fields, *Middle Ground*, 79.

70. Powers, "Black Charleston," 19.

71. Commonwealth v. Helen A. E. Briggs, July 12, 1862, Suit Papers, Hustings Court Suit Papers, LVA.

72. Petition of Jeremiah Willis for a Pass, February 4, 1839; Petition by A. Williams, To the Honorable S. C. Leakin Mayor, n.d., Mayor's Correspondence, BRG 9-2, BCA.

73. Minutes of the Conseil do Ville, May 19, 1804, in Le Glaunec, "Slave Migrations and Slave Control," 223.

74. Schermerhorn, *Money over Mastery*, 147.

75. Berlin, *Slaves Without Masters*, 219; Takagi, *Rearing Wolves*, 11, 26; Schnittman, "Slavery in Virginia's Urban Tobacco Industry," v.

76. Wade, *Slavery in the Cities*, 28–32; Douglass, *Narrative of the Life*, 38.

77. *Daily Picayune*, November 19, 1855.

78. To avoid prosecution, Lucas left the state of Louisiana. Schafer, *Becoming Free*, 117–18.

79. See chapter 4.

80. Schweninger made these observations for Richmond and a number of other cities in Virginia. United States Manuscript Slave Census, Richmond, 1st Ward, 1860, 1–2, 6; 2nd Ward, 56–57, in Schweninger, "Underside of Slavery."

81. See chapter 6.

82. Hustings Court Suit Papers, Ended Causes, March–October 1839, Commonwealth v. Robert Lacy, a Slave, September 12, 1839, LVA.

83. *Charleston Courier*, May 19, 1820.

84. *City Gazette and Commercial Daily Advertiser*, July 7, 1821; June 1, 1822.

85. *Charleston Courier*, May 7, 1829.

86. *City Gazette*, February 19, 1793, in Brown and Sims, *Fugitive Slave Advertisements*, xi.

87. *Charleston Courier*, March 26, 1822.

88. Records of the Charleston Police Department, Arrest Records and Morning Reports, Lower Ward 1855–1856, January 7, 12; February 25, 1856, CCPL.

89. Eckhard, *Digest of the Ordinances*, "Badges," CCPL; *City Gazette and Commercial Daily Advertiser*, July 21, 1800. The earliest legislation regarding slave badges was passed in the 1780s; the oldest physical slave badge that was found dates from 1800. Greene, Hutchins, and Hutchins, *Slave Badges and the Slave-Hire System*, 15.

90. *Charleston Courier*, January 29, 1848.

91. *City Gazette and Commercial Daily Advertiser*, September 1, 1812.

92. *Charleston Mercury*, July 31, 1833.

93. *Charleston Courier*, April 11, 1822.

94. *Charleston Mercury*, May 29, 1832.

95. Greene, "Slave Badges," 437.

96. Anonymous [Matthews], *Recollections of Slavery*, October 21, 1838.

97. Johnson, *Experience of a Slave*, 25.

98. Augustin, *General Digest of the Ordinances*, 139, 141.

99. *Charleston Mercury*, November 8, 1827, in Franklin and Schweninger, *Runaway Slaves*, 230; Greene, Hutchins, and Hutchins, *Slave Badges and the Slave-Hire System*, 6; Dawson, "Copper Neck Tags"; Augustin, *General Digest of the Ordinances*, 139.

100. Foner, *American Freedom*, 19.

101. Schermerhorn, *Money over Mastery*, 169; Wade, *Slavery in the Cities*, 30.

102. Rockman, "Unfree Origins of American Capitalism," 345.

103. The classifications "working classes" and "working class" came up in the American North for the first time in the 1820s. Blumin, *Emergence of the Middle Class*, 242.

104. Merritt, *Masterless Men*, 3; Möllers, *Kreolische Identität*, 100; Bagenal, *American Irish and their Influence*, 12–13; Anbinder, *Nativism and Slavery*, 5; Nau, *German People of New Orleans*, 9; Fields, *Middle Ground*, 44.

105. John William DeForest to Andrew DeForest, November 9, 1855, John William De-Forest Papers, Beinecke Rare Book and Manuscript Room, Yale University, in Johnson and Roark, *Black Masters*, 178.

106. In 1821, 21 percent of Irish immigrants were classified as unskilled laborers; in 1836, it was 60 percent. Of the "famine immigrants" who arrived after 1845, 80 to 90 percent were unskilled. Anbinder, *Nativism and Slavery*, 6–7.

107. Curry, *Free Black*, 25.

108. Olmsted, *Cotton Kingdom*, 231.

109. Olmsted, *Cotton Kingdom*, 41, 233. Hotel work was a good option for runaways in Baltimore. In 1853, when Henry Camp was already off for five months, his owner advertised: "He is an excellent waiter, and is supposed to be at some large Hotel acting in that capacity." *Sun*, November 24, 1853.

110. Olmsted, *Seaboard Slave States*, 48.

111. *Daily Journal*, July 20, 1856 [?]. Caulking was an occupation fiercely contested between Black and White men in the 1850s in Baltimore. See *Sun*, May 14, 18, 21, 25; June 28, 29; July 8; November 4, 1858; June 3,4, 7, 29, 1859; *Baltimore American*, February 12; July 8; October 11, 1858; *American and Commercial Daily Advertiser*, July 8, 1858.

112. For example, William Walden, John Peyton, Churchill Berry, John R. Tanesly, and Charles E. Dodge to the General Assembly of Virginia, December 9, 1831, Culpeper County, Virginia, Legislative Petitions, VSA, Race and Slavery Petitions Project, Series 1, Legislative Petitions, LOC.

113. This was only one part of the story. Native and foreign-born Whites did move against Black workers but native Whites likewise acted against foreigners, for instance, by forming violent gangs. Berlin and Gutman, "Natives and Immigrants," 1197.

114. Cullen, *American Dream*, 69.

115. Rubin, "Black Nativism," 198–99.

116. *Sun*, May 18, 1853.

117. Cole, "Servants and Slaves," 62; Rockman, *Scraping By*, 115.

118. *Charleston Daily Courier*, December 15, 1859.

119. Hoerder, "Gendered Labour Migration," 40.

120. Takagi, *Rearing Wolves*, 88.

121. Pinckney, *Reflections*, 18.

122. Thompson, *Working on the Dock*, 115.

123. Olson, *Baltimore*, 120.

124. Mohl, "Industrial Town and City," 6, 8–9.

125. Rockman, *Scraping By*, 47.

126. *Sun*, August 11, 1838. Although White and Black men largely executed the same tasks, there were physically kept apart from each other. Schermerhorn, *Money over Mastery*, 168.

127. Boney, Hume, and Zafar, *Autobiography of George Teamoh*, 82.

128. Takagi, *Rearing Wolves*, 32–33.

129. Rockman, *Scraping By*, 4; Fields, *Middle Ground*, 67; Brass, "Some Observations on Unfree Labour," 73.

130. Olson, *Baltimore*, 119.

131. Eckhard, *Digest of the Ordinances*, "Negroes," CCPL. This was actually a raise from 81 cents set in 1817.

132. Augustin, *General Digest,* 141.

133. White draymen petitioned the City Council of Charleston in 1854 to ask for an increase in the rates that had been established by law in 1837. Their petition was rejected. Thompson, *Working on the Dock,* 115.

134. Douglass, *Narrative of the Life,* 98.

135. Goldfield, "Black Life," 134–35.

136. Boney, Hume, and Zafar, *Autobiography of George Teamoh,* 90–91.

137. Takagi, *Rearing Wolves,* 23.

138. Ford Family Papers, 1809–1968, Manuscripts P, SCLC.

139. Lobo and Stotz, "Formação do operariado," 57, referenced in Mattos, *Laborers and Enslaved Workers,* 22.

140. Whitlock spent between $3 and $3.50 on board and rent and was, hence, able to save money and start his own business. Philip Whitlock Memoirs, Mss 5: IW5905: I, 67, 71, 74–75, VHS.

141. Du Bois, *Black Reconstruction in America,* 700–701; Roediger, *Wages of Whiteness.*

142. Rockman, *Scraping By,* 140; Naragon, "Ballots, Bullets, and Blood," 48.

143. Curry, *Free Black,* 23; Berlin, "Free Negro Caste," 308; Johnson and Roark, *Black Masters,* 60–61.

144. Bromme, *Reisen durch die Vereinigten Staaten,* 148–52, 155–56, JFK. But Germans also often came with tools because they were farmers and were planning to seek a future in this occupation. Brauns, *Ideen über die Auswanderung nach Amerika,* 564, JFK.

145. *American Christian Expositor,* November 1, 1832. Maryland did introduce a head tax of $1.50 for immigrants in 1831. *Niles' Register,* April 23, 1831, in Olson, *Baltimore,* 91.

146. Merritt, *Masterless Men,* 169.

147. Schafer, *Becoming Free,* 162; Berlin, "Free Negro Caste," 308; Bogger, *Free Blacks in Norfolk,* 60; Myers, *Forging Freedom,* 121; Phillips, *Freedom's Port,* 98–100, 155.

148. *Planter's Advocate,* February 22, 1860, in Fields, *Middle Ground,* 79.

149. Steinfeld and Engerman, "Labor—Free and Coerced?," 109–10.

150. Davis, *Inhuman Bondage,* 144. Davis used this formulation to point out that after the American Revolution, slavery became a form of exploitation that was no longer accepted by many Americans.

Chapter Six

1. Louisiana, First District Court (Orleans Parish), General Dockets, 1846–1880, v. 2 (February 7, 1850–December 24, 1856), #4666–12588; v. 3 (January 1, 1857–January 6, 1865), #12589–16369, VSA350, NOPL; Records of Prisoners Committed to the Parish Prison, 1852–1862, June 18, 1852–May 10, 1862, TX420, NOPL.

2. Kolchin, *American Slavery,* 35.

3. Events such as the Missouri Compromise of 1820, the Denmark Vesey insurrection, and the Charleston port's total dependence on cotton brought insecurities. The end of the Age of Sail took away the necessity for ships to stop at Charleston and the harbor was not deep enough to allow large vessels to dock at the city's wharves. Planters from the hinterland migrated west into the new Cotton Kingdom. Moreover, New York emerged as an intermediary between Charleston and Europe,

which reduced the profit margins for Charleston's merchants. Thompson, *Working on the Dock*, 4, 6, 37, 61.

4. Rosenwaike, *On the Edge of Greatness*, 68.

5. Proceedings of the City Council of Charleston, S.C., 1859 I, Thirty-First Regular Meeting, Council Chamber, January 4, 1859, reprint in *Daily Courier*, January 6, 1859, CCPL. By that time, the police force was composed of one chief, two captains, six lieutenants, four orderly sergeants, and 150 privates. In 1836, the City Guard had had one captain, three lieutenants, two orderly sergeants, eight corporals, 90 privates, two drummers, and two fifers. Records of the Charleston Police Department, Police Department Historic Files, 1855–1991, CCPL.

6. Eckhard, *Digest of the Ordinances*, "Guard (City)," CCPL.

7. Miller, "Feeding the Workhouse," 9; Paton, *No Bond but the Law*.

8. Records of the Charleston Police Department, Arrest Records and Morning Reports, Lower Ward 1855–1856, CCPL.

9. Eckhard, *Digest of the Ordinances*, "Work House," CCPL.

10. *City Gazette and Commercial Daily Advertiser*, July 21, 1800.

11. Testimony of Angelina Grimké Weld (April 6, 1839), in *American Slavery As It Is*, 53–54.

12. Testimony of Angelina Grimké Weld, 53–54.

13. McInnis, *Politics of Taste*, 226; Testimony of Angelina Grimké Weld, 53–54.

14. Paton, *No Bond but the Law*, 83, 88–89.

15. *Charleston Courier*, August 11, 1849, in Smalls, "Behind Workhouse Walls," 85.

16. Eckhard, *Digest of the Ordinances*, "Work House," CCPL.

17. Anonymous [Matthews], *Recollections of Slavery*, September 13, 1838.

18. Proceedings of the City Council of Charleston, SC, 1859 I; Charleston (SC) City Council, Proceedings of Council, POC-002 M: 1859–1870, CCPL.

19. Koger, *Black Slaveowners*, 92.

20. Records of the Charleston Police Department, Arrest Records and Morning Reports, Lower Ward 1855–1856, February 25, 1856, CCPL.

21. Charleston (SC), City Council, Proceedings of Council POC-001 M: 18 21-2, CCPL.

22. Anderson, *Life and Narrative*, 20–22.

23. Walker, *No More, No More*, 28–30.

24. Bremer, *Homes of the New World*, 211.

25. Paton, *No Bond but the Law*, 11.

26. Brown, *Slave Life in Georgia*, 104–5.

27. Hobsbawm, *Age of Capital*, 210–11.

28. Marler, *Merchants' Capital*, 57, 60, 64; Dessens, "New Orleans, LA," 106–7.

29. Fields, *Middle Ground*, 41–42.

30. Fogel, *Without Consent or Contract*, 87.

31. Marler, *Merchants' Capital*, 54.

32. Olson, *Baltimore*, 108–9; Fields, *Middle Ground*, 41–42; Hobsbawm, *Age of Capital*, 213–14.

33. Fields, *Middle Ground*, 43, 48.

34. Kerr-Ritchie, *Tobacco South*, 14, 18–19; Morgan, *Emancipation in Virginia's Tobacco Belt*, 24, 57–58.

35. Tomich, "Second Slavery and World Capitalism," 483.

36. Fields, *Middle Ground*, 17, 19–20.

37. Fields, *Middle Ground*, 20.

38. In total, Seamen Acts were passed in South Carolina, North Carolina, Georgia, Florida, Alabama, Mississippi, Louisiana, and Texas. Schoeppner, "Peculiar Quarantines," 559. W. Jeffrey Bolster has claimed that 10,000 sailors felt the direct effects of this legislation. Bolster, *Black Jacks*, 206.

39. Thompson, *Working on the Dock*, 68.

40. Schoeppner, "Peculiar Quarantines," 571.

41. Tansey, "Out-of-State Free Blacks," 372; Marler, *Merchants' Capital*, 59.

42. Enriched through trade, production, and finance, the bourgeoisie came to be the most powerful economic elite from the mid-nineteenth century onward. They were the first elite not to rely on birthrights and privilege. Beckert, *Monied Metropolis*, 3–4.

43. Goldfield, "Black Life," 126.

44. Berlin and Gutman, "Natives and Immigrants," 1184; Wells, *Southern Middle Class*, 168.

45. Dahl, "North of the South."

46. Rockman, "Unfree Origins," 360.

47. Naragon, "Ballots, Bullets, and Blood," 16. The manufacturing value per capita in New Orleans was less than one-third of that in Richmond. Charleston's output, in turn, was slightly higher than one-fourth of New Orleans's. Bateman and Weiss, *Deplorable Scarcity*, 22.

48. Hoffman, *Race, Class, and Power*, 18.

49. Naragon, "Ballots, Bullets, and Blood," 16.

50. Horse, *Ordinances of the City of Charleston*.

51. Kimball, *American City*, 38. See particularly the organization of churches for Black poor relief, as in Raboteau, *Slave Religion*; Green, *Business of Relief*.

52. Rockman, "Unfree Origins," 360.

53. To the Honb Senate & Representatives of the State of South Carolina, Colleton Parish/District, South Carolina, Petition by I. Raven Mathews Sr. et al., December 7, 1854, Accession #11385404, Race and Slavery Petitions Project, Series 1, Legislative Petitions.

54. Exceptions are the disputes about runaway slaves being harbored and employed on board ships and vessels. This reflects the concern about slaves attempting to flee to the northern states.

55. Missouri, Supreme Court, St. Louis: State v. Henke and Henke, October 1853, Missouri State Archives, in *Reports of Cases Argued and Decided*, 19:226–27.

56. Kimball, *American City*, 113–14.

57. Hoffman, *Race, Class, and Power*, 18.

58. Laws of Maryland, 1806, ch. 81, Vol. 192, 693; 1831, ch. 323. Vol. 141, 1068, 1115; 1860, Art. 66, Vol. 145, 450–53, in *Absconders, Runaways and Other Fugitives*, 51–52, 61, 67, 72.

59. Baltimore City Jail (Runaway Docket), 1836–1850, MSA; Fields, *Middle Ground*, 66–67.

60. *Sun*, October 16, 1849; *Cecil Whig*, July 24, 1858, in James L. Bowers (b. 1810–d. 1882), Accomplice to Slave Flight, Kent County, Maryland, 1858, SC 5496-8991, MSA.

61. Spitzer, "Rationalization of Crime Control," 190; Spitzer and Scull, "Privatization and Capitalist Development," 20, 23; Potter, "History of Policing." This understanding of the police wore on into the late nineteenth century: The police "shall strictly watch the con-

duct of all persons of known bad character, and in such manner that it will be evident to said persons that they are watched," was the order for the Charleston police in the 1880s. *Rules and Regulations for the General Government of the Police Department*, 29, CCPL.

62. Potter, "History of Policing."

63. *Daily Picayune*, October 27, 1858.

64. Daybook of the Richmond Police Guard, February 15, 1844, UVA.

65. Rousey, "Hibernian Leatherheads," 63, 69.

66. Executive Papers, Governor Randolph Executive Papers, Box 2, July 3, 1820; Condemned Blacks Executed or Transported, LVA; Takagi, *Rearing Wolves*, 113.

67. Before transportation, the slaves were valued by an independent observer and their owners were reimbursed for the lost investment. Condemned Blacks Executed or Transported, 19 January; 8 April; 9 August 1833, LVA. A total of 455 enslaved men and women saw their death sentences commuted to sale and transportation between 1815 and 1846. Forret, *William's Gang*, 56.

68. Forret, *William's Gang*, 10.

69. Condemned Blacks Executed or Transported, 18 February 1833, LVA.

70. For George's and similar cases: Condemned Blacks Executed or Transported, 29 July; 8 June 1839; 11 July 1842; 14 November 1841, LVA.

71. Condemned Blacks Executed or Transported, 7 September 1859, LVA. The same punishment expected Charles, Miles, Alberta, and Nareissa, all valued between $1,100 and $1,300. Condemned Blacks Executed or Transported, 22 September; 15, 23 November 1859; 25 April 1860, LVA.

72. Secretary of Commonwealth Executive Journal Indexes, Governor David Campbell, Annual Speech, 2 December 1839, LVA.

73. Walker, *No More, No More*, 29; *Report of the Board of Directors of the Louisiana Penitentiary*, Report for the year 1853, HML.

74. Hall, "Public Slaves," 532; Hall, "Slaves of the State," 19.

75. Hall, "Slaves of the State," 19–20, 32–33.

76. Weld, *American Slavery As It Is*, 75; Walker, *No More, No More*, 29.

77. Haley, *No Mercy Here*; Childs, *Slaves of the State*.

78. *Annual Report of the State Engineer to the Legislature of the State of Louisiana*, 24.

79. Greiner, *Louisiana Digest, Embracing the Laws of the Legislature*, I:518.

80. Hall, "Public Slaves," 567–68.

81. *The Daily Advocate*, October 18, 1855; *Journal of the House of Representatives of the State of Louisiana*. First Session—Twelfth Legislature, March 27, 1835, HML.

82. *Journal of the First Municipality of the City of New Orleans*, June 22; August 24, 1840, LaRC. The death rates on the public works were immense. "Fellow Citizens of the Senate and of the House of Representatives," Speech by A. Mouton, January 1, 1844, *Official Journal of the Proceedings of the House of Representatives of the State of Louisiana*. Second Session—Sixteenth Legislature, Journals House of Representatives Louisiana, HML.

83. Johnson, *Slavery's Metropolis*, 127.

84. Takagi, *Rearing Wolves*, 79.

85. Boney, Hume, and Zafar, *Autobiography of George Teamoh*, 82–83.

86. Bibb, *Narrative of the Life and Adventures*, 88–89; Birch and Buchanan, "Tyrant's Law," 32.

87. *Journal of the First Municipality of the City of New Orleans,* 6 August 1838, LaRC.

88. "Fellow Citizens of the Senate and of the House of Representatives," Speech by A. Mouton, January 1, 1844, *Official Journal of the Proceedings of the House of Representatives of the State of Louisiana.* Second Session—Sixteenth Legislature, Journals House of Representatives Louisiana, HML.

89. Birch and Buchanan, "Tyrant's Law," 27.

90. Paton, *No Bond but the Law,* 29.

91. John T. Rawlins to the Honorable Members of the Legislature of Virginia, January 6, 1824, Caroline County, Virginia, Accession #11682405, Legislative Petitions, VSA, Race and Slavery Petitions Project, Series 1, Legislative Petitions, LOC.

92. Petition by Benjamin J. Cochran, Jailer of Abbeville District, Petition and Supporting Papers Asking Compensation for Tending to Daphney, a Runaway Slave, Whose Master Has Not Claimed Her, and Who Could Not Be Sold Due to Old Age, 1857, SCDAH.

93. To the Honorable the Speaker and Members of the House of Representatives of the Said State, Kershaw Parish/District, South Carolina, Petition by William Love, November 1820, Accession #11382001, Race and Slavery Petitions Project, Series 1, Legislative Petitions.

94. *Journal of the House of Representatives of the State of Louisiana.* First Session—Seventeenth Legislature, February 3, 1845, HML.

95. *Journal of the House of Representatives of the State of Louisiana.* First Session—Seventeenth Legislature, February 3, 1845, HML.

96. Ch. 171, Laws of 1824, in Runaway Docket, Baltimore City and County, Guide to Government Records, MSA.

97. Laws of Maryland, 1831, ch. 323, Vol. 141, 1068, in *Absconders, Runaways and Other Fugitives,* 61; Wright, *Free Negro in Maryland,* 133.

98. Virginia Department of Corrections, Brief History; Maryland State Penitentiary, MSA SC 5496-30976, Jail, Baltimore City, Maryland, MSA; *Journal of the House of Representatives of the State of Louisiana.* First Session—Twelfth Legislature, January 5, 1835, HML; *Constitution of South Carolina,* 92–93.

99. Forret, *William's Gang,* 257.

100. Craig, *Craig's Business Directory,* 91, MSA.

101. "Fellow Citizens of the Senate and of the House of Representatives," Speech by A. Mouton, January 1, 1844, HML.

102. Rubin, *Deviant Prison;* Speech by W. M. Smith, *Journal of the House of Delegates of Virginia,* 10, LVA.

103. Fields, *Middle Ground,* 71.

104. John G. Gamble to the Delegates and Senators of the Legislature of Virginia, in General Assembly Convened, January 1825, Richmond City, Virginia, Richmond City, Virginia, Accession #11682502, Legislative Petitions, VSA, Race and Slavery Petitions Project, Series 1, Legislative Petitions, LOC.

105. Rockman, "Unfree Origins," 354.

106. Forret, *William's Gang,* 258.

107. To the Honorable the President and Members of the Senate of S. Carolina, Petition of Sundry Mechanics of the City of Charleston, n.d., S165015, Petitions to the General Assembly, SCDAH.

108. Curry, *Free Black*, 17.

109. Pinckney, *Reflections*, 19.

110. Thompson, *Working on the Dock*, 99–100.

111. Sinha, *Counterrevolution of Slavery*, 1–2, 135.

112. Berlin and Gutman, "Natives and Immigrants," 1185.

113. Hoffman, *Race, Class, and Power*, 21–22; Sinha, *Counterrevolution of Slavery*, 135.

114. Takagi, *Rearing Wolves*, 26, 86; Kimball, *American City*, xxi, 19, 167.

115. Jacobs, *Free Negro Question in Maryland*, 12–13, 15, MSA.

116. *Sun*, June 10, 1859.

117. The Inaugural Address of Thomas H. Hicks, Governor of Maryland, delivered in the Senate Chamber, at Annapolis, Wednesday, January 13, 1858, MSA.

118. Members of the lower classes did not succeed at accessing all levels of the government. Grand juries, for instance, remained dominated by slaveholders. Thompson, *Working on the Dock*, 21, 119.

119. Fields, "Ideology and Race," 143; Rockman, *Scraping By*, 14; Naragon, "Ballots, Bullets, and Blood," 17.

120. de Tocqueville, *Democracy in America*, 1.

121. Towers, *Urban South and the Coming of the Civil War*, 1, 4; Campbell, *Slavery on Trial*, 48.

122. Roediger, *Wages of Whiteness*, 67–68; Rockman, *Scraping By*, 50.

123. Naragon, "Ballots, Bullets, and Blood," 4.

124. Hobsbawm, *Age of Capital*, 98–99, 104.

125. Latimore, "Closer to Slavery."

126. *Richmond Dispatch*, September 3, October 11, December 3, 1853, in Campbell, *Slavery on Trial*, 28.

127. Richmond (VA), City Sergeant, Mss 3R415661, Section 1, Register 1841–1846, VHS.

128. Richmond (VA), City Sergeant, Mss 3R415661, Section 1, Register 1841–1846, VHS.

129. Latimore, "Closer to Slavery," 119.

130. Petition by Society of Friends, December 31, 1844, Legislative Petitions, LVA.

131. Latimore, "Closer to Slavery," 120, 124.

132. Latimore, "Closer to Slavery," 121, 127.

133. *Charleston Mercury*, December 10, 1859.

134. Proceedings of the City Council of Charleston, S.C., 1859 I; Charleston (S.C.) City Council, Proceedings of Council, POC-002 M: 1859–1870, CCPL.

135. *Charleston Courier*, August 9, 1860.

136. Myers, *Forging Freedom*, 83.

137. Sweeney, "Market Marronage," 214.

138. Thompson, *Working on the Dock*, 119–20, 123.

139. Johnson and Roark, *Black Masters*, 236–37, 274–75.

140. *Richmond Enquirer*, November 16, 1858.

141. Numbers taken from Green, "Black Tobacco Factory Workers," 195–96.

142. Campbell, *Slavery on Trial*, 156.

143. Wade, *Slavery in the Cities*, 218–19.

144. An Act Relative to Free Persons of Color Entering This State from Other States or Foreign Countries, March 15, 1959, Louisiana Acts 1859, 70–72, in Schafer, *Becoming Free*, 140.

145. Records of Prisoners Committed to the Parish Prison, 1852–1862, June 18, 1852–May 10, 1862, TX420, NOPL.

146. Schafer, *Becoming Free*, 134, 137–38, 141–42.

147. Wade, *Slavery in the Cities*, 218–19.

148. Auditor of Public Acts Fugitive Slave Fund Claims, Luther B. Kurtz, June 17, 1857, November 25, 1857; Edward Lee, April 15, July 6, 1858, LVA.

149. Commonwealth v. Eliza Ann Johnson, May 16, 1861, Suit Papers, Hustings Court Suit Papers, LVA.

150. This is testified to, for instance, in the private conversations of a member of the Charleston free Black elite. Johnsen to Dear Henry, August 29, 1860, Ellison Family Papers, SCLC.

151. Spooner, "This Scheme is From God," 559–60; Berlin, *Slaves Without Masters*, 85–86.

152. Dred Scott v. Sandford, Primary Documents in American History, LOC.

Conclusion

1. Sinha, *Slave's Cause*, 1.

2. As a reference, more than 40 percent of highly educated migrants from non-EU countries and non-Schengen member states in employment in the European Union work below their qualifications. European Commission, Migration and Home Affairs, "Integration in the Labour Market."

3. Lind, "Sanctuary Cities."

Bibliography

Newspapers and Periodicals

American and Commercial Daily Advertiser (Baltimore, MD)
American Christian Expositor (New York)
Augusta Chronicle (Augusta, GA)
Baltimore American (Baltimore, MD)
Baltimore Gazette (Baltimore, MD)
Baltimore Patriot (Baltimore, MD)
Charleston Courier (Charleston, SC)
Charleston Daily Courier (Charleston, SC)
Charleston Mercury (Charleston, SC)
Daily Advocate (Baton Rouge, LA)
Daily Dispatch (Richmond, VA)
Daily Journal (Indianapolis, IN)
Daily National Intelligencer (Washington, DC)
Daily Picayune (New Orleans, LA)
Enquirer (Richmond, VA)
National Intelligencer and Washington Advertiser (Washington, DC)
Picayune (New Orleans, LA)
Richmond Dispatch (Richmond, VA)
Richmond Enquirer (Richmond, VA)
Southern Patriot (Charleston, SC)
Sun (Baltimore, MD)

Other Sources

An Act Relative to Free Persons of Color Entering This State from Other States or Foreign Countries. March 15, 1959. Louisiana Acts 1859. In Judith Kelleher Schafer, *Becoming Free, Remaining Free: Manumission and Enslavement in New Orleans, 1846–1862*, 140. Baton Rouge: Louisiana State University Press, 2003.

Adams, Ephraim Douglass. *Great Britain and the American Civil War*. New York: Diversion Books, 2014.

Ainsworth, Kyle. "Advertising Maranda: Runaway Slaves in Texas, 1835–1865." In *Fugitive Slaves and Spaces of Freedom in North America*, edited by Damian Alan Pargas, 197–231. Gainesville: University Press of Florida, 2018.

Alfred Huger to Henry D. Lesesne. December 8, 1858. Alfred Huger Letterpress Books. 1853–1863. William R. Perkins Library. Special Collections. Duke University, Durham, NC. In *Black Masters: A Free Family of Color in the Old South*, edited by Michael P. Johnson and James L. Roark, 192–93. New York and London: W. W. Norton & Company, 1984.

American Colonization Society, ed. *The African Repository, and Colonial Journal* 14:1 (1838).

Anbinder, Tyler. *Nativism and Slavery: The Northern Know-Nothings and the Politics of the 1850s*. New York and Oxford: Oxford University Press, 1992.

Anderson, William J. *Life and Narrative of William J. Anderson, Twenty-Four Years a Slave; Sold Eight Times! In Jail Sixty Times!! Whipped Three Hundred Times!!! Or The Dark Deeds of American Slavery Revealed. Containing Scriptural Views of the Origin of the Black and of the White man. Also, a Simple and Easy Plan to Abolish Slavery in the United States. Together with an Account of the Services of Colored Men in the Revolutionary War—Day and Date, and Interesting Facts*. Chicago: Daily Tribune, 1857.

Andrews, Ethan A. *Slavery and the Domestic Slave-Trade in the United States. In a Series of Letters Addressed to the Executive Committee of the American Union for the Relief and Improvement of the Colored Race.* Boston: Light & Stearns, 1836.

Annual Report of the State Engineer to the Legislature of the State of Louisiana. Baton Rouge: J. M. Taylor, 1859.

Anonymous [James Matthews]. *Recollections of Slavery by a Runaway Slave.* Originally published as *Recollections of Slavery.* In *Emancipator.* August–October 1838.

Aptheker, Herbert. "Maroons within the Present Limit of the United States." In *Maroon Societies: Rebel Slave Communities in the Americas,* edited by Richard Price, 151–68. Baltimore and London: Johns Hopkins University Press, 1979. Originally published in *Journal of Negro History* 24:2 (1939): 167–84.

Ashton, Susanna. "Re-collecting Jim. Discovering a Name and Slave Narrative's Continuing Truth." *Common-Place* 15:1 (2014). http://www.common-place-archives.org /vol-15/no-01/tales/#.XHorieQ1uUl. March 4, 2019.

Ashworth, John. *Slavery, Capitalism, and Politics in the Antebellum Republic.* Vol. 1, *Commerce and Compromise, 1820–1850.* Cambridge and New York: Cambridge University Press, 1995.

Auditor of Public Acts Fugitive Slave Fund Claims. LVA.

Augustin, D., Esq., ed. *A General Digest of the Ordinances and Resolutions of the Corporation of New-Orleans.* New Orleans: Jerome Bayon, 1831.

Ayers, Edward L., Lewis L. Gould, David M. Oshinsky, and Jean R. Soderlund. *American Passages: A History of the United States.* 4th ed. Wadsworth: Cengage Learning, 2010.

Bacci, Massimo Livi. *A Short History of Migration.* Cambridge: Polity, 2012.

Bagenal, Philip. *The American Irish and their Influence on Irish Politics.* London: Kegan Paul, Trench & Co., 1882.

Ball, Charles. *Fifty Years in Chains; or, The Life of an American Slave.* New York: H. Dayton, and Indianapolis: Asher & Company, 1859.

———. *Slavery in the United States. A Narrative of the Life and the Adventurers of Charles Ball, a Black Man, Who Lived Forty Years in Maryland, South Carolina and Georgia, as a Slave Under Various Masters, and was One Year in the Navy with Commodore Barney, During the Late War. Containing an Account of the Manners and Usages of the Planters and Slaveholders of the South—a Description of the Condition and Treatment of the Slaves, with Observations upon the State of Morals amongst the Cotton Planters, and the Perils and Sufferings of a Fugitive Slave, Who Twice Escaped from the Cotton Country.* New York: John S. Taylor, 1837.

"Baltimore City and County Jail Runaway and Accommodations Dockets, 1831–1864." In *Absconders, Runaways and Other Fugitives in the Baltimore City and County Jail,* edited by Jerry M. Hynson, 76–153. Westminster: Willow Bend Books, 2004.

Baltimore City Jail (Runaway Docket). 1836–1850. MSA.

Baltimore. Ordinances. In Richard C. Wade, *Slavery in the Cities: The South 1820–1860,* 249. London, Oxford, and New York: Oxford University Press, 1964.

Baptist, Edward E. *The Half Has Never Been Told: The Slave Migration that Shaped African America, the United States, and the Modern World.* New York: Basic Books, 2014.

———. "Toxic Debts, Liar Loans, Collateralized and Securitized Human Beings, and the Panic of 1837." In *Capitalism Takes Command: The Social Transformation of Nineteenth-Century America,* edited by Michael Zakim and Gary J. Kornblith, 69–92. Chicago: University of Chicago Press, 2011.

Bateman, Fred, and Thomas Weiss. *A Deplorable Scarcity: The Failure of Industrialization in the Slave Economy*. Chapel Hill: University of North Carolina Press, 1981.

Bayley, Solomon. *A Narrative of Some Remarkable Incidents in the Life of Solomon Bayley, Formerly a Slave in the State of Delaware, North America; Written by Himself, and Published for His Benefit; to Which Are Prefixed, a Few Remarks by Robert Hurnard*. London: Harvey and Darton, 1825.

Beckert, Sven. *Empire of Cotton: A Global History*. New York: Alfred A. Knopf, 2015.

———. *The Monied Metropolis. New York City and the Consolidation of the American Bourgeoisie, 1850–1896*. Cambridge: Cambridge University Press, 2001.

Bell, Frank. Vienna, Va. Interviewer Claude W. Anderson. n.d. Virginia State Library. In *Weevils in the Wheat: Interviews with Virginia Ex-Slaves*, edited by Charles L. Perdue, Thomas E. Barden, and Robert K. Phillips, 25–28. Charlottesville and London: University of Virginia Press, 1992. Originally published 1976.

Benson, Adolph, Fredrika Bremer, and Carrie Catt, eds. *America of the Fifties: Letters of Fredrika Bremer*. Selected and Edited by Adolph B. Benson. New York: American-Scandinavian Foundation; and London: Humphrey Milford Oxford University Press, 1924.

Berlin, Ira. *Generations of Captivity: A History of African American Slaves*. Cambridge, MA: Harvard University Press, 2003.

———. *Many Thousands Gone: The First Two Centuries of Slavery in North America*. Cambridge, MA, and London: Harvard University Press, 1998.

———. *Slaves Without Masters: The Free Negro in the Antebellum South*. New York: Pantheon Books, 1974.

———. "The Structure of the Free Negro Caste in the Antebellum United States." *Journal of Social History* 9:3 (1976): 297–318.

Berlin, Ira, and Herbert G. Gutman. "Natives and Immigrants, Free Men and Slaves: Urban Workingmen in the Antebellum American South." *American Historical Review* 88:5 (1983): 1175–1200.

Bibb, Henry. *Narrative of the Life and Adventures of Henry Bibb, An American Slave, Written by Himself*. New York, 1849.

Birch, Kelly, and Thomas Buchanan. "The Penalty of a Tyrant's Law: Landscapes of Incarceration during the Second Slavery." *Slavery & Abolition* 34:1 (2013): 22–38.

Blackburn, Robin. "Introduction." In *Paths to Freedom: Manumission in the Atlantic World*, edited by Rosemary Brana-Shute and Randy J. Sparks, 1–13. Columbia: University of South Carolina Press, 2009.

Blanchette, Thaddeus, and Cristiana Schettini. "Sex Work in Rio de Janeiro: Police Management without Regulation." In *Selling Sex in the City: A Global History of Prostitution, 1600s-2000s*, edited by Magaly Rodríguez García, Lex Heerma van Voss, and Elise van Nederveen Meerkerk, 490–516. Leiden and Boston: Brill, 2017.

Blassingame, John W. *The Slave Community: Plantation Life in the Antebellum South*. Oxford and New York: Oxford University Press, 1972.

———. "Using the Testimony of Ex-Slaves: Approaches and Problems." In *The Slave's Narrative*, edited by Charles T. Davis and Henry Louis Gates Jr., 78–97. Oxford and New York: Oxford University Press, 1991.

Blight, David. *Frederick Douglass: Prophet of Freedom*. New York: Simon & Schuster, 2018.

Bloch, Alice, and Sonia McKay. *Living on the Margins: Undocumented Migrants in a Global City*. Bristol and Chicago: Policy Press, 2016.

Blumin, Stuart M. *The Emergence of the Middle Class: Social Experience in the American City, 1760–1900*. Cambridge and New York: Cambridge University Press, 1989.

Bogger, Tommy. *Free Blacks in Norfolk, Virginia, 1790–1860: The Darker Side of Freedom*. Charlottesville and London: University Press of Virginia, 1997.

Boles, John B. *Black Southerners, 1619–1869*. Lexington: University Press of Kentucky, 1984.

Bolster, W. Jeffrey. *Black Jacks: African American Seamen in the Age of Sail*. Cambridge, MA: Harvard University Press, 1997.

Boney, F. N., Richard L. Hume, and Rafia Zafar. *God Made Man, Man Made the Slave: The Autobiography of George Teamoh*. Macon, GA: Mercer University Press, 1990. Written in 1874.

"Born in Slavery: Slave Narratives from the Federal Writers' Project, 1836–1838." LOC. https://www.loc.gov/collections/slave-narratives-from-the-federal-writers-project -1936-to-1938/about-this-collection/. August 15, 2019.

Bradford, S. Sidney. "The Negro Ironworker in Ante Bellum Virginia." In *The Making of Black America*. Vol. 1, *The Origins of Black Americans*, edited by August Meier and Elliott Rudwick, 4–27. New York: Atheneum, 1971. Originally published in *Journal of Southern History* 25:2 (1959): 194–206.

Brass, Tom. "Some Observations on Unfree Labour, Capitalist Restructuring, and Deproletarianization." In *Free and Unfree Labour. The Debate Continues*, edited by Tom Brass and Marcel van der Linden, 57–75. Berne: Peter Lang, 1997.

Brauns, Ernst. *Ideen über die Auswanderung nach Amerika; nebst Beiträgen zur genaueren Kenntnis seiner Bewohner und seines gegenwärtigen Zustandes. Nach eignen Ansichten und den neuesten Quellen und Hülfsmitteln*. Göttingen: Vandenhoeck and Ruprecht, 1827. JFK.

Bremer, Fredrika. *The Homes of the New World; Impressions of America*. Translated by Mary Howitt. Vol. 2. New York: Harper & Brothers, 1853.

Bromme, Traugott. *Gemälde von Nord-Amerika in allen Beziehungen von der Entdeckung an bis auf die neuste Zeit. Eine pittoreske Geographie für Alle, welche unterhaltende Belehrung suchen und ein Umfassendes Reise-Handbuch für Jene, welche in diesem Land wandern wollen*. Zweiter Band. Stuttgart: J. Scheible's Buchhandlung, 1842. JFK.

———. *Reisen durch die Vereinigten Staaten und Ober-Canada*. Dritter Band. Baltimore: T. Scheid & Co.; Dresden: Walthersche Hofbuchhandlung, 1834. JFK.

Brown, Elsa Barkley, and Gregg Kimball. "Mapping the Terrain of Black Richmond." *Journal of Urban History* 21:3 (1995): 296–346.

Brown, John. *Slave Life in Georgia: A Narrative of the Life, Sufferings, and Escape of John Brown, a Fugitive Slave, Now in England*, edited by L. A. Chamerovzow. London: W. M. Watts, 1855.

Buchanan, James. "Speech on the Slavery Question." 1836. In *Life of James Buchanan, Fifteenth President of the United States*. Vol. I, edited by George Ticknor Curtis, 315–18. New York: Harper & Brothers, 1883.

Buchanan, Thomas C. *Black Life on the Mississippi: Slaves, Free Blacks, and the Western Steamboat World*. Chapel Hill and London: University of North Carolina Press, 2004.

Buckler, Thomas H. *History of Epidemic Cholera, as it Appeared at the Baltimore City and County Alms-House, in the Summer of 1849, With Some Remarks on the Medical Topography and Diseases of this Region*. Baltimore: James Lucas, 1851.

Cain, Louis, and Sok Chul Hong. "Survival in 19th Century Cities: The Larger the City, the Smaller Your Chances." *Explorations in Economic History* 46:4 (2009): 450–63.

Cairns, David. *Youth Transitions, International Student Mobility and Spatial Reflexivity.* Basingstoke: Palgrave Macmillan, 2014.

Camp, Stephanie M. H. *Closer to Freedom: Enslaved Women and Everyday Resistance in the Plantation South.* Chapel Hill: University of North Carolina Press, 2004.

Campanella, Richard. "Culture Wars Led to New Orleans's Most Peculiar Experiment in City Management." *NOLA.com* (March 7, 2016). https://www.nola.com/homegarden /index.ssf/2016/03/relics_remain_of_new_orleans_m.html. January 27, 2019.

———. "The Turbulent History behind the Seven New Orleans Municipal Districts." *NOLA.com* (October 9, 2013). https://www.nola.com/entertainment_life/home _garden/article_931737d6-c922-5bd9-9062-80a7f5959d51.html. July 15, 2019.

Campbell, James M. *Slavery on Trial: Race, Class, and Criminal Justice in Antebellum Richmond, Virginia.* Gainesville: University Press of Florida, 2007.

Carter, Clarence Edwin, ed. *The Territorial Papers of the United States.* Vol. 9, *The Territory of New Orleans 1803–1812.* Washington, DC: Government Printing Office, 1940. HML.

Carter, Matilda. Hampton, Va. Interviewer Claude W. Anderson. January 4, 1937. Virginia State Library. In *Weevils in the Wheat: Interviews with Virginia Ex-Slaves,* edited by Charles L. Perdue, Thomas E. Barden, and Robert K. Phillips, 68–70. Charlottesville and London: University of Virginia Press, 1992. Originally published 1976.

Cecelski, David S. *The Waterman's Song: Slavery and Freedom in Maritime North Carolina.* Chapel Hill: University of North Carolina Press, 2001.

Cecil Whig. In James L. Bowers (b. 1810–d. 1882), Accomplice to Slave Flight. Kent County, Maryland. 1858. SC 5496-8991. MSA.

Chalhoub, Sidney. "The Precariousness of Freedom in a Slave Society (Brazil in the Nineteenth Century)." *International Review of Social History* 56:3 (2011): 405–39.

Charleston (S.C.). City Council. Proceedings of Council POC-001 M: 18 21-2. CCPL.

———. POC-002 M: 1859–1870. CCPL.

Charleston Times. In Michael D. Thompson, *Working on the Dock of the Bay. Labor and Emancipation in an Antebellum Southern Port,* 44. Columbia: University of South Carolina Press, 2015.

Childs, Dennis. *Slaves of the State: Black Incarceration from the Chain Gang to the Penitentiary.* Minneapolis: University of Minnesota Press, 2015.

City Gazette. In Thomas Brown and Leah Sims, *Fugitive Slave Advertisements in* The City Gazette, *Charleston, South Carolina, 1787–1797.* London: Lexington Books, 2015.

City Gazette and Commercial Daily Advertiser. Charleston, SC.

Cohen, Patricia Cline. *The Murder of Helen Jewett: The Life and Death of a Prostitute in Nineteenth-Century New York.* New York: Vintage Books, 1999.

Cohen's New Orleans & Lafayette Directory for 1851. New Orleans, 1851. Louisiana Division. NOPL. http://files.usgwarchives.net/la/orleans/history/directory/1851cdcd.txt. March 8, 2018.

Cole, Shawn. "Capitalism and Freedom: Manumissions and the Slave Market in Louisiana, 1725–1820." *Journal of Economic History* 65:4 (2005): 1008–27.

Cole, Stephanie. "Servants and Slaves: Domestic Service in the Border Cities, 1800–1850." PhD diss., University of Florida, 1994.

Commonwealth v. Eliza Ann Johnson. May 16, 1861. LVA. Suit Papers. Hustings Court Suit Papers. LVA.

Commonwealth v. Helen A. E. Briggs. July 12, 1862. Suit Papers. Hustings Court Suit Papers. LVA.

Condemned Blacks Executed or Transported. LVA.

The Constitution of South Carolina, Adopted April 16, 1868, and the Acts and Joint Resolutions of the General Assembly, Passed at the Special Session of 1868, Together with the Military Orders Therein Re-Enacted. Columbia: John W. Denny, 1868.

Copp, Roberta V.H. "O'Neall, John Belton." *South Carolina Encyclopedia.* Columbia, S.C.: University of South Carolina, Institute for Southern Studies (2016). https://www.scencyclopedia.org/sce/entries/oneall-john-belton/. March 9, 2022.

Cornelius, Janet Duitsman. *Slave Missions and the Black Church in the Antebellum South.* Columbia: University of South Carolina Press, 1999.

County Court Chancery Papers. February 19, 1855. LVA. In Race and Slavery Petitions Project. Series 2. County Court Petitions. University of North Carolina at Greensboro.

Cullen, Jim. *American Dream: A Short History of an Idea that Shaped a Nation.* Oxford and New York: Oxford University Press, 2003.

Curry, Leonard P. *The Free Black in Urban America, 1800–1850: The Shadow of the Dream.* Chicago: University of Chicago Press, 1981.

Craig, Daniel H. *Craig's Business Directory and Baltimore Almanac; for 1842.* Published Annually. Baltimore: J. Robinson, 1842. MSA.

Dahl, Alan Lewis. "The North of the South: Planters and the Transition to Capitalism in the Central Virginia Piedmont." PhD diss., University of Kentucky, 2010.

Dantas, Mariana L. R. *Black Townsmen: Urban Slavery and Freedom in the Eighteenth-Century Americas.* New York: Palgrave Macmillan, 2008.

David Gavin Diary. SCHS.

David Yates to Mother. July 30, 1824. Yates Family Papers. SCHS.

Davis, David Brion. *Inhuman Bondage: The Rise and Fall of Slavery in the New World.* Oxford and New York: Oxford University Press, 2006.

———. *The Problem of Slavery in the Age of Revolution, 1770–1823.* Oxford and New York: Oxford University Press, 1999.

Davis, Hugh. "American Colonization Society." In *Abolition and Antislavery: A Historical Encyclopedia of the American Mosaic,* edited by Peter Hinks and John McKivigan, 13–15. Santa Barbara and Denver: Greenwood, 2015.

Dawson, J. L., and Henry William DeSaussure, eds. *Census of the City of Charleston, South Carolina, for the Year 1848, Exhibiting the Condition and Prospects of the City, Illustrated by Many Statistical Details, Prepared under the Authority of the City Council.* Charleston: J. B. Nixon, 1849.

Dawson, Victoria. "Copper Neck Tags Evoke the Experience of American Slaves Hired Out as Part-Time Laborers." *Smithsonian Magazine* (February 2003). https://www.smithsonianmag.com/history/copper-neck-tags-evoke-experience-american-slaves-hired-out-part-time-laborers-76039831/. June 27, 2019.

Daybook of the Richmond Police Guard, 1834–1844. Alderman Library. Special Collections. University of Virginia. Transcribed in Leni Ashmore Sorensen. "Absconded: Fugitive Slaves in the Daybook of the Richmond Police Guard, 1834–1844." PhD diss., College of William and Mary, 2005.

DeBow, J. D. B., ed. *The Seventh Census of the United States: 1850. Embracing a Statistical View of Each of the States and Territories, Arranged by Counties, Towns, etc., Under the Following Divisions . . . with an Introduction, Embracing the Aggregate Tables for the United States Compared with Every Previous Census since 1790—Schedules and Laws of Congress Relating to the Census in the Same Period—Ratio Tables of Increase and Decrease of Cities and States, etc., by Sex and Ages, and Color—Table of Population of Every County, Town, Township, etc., in the United States, Alphabetically Arranged—Together with Some Explanatory Remarks, and an Appendix Embracing Notes upon the Tables of Each of the States.* Washington, DC: Robert Armstrong, 1853.

Delbanco, Andrew. *The War Before the War: Fugitive Slaves and the Struggle for America's Soul from the Revolution to the Civil War.* New York: Penguin Press, 2018.

Department of Commerce and Labor Bureau of the Census. *Heads of Families at the First Census of the United States in the Year 1790: South Carolina.* Washington, DC: Government Printing Office, 1908. https://www.census.gov/library/publications/1907/dec/heads-of-families.html. April 16, 2019.

Dessens, Nathalie. "New Orleans, LA, 1790–1828." In *Cities in American Political History,* edited by Richard Dilworth, 103–9. Los Angeles and London: SAGE, 2011.

Din, Gilbert C. *Spaniards, Planters, and Slaves: The Spanish Regulation of Slavery in Louisiana, 1763–1803.* College Station: Texas A&M University Press, 1999.

Diouf, Sylviane A. "Borderland Maroons." In *Fugitive Slaves and Spaces of Freedom in North America,* edited by Damian Alan Pargas, 168–96. Gainesville: University Press of Florida, 2018.

———. *Slavery's Exiles: The Story of the American Maroons.* New York and London: New York University Press, 2014.

Dittmar, Jeremiah, and Suresh Naidu. "Contested Property: Fugitive Slaves in the Antebellum U.S. South." Version 0.1. http://eh.net/eha/wp-content/uploads/2013/11/Dittmar.pdf. May 29, 2019.

Doddington, David Stefan. *Contesting Slave Masculinity in the American South.* Cambridge: Cambridge University Press, 2018.

Donaldson, Gary A. "A Window on Slave Culture: Dances at Congo Square in New Orleans, 1800–1862." *Journal of Negro History* 69:2 (1984): 63–72.

Douglass, Frederick. *The Life and Times of Frederick Douglass. Written by Himself. His Early Life as a Slave, his Escape from Bondage, and his Complete History to the Present Time.* Hartford: Park Publishing Co., 1881.

———. *Narrative of the Life of Frederick Douglass, an American Slave. Written by Himself.* Boston: Anti-Slavery Office, 1845.

Dred Scott v. Sandford. Primary Documents in American History. LOC (April 25, 2017). http://www.loc.gov/rr/program/bib/ourdocs/DredScott.html. October 18, 2017.

Drew, Benjamin. *A North-Side View of Slavery. The Refugee: Or the Narratives of Fugitive Slaves in Canada. Related by Themselves, with an Account of the History and Condition of the Colored Population of Upper Canada.* Boston: John P. Jewett & Company; Cleveland: Jewett, Proctor, and Worthington; New York: Sheldon, Lamport, and Blakeman; and London: Trübner & Co., 1856.

Du Bois, W. E. B. *Black Reconstruction in America, 1860–1880.* Introduction by David Levering Lewis. New York, London, Toronto, and Sydney: Free Press, 1992.

Dunn, Richard S. *A Tale of Two Plantations: Slave Life and Labor in Jamaica and Virginia.* Cambridge, MA: Harvard University Press, 2014.

Eckhard, George B., ed. *A Digest of the Ordinances of the City Council of Charleston, from the year 1783 to Oct. 1844. To which are annexed the Acts of the Legislature which relate exclusively to the City of Charleston.* Charleston: Walker & Burke, 1844. CCPL.

Elvira Jones to the Honorable the Speakers and Members of both Houses of the Legislature of the Commonwealth of Virginia. December 5, 1823. Richmond City, Virginia. Accession #11682304. Legislative Petitions. VSA. Race and Slavery Petitions Project. Series 1. Legislative Petitions. LOC.

Ernest, John. "Introduction." In *The Oxford Handbook of the African American Slave Narrative,* edited by John Ernest, 1–18. Oxford and New York: Oxford University Press, 2014.

European Commission, Migration and Home Affairs. "Integration in the Labour Market." https://ec.europa.eu/home-affairs/what-we-do/policies/legal-migration/integration /integration-labour-market_en. July 27, 2020.

Everett, Donald E. "Emigres and Militiamen: Free Persons of Color in New Orleans, 1803–1815." *Journal of Negro History* 38: 4 (1953): 377–402.

Executive Communications. The Speaker of the House of Delegates. December 4, 1820. LVA.

Executive Papers. Governor Randolph Executive Papers. Box 2. LVA.

Extract from the Negro Register. Chesterfield County Court. January 8, 1855. Gray Papers. VHS.

Federal Gazette and Baltimore Daily Advertiser. Baltimore, MD.

Fehrenbacher, Don E. *The Slaveholding Republic: An Account of the United States Government's Relations to Slavery,* edited by Ward M. McAfee. New York: Oxford University Press, 2001.

"Fellow Citizens of the Senate and of the House of Representatives." Speech by A. Mouton. January 1, 1844. *Official Journal of the Proceedings of the House of Representatives of the State of Louisiana.* Second Session—Sixteenth Legislature. Journals House of Representatives Louisiana. HML.

Fields, Barbara J. "Ideology and Race in American History." In *Region, Race, and Reconstruction. Essays in Honor of C. Vann Woodward,* edited by J. Morgan Kousser and James M. McPherson, 95–118. New York and Oxford: Oxford University Press, 1982.

———. *Slavery and Freedom on the Middle Ground. Maryland during the Nineteenth Century.* New Haven, CT and London: Yale University Press, 1985.

———. "Slavery, Race, and Ideology in the United States of America." *New Left Review* 181 (1990): 95–118.

Finch, Marianne. *An Englishwoman's Experience in America.* New York: Negro Universities Press, 1969. Originally published London: Richard Bentley, 1853.

First African Baptist Church (Richmond, Virginia). Minute Books. 1841–1930. LVA.

Flanigan, Daniel J. "Criminal Procedure in Slave Trials in the Antebellum South." *Journal of Southern History* 40:4 (1974): 537–64.

Flournoy, H. W., ed. *House of Delegates, Senate & Virginia State Papers, Calendar of Virginia State Papers and Other Manuscripts from January 1, 1799, to December 31, 1807, Preserved in the Capitol, at Richmond.* Vol. 9: Richmond, 1890. LVA.

Fogel, Robert William. *Without Consent or Contract: The Rise and Fall of American Slavery.* New York: W. W. Norton, 1989.

Follett, Richard. *The Sugar Masters: Planters and Slaves in Louisiana's Cane World,*
    1820–1860. Baton Rouge: Louisiana State University Press, 2005.

Foner, Eric. "African Americans and the Story of American Freedom." *Souls* 1:1 (1999):
    16–22.

———. *Gateway to Freedom: The Hidden History of the Underground Railroad*. New York
    and London: W. W. Norton, 2015.

———. *The Story of American Freedom*. New York and London: W. W. Norton & Company,
    1998.

Foner, Laura. "The Free People of Color in Louisiana and St. Domingue: A Comparative
    Portrait of Two Three-Caste Slave Societies." *Journal of Social History* 3:4 (1970):
    406–30.

Foner, Philip S. "A Tribune of His People." In *Frederick Douglass on Slavery and the Civil
    War. Selections from His Writings*, edited by Philip S. Foner, 1–29. Mineola, NY: Dover
    Publications, 2003.

Ford, Lacy K. *Deliver Us from Evil: The Slavery Question in the Old South*. Oxford: Oxford
    University Press, 2009.

Ford Family Papers. 1809–1968. Manuscripts P. SCLC.

Forret, Jeff. "Slaves, Poor Whites, and the Underground Economy of the Rural Carolinas."
    Journal of Southern History 70:4 (2004): 783–824.

———. *William's Gang: A Notorious Slave Trader and his Cargo of Black Convicts*.
    Cambridge: Cambridge University Press, 2020.

Franklin, John Hope. *From Slavery to Freedom: A History of the American Negro*. New York:
    Alfred A. Knopf, 1947.

Franklin, John Hope, and Loren Schweninger. *Runaway Slaves: Rebels on the Plantation*.
    Oxford and London: Oxford University Press, 1999.

French Statements of Alexis Bougny and Celestín Villemont. April 23, 1810. General
    Manuscripts. January 18, 1808–December 21, 1811. John Minor Wisdom Collection.
    LaRC.

Gara, Larry. *The Liberty Line: The Legend of the Underground Railroad*. Lexington:
    University Press of Kentucky, 1996.

Geggus, David Patrick. *The Impact of the Haitian Revolution in the Atlantic World*.
    Columbia: University of South Carolina Press, 2001.

General Assembly. "An ACT to amend the several laws concerning slaves." 1806.
    Transcribed from *The Statutes at Large of Virginia, from October Session 1792, to
    December Session 1806*, edited by Samuel Shepherd. Richmond: Samuel Shepherd, 1836.
    In *Encyclopedia Virginia*, July 31, 2012. http://www.encyclopediavirginia.org/_An_ACT
    _to_amend_the_several_laws_concerning_slaves_1806. October 26, 2016.

Gilbert Hunt, William B. Ballandine, Isham Ellis, Harison Dendridge, and James
    Greenhow to the Honorable the Legislature of Virginia. December 1834. Richmond
    City, Virginia. Accession #11683411. Legislative Petitions, VSA. Race and Slavery
    Petitions Project. Series 1. Legislative Petitions. LOC.

Ginsburg, Rebecca. "Escaping through a Black Landscape." In *Cabin, Quarter, Plantation:
    Architecture and Landscapes of North American Slavery*, edited by Clifton Ellis and
    Rebecca Ginsburg, 51–66. New Haven, CT and London: Yale University Press, 2010.

———. "Freedom and the Slave Landscape." *Landscape Journal* 26:1 (2007): 36–44.

Goldfield, David. "Black Life in Old South Cities." In *Before Freedom Came: African-American Life in the Antebellum South,* edited by Edward Campbell Jr. and Kym Rice, 123–53. Richmond: Museum of the Confederacy, 1991.

Goldin, Claudia Dale. *Urban Slavery in the American South, 1820–1860: A Quantitative History.* Chicago: University of Chicago Press, 1976.

Gordon, David M., Richard Edwards, and Michael Reich. *Segmented Work, Divided Workers: The Historical Transformation of Labor in the United States.* Cambridge, New York, and Melbourne: Cambridge University Press, 1986. Originally published 1982.

Governor and Council (Pardon Papers). S1061. 1775–1836. MSA.

Grandy, Moses. *Narrative of the Life of Moses Grandy; Late a Slave in the United States of America.* London: C. Gilpin, 1843.

Green, Rodney D. "Black Tobacco Factory Workers and Social Conflict in Antebellum Richmond: Were Slavery and Urban Industry Really Compatible?" *Slavery & Abolition* 8:2 (1987): 183–203.

Greene, Harlan. "Slave Badges." In *World of a Slave: Encyclopedia of the Material Life of Slaves in the United States.* Vol. 1: A–I, edited by Martha B. Katz-Hyman and Kym S. Rice, 434–38. Santa Barbara, Denver, and Oxford: Greenwood, 2010.

Greene, Harlan, Harry S. Hutchins Jr., and Brian E. Hutchins. *Slave Badges and the Slave-Hire System in Charleston, South Carolina, 1783–1865.* Jefferson and London: McFarland, 2008.

Greiner, Meinrad, ed. *The Louisiana Digest, Embracing the Laws of the Legislature of a General Nature, Enacted from the Year 1804 to 1841, Inclusive, and in Force at this Last Period. Also, an Abstract of the Decisions of the Supreme Court of Louisiana on the Statutory Law, Arranged under the Appropriate Articles in the Digest.* Vol. 1. New Orleans: Benjamin Levy, 1841.

Grimes, William. *Life of William Grimes, the Runaway Slave,* edited by William L. Andrews and Regina E. Mason. Oxford and New York: Oxford University Press, 2008. Originally published as *Life of William Grimes, the Runaway Slave, Brought Down to the Present Time. Written by Himself.* New Haven, CT: Published by the Author, 1855.

Gutman, Herbert G. *The Black Family in Slavery and Freedom, 1750–1925.* New York: Vintage, 1976.

Hadden, Sally E. *Slave Patrols: Law and Violence in Virginia and the Carolinas.* Cambridge, MA and London: Harvard University Press, 2001.

Haley, Sarah. *No Mercy Here: Gender, Punishment, and the Making of Jim Crow Modernity.* Chapel Hill: University of North Carolina Press, 2016.

Hall, Aaron. "Public Slaves and State Engineers: Modern Statecraft on Louisiana's Waterways, 1833–1861." *Journal of Southern History* 85:3 (2019): 531–76.

———. "Slaves of the State: Infrastructure and Governance through Slavery in the Antebellum South." *Journal of American History* 106:1 (2019): 19–46.

Hall, Robert L. "Slave Resistance in Baltimore City and County, 1747–1790." *Maryland Historical Magazine* 84:4 (1989): 305–18.

Hammond, Caroline (A Fugitive). Interview. 1938. In *Federal Writers' Project: Slave Narrative Project.* Vol. 8: Maryland. Washington, 1941. Manuscript/Mixed Material. LOC. https://www.loc.gov/item/mesn080/. February 20, 2019.

Hanchett, Thomas W. *Sorting Out the New South City: Race, Class, and Urban Development in Charlotte, 1875–1975.* Chapel Hill: University of North Carolina Press, 1998.

"Harriet 'Rit' Ross, Caroline County." Biographical Series. MSA. https://msa.maryland
.gov/megafile/msa/speccol/sc5400/sc5496/008400/008444/html/008444bio.html.
September 21, 2018.

Harring, Sidney. *Policing in a Class Society: The Experience of American Cities, 1865–1915.*
New Brunswick, NJ: Rutgers University Press, 1983.

Harris, J. William. *The Making of the American South: A Short History, 1500–1877.* Oxford:
Blackwell, 2006.

Heisler, Barbara Schmitter. "The Sociology of Immigration: From Assimilation to
Segmented Integration, from the American Experience to the Global Arena." In
Migration Theory: Talking Across Disciplines, edited by Caroline B. Brettell and James F.
Hollifield, 77–96. New York and London: Routledge, 2000.

Helo, Ari. *Thomas Jefferson's Ethics and the Politics of Human Progress: The Morality of a
Slaveholder.* Cambridge: Cambridge University Press, 2013.

Hemphill, Katie M. *Bawdy City: Commercial Sex and Regulation in Baltimore, 1790–1915.*
New York: Cambridge University Press, 2020.

Hening, William Waller, ed. *The Statutes at Large; Being a Collection of all the Laws of
Virginia, From the First Session of the Legislature in the Year 1619.* Vol. 4. Richmond:
W. W. Gray, 1820.

Higginbotham, A. Leon, Jr. *In the Matter of Color: Race and the American Legal Process. The
Colonial Period.* New York and Oxford: Oxford University Press, 1978.

Hill, Christopher. *Liberty Against the Law: Some Seventeenth-Century Controversies.*
London: Allen Lane, 1996.

Hill, Daniel G. *Freedom Seekers: Blacks in Early Canada.* Toronto: Stodaart, 1992.

Historians against Slavery. "HAS Definition of Slavery." https://www.historiansagainstslavery
.org/main/about-us/. October 11, 2020.

"History of the Richmond Police Department." Richmond, Virginia. http://www.ci
.richmond.va.us/Police/HistoryPoliceDepartment.aspx. July 5, 2019.

Hobsbawm, Eric J. *The Age of Capital, 1848–1875.* New York: Charles Scribner's Sons, 1975.

Hodge, Willis Augustus. "The Autobiography of Willis Augustus Hodge, a Free Man of
Color. Excerpts." *National Humanities Center* (2008). http://nationalhumanitiescenter
.org/pds/maai/identity/text3/hodgesfreeman.pdf. March 12, 2019. Reference to
Gatewood, Willard B., Jr. ed. *Free Man of Color: The Autobiography of Willis Augustus
Hodge.* Knoxville: University of Tennessee Press, 1982. Originally published 1896.

Hodges, Graham Russell Gao. *Taxi! A Social History of the New York City Cabdriver.* New
York: New York University Press, 2012.

Hoerder, Dirk. "Transcultural Approaches to Gendered Labour Migration: From the
Nineteenth-Century Proletarian to Twenty-First Century Caregiver Mass Migrations."
In *Proletarian and Gendered Mass Migrations: A Global Perspective on Continuities and
Discontinuities from the 19th to the 21st Centuries,* edited by Dirk Hoerder and Amarijt
Kaur, 19–64. Leiden and Boston: Brill, 2013.

Hoffman, Steven J. *Race, Class, and Power in the Building of Richmond, 1870–1920.* Jefferson
and London: McFarland & Company, 2004.

To the Honb Senate & Representatives of the State of South Carolina. Colleton Parish/
District, South Carolina. Petition by I. Raven Mathews Sr. et al. December 7, 1854.
Accession #11385404. Race and Slavery Petitions Project. Series 1. Legislative Petitions.

To the Honorable the President and Members of the Senate of S. Carolina. Petition of Sundry Mechanics of the City of Charleston. n.d. S165015. Petitions to the General Assembly. SCDAH.

To the Honorable the Speaker and Members of the House of Representatives of the Said State. Kershaw Parish/District, South Carolina. Petition by William Love. November 1820. Accession #11382001. Race and Slavery Petitions Project. Series 1. Legislative Petitions.

Horse, J. R., ed. *Ordinances of the City of Charleston, from the 14th of September 1854, to the 1st of December 1859; and the Acts of the General Assembly Relating to the City Council of Charleston, and the City of Charleston, During the Same Period.* Charleston, 1854.

House of Delegates. Senate & Virginia State Papers. Annual Messages. *Journal of the House of Delegates of Virginia. Session 1846–1847.* Speech by W. M. Smith. Richmond: Manuel Shepherd, 1846. LVA.

Howard District Register of Wills (Petitions). Petition of Charles G. Haslap. February 9, 1847. Schweninger Collection. MSA.

Hughes, Louis. *Thirty Years a Slave. From Bondage to Freedom: The Institution of Slavery as Seen on the Plantation and in the Home of the Planter. Autobiography of Louis Hughes.* Milwaukee: South Side Printing Company, 1897.

Hummel, Jeffrey Rogers. *Emancipating Slaves, Enslaving Free Men: A History of the American Civil War.* Chicago: Open Court, 2014. Originally published 1996.

Hustings Court Minutes. LVA.

Hustings Court Suit Papers. Ended Causes. City Jail—Report Concerning. LVA.

———. Ended Causes. March–October 1839.

———. Commonwealth v. Robert Lacy, a Slave. September 12, 1839. LVA.

Hutchins, Zachary. "No Author, Recollections of Slavery by a Runaway Slave." *Documenting the American South.* https://docsouth.unc.edu/neh/runaway/summary .html. March 12, 2019.

The Inaugural Address of Thomas H. Hicks, Governor of Maryland. Delivered in the Senate Chamber, at Annapolis. January 13, 1858. MSA.

Ingraham, Joseph Holt. *The South-West. By a Yankee.* Vol. 2. New York: Harper & Brothers, 1835.

Jacobs, Col. C. W. *The Free Negro Question in Maryland.* Baltimore: John W. Woods, 1859. MHS.

Jacobs, Harriet Ann. *Incidents in the Life of a Slave Girl. Written by Herself,* edited by Lydia Maria Child. Boston: 1861.

James Steer to John Minor. February 23, 1818. William J. Minor and Family Papers. HML. In Leslie Howard Owens. *This Species of Property: Slave Life and Culture in the Old South,* 16. Oxford and New York: Oxford University Press, 1976.

Jefferson, Thomas. "Notes on the State of Virginia." In *The Oxford Book of the American South. Testimony, Memory, and Fiction,* edited by Edward L. Ayers and Bradley C. Mittendorf, 13–17. New York and Oxford: Oxford University Press, 1997.

John Francis Delorme Petition. 1801. S165015. Petitions to the General Assembly. SCDAH.

John G. Gamble to the Delegates and Senators of the Legislature of Virginia, in General Assembly Convened. January 1825. Richmond City, Virginia. Accession #11682502. Legislative Petitions. VSA. Race and Slavery Petitions Project. Series 1. Legislative Petitions. LOC.

John Miller v. Negro Richard. August 3, 1847. Anne Arundel County Register of Will. Orders and Petitions 1840–1851, 201–202. MSA.

Johnson, Michael P. "Runaway Slaves and the Slave Communities in South Carolina, 1799 to 1830." *William & Mary Quarterly* 38:3 (1981): 418–41.

Johnson, Michael P., and James L. Roark. *Black Masters: A Free Family of Color in the Old South*. New York and London: W. W. Norton & Company, 1984.

Johnson, Rashauna. *Slavery's Metropolis: Unfree Labor in New Orleans During the Age of Revolutions*. Cambridge: Cambridge University Press, 2016.

Johnson, Walter. *River of Dark Dreams: Slavery and Empire in the Cotton Kingdom*. Cambridge, MA: Harvard University Press, 2013.

John T. Rawlins to the Honorable Members of the Legislature of Virginia. January 6, 1824. Caroline County, Virginia. Accession #11682405. Legislative Petitions. VSA. Race and Slavery Petitions Project, Series 1. Legislative Petitions. LOC.

John Watkins to Secretary Graham. September 6, 1805. In *The Territorial Papers of the United States. Compiled and Edited by Clarence Edwin Carter*. Vol. IX: The Territory of New Orleans 1803–1812, edited by Clarence E. Carter, 503. Washington, DC: Government Printing Office, 1940. HML.

John William DeForest to Andrew DeForest. November 9, 1855. John William DeForest Papers. In Michael P. Johnson and James L. Roark, *Black Masters: A Free Family of Color in the Old South*, 178. New York and London: W. W. Norton & Company, 1984.

Johnsen to Dear Henry. August 29, 1860. Ellison Family Papers. SCLC.

Johnson, John Andrew. *The Experience of a Slave in South Carolina*. London: Passmore & Alabaster, 1862.

Johnson, William I., Jr. Richmond, Va. Interviewer Milton L. Randolph. May 28, 1937. Virginia State Library. In *Weevils in the Wheat: Interviews with Virginia Ex-Slaves*, edited by Charles L. Perdue, Thomas E. Barden, and Robert K. Phillips, 165–79. Charlottesville and London: University of Virginia Press, 1992. Originally published 1976.

Jones, Martha S. *Birthright Citizens: A History of Race and Rights in Antebellum America*. New York and Cambridge: Cambridge University Press, 2018.

Journal of Dugald McCall. 918 Box 1. Cross Keys Plantation. LaRC.

Journal of the First Municipality of the City of New Orleans, Containing the Seatings, Reports, Ordinances and Resolutions, From the 10th August 1836 to the 19 November 1836. New Orleans: J. Bayon, 1836. LaRC.

Journal of the House of Representatives of the State of Louisiana. First Session—Seventeenth Legislature. HML.

———. First Session—Twelfth Legislature. HML.

Kantrowitz, Stephen D. *More than Freedom: Fighting for Black Citizenship in a White Republic, 1829–1889*. New York: Penguin, 2012.

Kaye, Anthony E. "Neighborhoods and Solidarity in the Natchez District of Mississippi: Rethinking the Antebellum Slave Community." *Slavery & Abolition* 23:1 (2002): 1–24.

Keckley, Elizabeth. *Behind the Scenes, or, Thirty Years a Slave, and Four Years in the White House*. New York: G. W. Carleton & Co., 1868.

Kennedy, Joseph C. G., ed. *Population of the United States in 1860; Compiled from the Original Returns of the Eighth Census under the Secretary of the Interior.* Washington, DC: Government Printing Office, 1864.

Kennedy, Lionel H., and Thomas Parker. *An Official Report of the Trials of Sundry Negroes, Charged with an Attempt to Raise an Insurrection in the State of South-Carolina: Preceded by an Introduction and Narrative; and in an Appendix, a Report of the Trials of Four White Persons, on Indictments for Attempting to Excite the Slaves to Insurrection.* Charleston: James R. Schenk, 1822. LOC.

Kenny, Nicolas, and Rebecca Madgin. "'Every Time I Describe a City': Urban History as Comparative and Transnational Practice." In *Cities Beyond Borders: Comparative and Transnational Approaches to Urban History*, edited by Nicolas Kenny and Rebecca Madgin, 3–26. Farnham and Burlington: Ashgate, 2015.

Kerr-Ritchie, Jeffrey R. *Freedpeople in the Tobacco South, Virginia 1860–1900.* Chapel Hill: University of North Carolina Press, 1999.

Kimball, Gregg D. *American City, Southern Place: A Cultural History of Antebellum Richmond.* Athens and London: University of Georgia Press, 2000.

King, Wilma. *The Essence of Liberty: Free Black Women During the Slave Era.* Columbia and London: University of Missouri Press, 2006.

Koger, Larry. *Black Slaveowners: Free Black Slave Masters in South Carolina, 1790–1860.* Jefferson and London: McFarland, 2014.

Kok, Jan. "The Family Factor in Migration Decisions." In *Migration History in World History: Multidisciplinary Approaches*, edited by Jan Lucassen, Leo Lucassen, and Patrick Manning, 215–50. Leiden and Boston: Brill, 2010.

Kolchin, Peter. *American Slavery 1619–1877.* New York: Hill and Wang, 1994.

Kotlikoff, Laurence J., and Anton Rupert. "The Manumission of Slaves in New Orleans, 1827–1846." *Southern Studies* 19:2 (1980): 172–81.

Kulikoff, Allan. *Tobacco and Slaves: The Development of Southern Cultures in the Chesapeake, 1680–1800.* Chapel Hill and London: University of North Carolina Press, 1986.

Landers, Jane. *Black Society in Spanish Florida.* Urbana and Chicago: University of Illinois Press, 1999.

Landsford, Tom. "Manumission." In *Encyclopedia of Emancipation and Abolition in the Transatlantic World*, edited by Junius P. Rodriguez, 357. London and New York: Routledge, 2007.

Lane, Lunsford. *The Narrative of Lunsford Lane, Formerly of Raleigh, N.C. Embracing an Account of His Early Life, the Redemption by Purchase of Himself and Family from Slavery, and His Banishment from the Place of His Birth for the Crime of Wearing a Colored Skin.* Boston: J. G. Torrey, 1842.

Latimore, Carey, IV. "A Step Closer to Slavery? Free African Americans, Industrialization, Social Control and Residency in Richmond City, 1850–1860." *Slavery & Abolition* 33:1 (2011): 119–37.

Latrobe, Benjamin Henry Boneval. *The Journal of Latrobe. Being the Notes and Sketches of an Architect, Naturalist and Traveler in the United States from 1796 to 1820.* With an Introduction by J. H. B. Latrobe. New York: D. Appleton and Company, 1905. Originally published 1876.

Laws of Maryland. 1796. Ch. 67. Vol. 105, 253. In Proceedings and Acts of the General Assembly. 1796. https://msa.maryland.gov/megafile/msa/speccol/sc2900/sc2908 /000001/000105/html/am105–253.html. December 5, 2018.

———. 1806. Ch. 81. Vol. 192, 693. In *Absconders, Runaways and Other Fugitives in the Baltimore City and County Jail*, edited by Jerry M. Hynson, 51–52. Westminster, MD: Willow Bend Books, 2004.

———. 1817. Ch. 112. Early State Records Online. MSA. http://msa.maryland.gov /megafile/msa/speccol/sc4800/sc4872/003183/html/m3183-0375.html. May 23, 2017.

———. 1818. Ch. 157, 615. https://msa.maryland.gov/megafile/msa/speccol/sc4800 /sc4872/003183/html/m3183-0615.html. December 5, 2018.

———. 1824. Ch. 85. Vol. 141, 807. In *Absconders, Runaways and Other Fugitives in the Baltimore City and County Jail*, edited by Jerry M. Hynson, 59. Westminster, MD: Willow Bend Books, 2004.

———. 1824. Ch. 171. In Runaway Docket. Baltimore City and County. Guide to Government Records, MSA.

———. 1831. Ch. 281. In Barbara Fields. *Slavery and Freedom on the Middle Ground. Maryland during the Nineteenth Century*, 36–37. New Haven, CT and London: Yale University Press, 1985.

———. 1831. Ch. 323. Vol. 141, 1068. In *Absconders, Runaways and Other Fugitives in the Baltimore City and County Jail*, edited by Jerry M. Hynson, 61. Westminster, MD: Willow Bend Books, 2004.

———. 1832. Ch. 111. Vol. 141, 1115. In *Absconders, Runaways and Other Fugitives in the Baltimore City and County Jail*, edited by Jerry M. Hynson, 67. Westminster, MD: Willow Bend Books, 2004.

———. 1860. Art. 66. Vol. 145, 450–53. In *Absconders, Runaways and Other Fugitives in the Baltimore City and County Jail*, edited by Jerry M. Hynson, 72. Westminster, MD: Willow Bend Books, 2004.

———. Session Laws. 1849. Ch. 296, 373–74. https://msa.maryland.gov/megafile /msa/speccol/sc2900/sc2908/000001/000613/html/am613–374.html. December 5, 2018.

Legacy of Slavery in Maryland. "History of Runaways." MSA. http://slavery.msa .maryland.gov/html/research/histlaw.html. January 25, 2019.

Legislative Petitions. LVA.

Legislative Petitions. SCDAH.

Le Glaunec, Jean-Pierre. "Slave Migrations and Slave Control in Spanish and Early American New Orleans." In *Empires of the Imagination: Transatlantic Histories of the Louisiana Purchase*, edited by Peter J. Kastor and François Weil, 204–38. Charlottesville and London: University of Virginia Press, 2009.

Lewis L. Stiff to William Gray. May 25, 1842. Gray Papers. VHS.

Lewis, Ronald L. "Slavery in the Chesapeake Iron Industry, 1716–1865." PhD diss., University of Akron, 1974.

Lexington Intelligence. In Damian Alan Pargas. "Seeking Freedom in the Midst of Slavery: Fugitive Slaves in the Antebellum South." In *Fugitive Slaves and Spaces of Freedom in North America*, edited by Damian Alan Pargas, 123. Gainesville: University Press of Florida, 2018.

Libby, David. *Slavery and Frontier Mississippi, 1720–1835.* Jackson: University Press of Mississippi, 2003.

Lind, Dara. "Sanctuary Cities, Explained: The Stereotype and the Reality." *Vox* (March 8, 2018). https://www.vox.com/policy-and-politics/2018/3/8/17091984/sanctuary-cities-city-state-illegal-immigration-sessions. September 3, 2018.

Litwack, Leon. *North of Slavery: The Negro in the Free States, 1790–1860.* Chicago: University of Chicago Press, 1961.

Lobo, Eulália L., and Eduardo N. Stotz. "Formação do operariado e movimento operário no Rio de Janeiro, 1870–1894." *Estudos Econômicos* 15 (1985): 49–88. Referenced in Marcelo Badaró Mattos, *Laborers and Enslaved Workers: Experiences in Common in the Making of Rio de Janeiro's Working Class, 1850–1920,* 22. New York and Oxford: Berghahn Books, 2017.

Louisiana. First District Court (Orleans Parish). General Dockets. 1846–1880. Vol. 2 (February 7, 1850–December 24, 1856). #4666–12588. VSA350. NOPL.

———. Vol. 3 (January 1, 1857–January 6, 1865). #12589–16369. VSA350. NOPL.

Lundman, Robert J. *Police and Policing: An Introduction.* New York: Holt, Reinhart & Winston, 1980.

Lusk v. Swon. June 1854. Docket #2852. Historical Archives of the Supreme Court of Louisiana. EKL.

Marciaq v. H. M. Wright. May 1857, January 1858. Docket #4645. Historical Archives of the Supreme Court of Louisiana. EKL.

Mareite, Thomas. "Conditional Freedom: Free Soil and Fugitive Slaves from the US South to Mexico's Northeast, 1803–1861." PhD diss., Leiden University, 2020.

Marler, Scott P. *The Merchants' Capital: New Orleans and the Political Economy of the Nineteenth-Century South.* New York: Cambridge University Press, 2013.

Marshall, Amani. "Enslaved Women Runaways in South Carolina, 1820–1865." PhD diss., Indiana University, 2007.

———. "'They Will Endeavor to Pass for Free': Enslaved Runaways' Performances of Freedom in Antebellum South Carolina." *Slavery & Abolition* 31:2 (2010): 161–80.

Martin, Jonathan D. *Divided Mastery: Slave Hiring in the American South.* Cambridge, MA and London: Harvard University Press, 2004.

Mary C. Spence Petition. Baltimore County, Maryland. November 15, 1826. Race and Slavery Petitions Project. Series 2. County Court Petitions. University of North Carolina at Greensboro. Schweninger Collection. MSA.

Matchett's Baltimore Director, Corrected up to June 1831. Containing (With, or Without) A Plan of the City; With Reference to the Public Buildings. Baltimore, 1831. MSA.

Maryland State Penitentiary. MSA SC 5496-30976. Jail. Baltimore City, Maryland. MSA. https://msa.maryland.gov/megafile/msa/speccol/sc5400/sc5496/030900/030976/html/030976bio.html. March 21, 2019.

Mayor's Court Docket Book. Valentine Museum, Richmond. In James M. Campbell, *Slavery on Trial: Race, Class, and Criminal Justice in Antebellum Richmond, Virginia,* 30–31. Gainesville: University Press of Florida, 2007.

McCurry, Stephanie. *Masters of Small Worlds: Yeoman Households, Gender Relations, and the Political Culture of the Antebellum South Carolina Low Country.* New York and Oxford: Oxford University Press, 1997.

McInnis, Maurie D. *The Politics of Taste in Antebellum Charleston.* Chapel Hill: University of North Carolina Press, 2005.

McKittrick, Katherine. *Demonic Grounds: Black Women and the Cartographies of Struggle.* Minneapolis: University of Minnesota Press, 2006.

McMaster v. Beckwith, April 1831. Docket #2017. Historical Archives of the Supreme Court of Louisiana. EKL.

McMichael, Andrew. *Atlantic Loyalties: Americans in Spanish West Florida, 1785–1810.* Athens and London: University of Georgia Press, 2008.

Meaders, Daniel E. "South Carolina Fugitives as Viewed Through Local Colonial Newspapers with Emphasis on Runaway Notices 1732–1801." *Journal of Negro History* 60:2 (1975): 288–319.

Meier, August, and Elliott Rudwick. *From Plantation to Ghetto.* New York: Hill and Wang, 1966.

Melish, Joanne Pope. *Disowning Slavery: Gradual Emancipation and "Race" in New England, 1780–1860.* Ithaca, NY: Cornell University Press, 1998.

Merritt, Keri Leigh. *Masterless Men: Poor Whites and Slavery in the Antebellum South.* Cambridge: Cambridge University Press, 2017.

Miller, Ian. "Feeding the Workhouse: The Institutional and Ideological Functions of Food in Britain, ca. 1834–70." *Journal of British Studies* 52 (2013): 1–23.

Miller, Joseph C. *The Problem of Slavery as History: A Global Approach.* New Haven, CT and London: Yale University Press, 2012.

Minutes of the Conseil do Ville. May 19, 1804. In Jean-Pierre Le Glaunec, "Slave Migrations and Slave Control in Spanish and Early American New Orleans." In *Empires of the Imagination: Transatlantic Histories of the Louisiana Purchase*, edited by Peter J. Kastor and François Weil, 223. Charlottesville and London: University of Virginia Press, 2009.

Missouri Supreme Court, St. Louis: State v. Henke and Henke. October 1853. Missouri State Archives. In *Reports of Cases Argued and Decided in the Supreme Court of Missouri* Vol. 19: *1853–1854*, edited by Samuel A. Bennett, 226–27. Saint Louis: Chambers & Knapp, 1855.

Möllers, Nina. *Kreolische Identität: Eine Amerikanische 'Rassengeschichte' zwischen Schwarz und Weiß: Die Free People of Color in New Orleans.* Bielefeld: Transcript, 2008.

Mohl, Raymond A. "The Industrial Town and City: Introduction." In *The Making of Urban America*, edited by Raymond A. Mohl, 3–11. Wilmington, DE: Scholarly Resources, 1988.

Morgan, Lynda J. *Emancipation in Virginia's Tobacco Belt, 1850–1870.* Athens: University of Georgia Press, 1992.

Morgan, Philip. "Three Planters and Their Slaves: Perspectives on Slavery in Virginia, South Carolina, and Jamaica, 1750–1790." In *Race and Family in the Colonial South*, edited by Winthrop D. Jordan and Sheila L. Skemp, 37–80. Jackson: University Press of Mississippi, 1987.

Morris, Thomas D. *Southern Slavery and the Law, 1619–1860.* Chapel Hill: University of North Carolina Press, 1996.

Motte Plantation Record Book. Record Book, July–December 1854. SCLC.

———. Plantation Exeter. Work Book, January 1856. Dr. J. B. Motte. SCLC.

Mullin, Gerald W. *Flight and Rebellion: Slave Resistance in Eighteenth-Century Virginia.* Oxford and New York: Oxford University Press, 1972.

Mullin, Michael. *Africa in America: Slave Acculturation and Resistance in the American South and the British Caribbean, 1736–1831*. Urbana and Chicago: University of Illinois Press, 1992.

Murray, John E. "Poor Mothers, Stepmothers, and Foster Mothers in Early Republic and Antebellum Charleston." *Journal of the Early Republic* 32:3 (2012): 463–92.

Myers, Amrita Chakrabarti. *Forging Freedom: Black Women and the Pursuit of Liberty in Antebellum Charleston*. Chapel Hill: University of North Carolina Press, 2011.

Naragon, Michael Douglas. "Ballots, Bullets, and Blood: The Political Transformation of Richmond, Virginia, 1850–1874." PhD diss., University of Pittsburgh, 1996.

Nashville Union and American. In Ira Berlin, "The Structure of the Free Negro Caste in the Antebellum United States." *Journal of Social History* 9:3 (1976): 307.

"Nat Turner's Rebellion, 1831." Gilder Lehrman Institute of American History. https://www.gilderlehrman.org/content/nat-turner%E2%80%99s-rebellion-1831. August 28, 2019.

Nau, Frederick. *The German People of New Orleans, 1850–1900*. Leiden: E. J. Brill, 1958.

Newman, Simon P. "Rethinking Runaways in the British Atlantic World: Britain, the Caribbean, West Africa and North America." *Slavery & Abolition* 38:1 (2017): 49–75.

New Orleans (La.) Police Jail of the Third Municipality. Daily Reports, 1838–1840 (February 1, 1838–April 30, 1839). TX205. 1838–1840. NOPL.

Nicholson, Andrea, Minh Dang, and Zoe Trodd. "A Full Freedom: Contemporary Survivors' Definitions of Slavery." *Human Rights Law Review* 18 (2018): 689–704.

Niles' Register. April 23, 1831. In Sherry H. Olson, *Baltimore: The Building of an American City*, 91. Baltimore and London: Johns Hopkins University Press, 1997. Originally published 1980.

Norman, Benjamin Moore. *Norman's New Orleans and Environs: Containing a Brief Historical Sketch of the Territory and State of Louisiana, and the City of New Orleans, from the Earliest Period to the Present Time: Presenting a Complete Guide to all Subjects of General Interest in the Southern Metropolis; With a Correct and Improved Plan of the City, Pictorial Illustrations of Public Buildings, Etc*. New Orleans: B. M. Norman, 1845.

Northup, Solomon. *Twelve Years a Slave: Narrative of Solomon Northup, a Citizen of New-York, Kidnapped in Washington City in 1841, and Rescued in 1853, from a Cotton Plantation near the Red River in Louisiana*. Auburn, NY: Derby and Miller; Buffalo: Derby, Orton and Mulligan; and London: Sampson Low, Son & Company, 1853.

Oakes, James. *The Ruling Race: A History of American Slaveholders*. New York: Vintage Books, 1982.

O'Donovan, Susan E. *Becoming Free in the Cotton South*. Cambridge, MA and London: Harvard University Press, 2007.

Olmstead, Alan L., and Paul W. Rhode. "Biological Innovation and Productivity Growth in the Antebellum Cotton Economy." *Journal of Economic History* 68:4 (2008): 1123–71.

Olmsted, Frederick Law. *The Cotton Kingdom: A Traveller's Observations on Cotton and Slavery in the American Slave States. Based Upon Three Former Volumes of Journeys and Investigations by the Same Author*. Vol. 1. New York: Mason Brothers; and London: Sampson Low, Son, & Co., 1862.

———. *A Journey in the Seaboard Slave States; With Remarks on Their Economy*. London: Sampson, Low, Son & Co.; and New York: Dix and Edwards, 1856.

———. *Our Slave States*. Vol. III: *A Journey in the Back Country*. New York: Mason Brothers, 1860.

Olson, Sherry H. *Baltimore: The Building of an American City*. Baltimore and London: Johns Hopkins University Press, 1997. Originally published 1980.

Olwell, Robert. "Becoming Free: Manumission and the Genesis of a Free Black Community in South Carolina, 1740–90." In *Against the Odds: Free Blacks in the Slave Societies of the Americas*, edited by Jane G. Landers, 1–19. New York and London: Routledge, 1996.

Papademetriou, Demetrios G. "The Global Struggle with Illegal Migration: No End in Sight." *Migration Information Source* (September 1, 2005). https://www.migrationpolicy.org/article/global-struggle-illegal-migration-no-end-sight. February 2, 2019.

Pargas, Damian Alan. *Slavery and Forced Migration in the Antebellum South*. New York: Cambridge University Press, 2015.

———. "Seeking Freedom in the Midst of Slavery: Fugitive Slaves in the Antebellum South." In *Fugitive Slaves and Spaces of Freedom in North America*, edited by Damian Alan Pargas, 116–36. Gainesville: University Press of Florida, 2018.

Parker, Freddie L. *Running for Freedom: Slave Runaways in North Carolina, 1775–1840*. New York: Garland, 1993.

Paton, Diana. *No Bond but the Law: Punishment, Race, and Gender in Jamaican State Formation, 1780–1870*. Durham, NC: Duke University Press, 2004.

———. "Punishment, Crime, and the Bodies of Slaves in Eighteenth-Century Jamaica." *Journal of Social History* 34:4 (2001): 923–54.

Patterson, Orlando. *Slavery and Social Death: A Comparative Study*. Cambridge, MA and London: Harvard University Press, 1982.

Payne, Daniel A. *History of the African Methodist Episcopal Church*, edited by C. S. Smith. Nashville: Publishing House of the A.M.E. Sunday-School Union, 1891. HML.

Pease, Jane H., and William H. Pease. "Social Structure and the Potential for Urban Change: Boston and Charleston in the 1830s." *Journal of Urban History* 8 (1982): 171–95.

Petition by A. Williams. To the Honorable S. C. Leakin Mayor. n.d. Mayor's Correspondence. BRG 9-2. BCA.

Petition by Benjamin J. Cochran, Jailer of Abbeville District. Petition and Supporting Papers Asking Compensation for Tending to Daphney, a Runaway Slave, Whose Master Has Not Claimed Her, and Who Could Not Be Sold Due to Old Age. 1857. SCDAH.

Petition by Citizens from Berkeley County. January 16, 1838. Legislative Petitions. LVA.

Petition by Edward Brailsford. November 26, 1816. Legislative Petitions. SCDAH.

Petition by Edward R. Ware, Physician, Resident of Athens, Clark County, GA. November 28, 1855. SCDAH.

Petition by Ruben Burton. Henrico County. December 21, 1825. Legislative Petitions. LVA.

Petition by Society of Friends. December 31, 1844. Legislative Petitions. LVA.

Petition of Jeremiah Willis for a Pass. February 4, 1839. Mayor's Correspondence. BRG 9-2, BCA.

Philip Whitlock Memoirs. Mss 5: IW5905: I. VHS.

Phillips, Christopher. *Freedom's Port: The African American Community of Baltimore, 1790–1860*. Urbana and Chicago: University of Illinois Press, 1997.

Pinckney, Thomas. *Reflections Occasioned by the Late Disturbances in Charleston. By Achates.* Charleston: A. E. Miller, 1822.

Pluskota, Marion. "'We Use Our Bodies to Work Hard, So We Need to Get Legitimate Workers' Rights': Labour Relations in Prostitution, 1600–2010." In *Selling Sex in the City: A Global History of Prostitution, 1600s–2000s,* edited by Magaly Rodríguez García, Lex Heerma van Voss, and Elise van Nederveen Meerkerk, 653–76. Leiden and Boston: Brill, 2017.

Police Jail Daily Reports. 1820–1840. New Orleans (La.) Police Jail/Parish Prison. NOPL.

Population of Virginia—1810. http://www.virginiaplaces.org/population/pop1810numbers .html. January 8, 2019.

Potter, Gary. "The History of Policing in the United States." *EKU Online.* https:// plsonline.eku.edu/sites/plsonline.eku.edu/files/the-history-of-policing-in-us.pdf. January 24, 2019.

Powers, Bernard Edward Jr. "Black Charleston: A Social History, 1822–1885." PhD diss., Northwestern University, 1982.

Presentment of Grant Jury of Charleston District. October 1820, March 1856. Legislative Petitions. SCDAH.

Proceedings of the City Council of Charleston, SC. 1859 I. CCPL.

———. Thirty-First Regular Meeting, Council Chamber. In *Daily Courier.* January 6, 1859. CCPL.

Rabinowitz, Howard N. *Race Relations in the Urban South, 1865–1890.* Foreword by George M. Fredrickson. Athens and London: University of Georgia Press, 1996. Originally published New York: Oxford University Press, 1978.

Raboteau, Albert J. *Slave Religion: The "Invisible Institution" in the Antebellum South.* Oxford and New York: Oxford University Press, 2004.

Randall, Carol Anna. Newport News, VA. Interviewer unknown. n.d. In Virginia Writers' Program. *The Negro in Virginia.* New York: Hastings House, 1940, 171. In *Weevils in the Wheat: Interviews with Virginia Ex-Slaves,* edited by Charles L. Perdue, Thomas E. Barden, and Robert K. Phillips. Charlottesville and London: University of Virginia Press, 1992, 236. Originally published 1976.

Records of Prisoners Committed to the Parish Prison. 1852–1862. June 18, 1852–May 10, 1862. TX420. NOPL.

Records of the Charleston Police Department. 1855–1991. CCPL.

———. Arrest Records and Morning Reports. Lower Ward 1855–1856. CCPL.

———. Police Department Historic Files. 1855–1991. CCPL.

Redpath, James. *The Roving Editor: or, Talks with Slaves in the Southern States.* New York: A. B. Burdick, 1859.

Report of the Board of Directors of the Louisiana Penitentiary. New Orleans: Emile La Sere, 1854. HML.

Return of the Whole Number of Persons within the Several Districts of the United States, According to "An Act Providing for the Enumeration of the Inhabitants of the United States." Philadelphia: Childs and Swaine, 1791.

Richard West Flournoy to William Gray. October 10, 1855. Gray Papers. VHS.

Richmond (VA.). City Sergeant. Mss 3R415661. Section 1. Register 1841–1846. VHS.

Robinson, William H. *From Log Cabin to the Pulpit, or, Fifteen Years in Slavery.* 3rd ed. Eau Claire, WI: James H. Tifft, 1913.

Rockman, Seth. *Scraping By: Wage Labor, Slavery, and Survival in Early Baltimore.* Baltimore: Johns Hopkins University Press, 2009.

———. "Unfree Origins of American Capitalism." In *The Economy of Early America. Historical Perspectives and New Directions,* edited by Cathy Matson, 335–61. University Park: Pennsylvania State University Press, 2006.

Roediger, David R. *The Wages of Whiteness: Race and the Making of the American Working Class.* London and New York: Verso, 1991.

Rood, Daniel B. *The Reinvention of Atlantic Slavery: Technology, Labor, Race, and Capitalism in the Greater Caribbean.* New York: Oxford University Press, 2017.

Rousey, Dennis C. "'Hibernian Leatherheads': Irish Cops in New Orleans, 1830–1880." *Journal of Urban History* 10:1 (1983): 61–84.

———. *Policing the Southern City: New Orleans, 1805–1889.* Baton Rouge and London: Louisiana State University Press, 1996.

Rodriguez, Junius P. "Ripe for Revolt: Louisiana and the Tradition of Slave Insurrection, 1803–1865." PhD diss., Auburn University, 1992.

Rosenwaike, Ira. *On the Edge of Greatness: A Portrait of American Jewry in the Early National Period.* Cincinnati: American Jewish Archives, 1985.

Rubin, Ashley T. *The Deviant Prison: Philadelphia's Eastern State Penitentiary and the Origins of America's Modern Penal System, 1829–1913.* Cambridge and New York: Cambridge University Press, 2021.

Rubin, Jay. "Black Nativism: The European Immigrant in Negro Thought, 1830–1860." *Phylon* 39:3 (1978): 198–99.

Rules and Regulations for the General Government of the Police Department of the City of Charleston. Charleston: Walker & Evans, 1884. CCPL.

Rumbaut, Rubén G., Katie Dingeman, and Anthony Robles. "Immigration and Crime and the Criminalization of Immigration." In *The Routledge International Handbook of Migration Studies,* edited by Steven J. Gold and Stephanie J. Nawyn, 472–82. New York: Routledge, 2019.

Russell, Robert. *North America, Its Agriculture and Climate, Containing Observations on the Agriculture and Climate of Canada, the United States, and the Island of Cuba.* Edinburgh: Adam and Charles Black, 1857.

Ryden, David. "Manumission." *Oxford Bibliographies* (September 30, 2013). https://www .oxfordbibliographies.com/view/document/obo-9780199730414/obo-9780199730414 -0194.xml. July 19, 2019.

Samuel G. Lipey [?] to Jonathan Jordan. June 18, 1842. Jordan and Twiggs Family Papers. SCLC.

"Sanitary Report of Baltimore." *Ordinances of the Mayor and City Council of Baltimore* (1850), 208–9. In *Slaves Without Masters: The Free Negro in the Antebellum South,* 258. New York: Pantheon Books, 1974.

Schafer, Judith Kelleher. *Becoming Free, Remaining Free: Manumission and Enslavement in New Orleans, 1846–1862.* Baton Rouge: Louisiana State University Press, 2003.

———. *Brothels, Depravity, and Abandoned Women: Illegal Sex in Antebellum New Orleans.* Baton Rouge: Louisiana State University Press, 2009.

———. "New Orleans Slavery in 1850 as Seen in Advertisements." *Journal of Southern History* 47:1 (1981): 33–56.

Schermerhorn, Calvin. *Money over Mastery, Family over Freedom: Slavery in the Antebellum Upper South*. Baltimore: Johns Hopkins University Press, 2011.

Schnittman, Suzanne Gehring. "Slavery in Virginia's Urban Tobacco Industry—1840–1860." PhD diss., University of Rochester, 1986.

Schoeppner, Michael. "Peculiar Quarantines: The Seamen Acts and the Regulatory Authority in the Antebellum South." *Laws & History Review* 31:3 (2013): 559–86.

Schrover, Marlou. "Labour Migration." In *Handbook Global History of Work*, edited by Marcel van der Linden and Karin Hofmeester, 443–78. Berlin and Boston: De Gruyter, 2018.

Schultz, Stanley K., and Clay McShane. "To Engineer the Metropolis: Sewers, Sanitation, and City Planning in Late Nineteenth-Century America." In *The Making of Urban America*, edited by Raymond A. Mohl, 81–98. Wilmington, DE: SR Books, 1988.

Schweninger, Loren. "Prosperous Blacks in the South, 1790–1880." *American Historical Review* 95:1 (1990): 31–56.

———. "The Underside of Slavery: The Internal Economy, Self-Hire, and Quasi-Freedom in Virginia, 1780–1865." *Slavery & Abolition* 12:2 (1991): 1–22.

Scott, James C. *Dominance and the Arts of Resistance: Hidden Transcripts*. New Haven, CT: Yale University Press, 1990.

Secretary of Commonwealth Executive Journal Indexes, Governor David Campbell, Annual Speech, 2 December 1839. LVA.

Selfa, Lance. *The Democrats: A Critical History*. Chicago: Haymarket Books, 2008.

Sheldon, Marianne Buroff. "Black-White Relations in Richmond, Virginia." *Journal of Southern History* 45:1 (1979): 27–44.

Sinha, Manisha. *The Counterrevolution of Slavery: Politics and Ideology in Antebellum South Carolina*. Chapel Hill: University of North Carolina Press, 2000.

———. *The Slave's Cause: A History of Abolition*. New Haven, CT: Yale University Press, 2016.

Sio, Arnold A. "Interpretations of Slavery: The Slave Status in the Americas." In *Slavery in the New World: A Reader in Comparative History*, edited by Laura Foner and Eugene D. Genovese, 96–112. Englewood Cliffs, NJ: Prentice-Hall, 1969. Originally published in *Comparative Studies in Society and History* 7:3 (1965): 289–308.

Smalls, Samanthis Quantrellis. "Behind Workhouse Walls: The Public Regulation of Slavery in Charleston, 1730–1850." PhD diss., Duke University, 2015.

Sorensen, Leni Ashmore. "Absconded: Fugitive Slaves in the Daybook of the Richmond Police Guard, 1834–1844." PhD diss., College of William and Mary, 2005.

Southern Recorder. In Richard C. Wade, *Slavery in the Cities: The South 1820–1860*, 150. London, Oxford, and New York: Oxford University Press, 1964.

Spady, James O'Neil. "Power and Confession: On the Credibility of the Earliest Reports of the Denmark Vesey Slave Conspiracy." *William & Mary Quarterly* 68:2 (2011): 287–304.

Spain, Daphne. "Race Relations and Residential Segregation in New Orleans: Two Centuries of Paradox." *Annals of the American Academy of Political and Social Science* 441 (1979): 82–96.

Spalding v. Taylor et al. June 1846. In *Louisiana Annual Reports, Reports of Cases Argued and Determined in the Supreme Court of Louisiana*. Vol. I: *From the Reorganization of the Court under the Constitution of 1845, to the 31st of December, 1846*, edited by Merritt M. Robinson, 195–97. New Orleans: Thomas Bea, 1847.

Spitzer, Stephen. "The Rationalization of Crime Control in Capitalist Society." *Contemporary Crises* 3:1 (1979): 187–206.

Spitzer, Stephen, and Andrew Scull. "Privatization and Capitalist Development: The Case of the Private Police." *Social Problems* 25:1 (1977): 18–29.

Spooner, Matthew. "'I Know This Scheme is From God': Toward a Reconsideration of the Origins of the American Colonization Society." *Slavery & Abolition* 35:4 (2014): 559–75.

Sprague, Rosetta Douglass. *Anna Murray Douglass, My Mother As I Recall Her* (1900). Manuscript/Mixed Material. LOC. https://www.loc.gov/item/mfd.02007/. January 26, 2017.

Stampp, Kenneth. *The Peculiar Institution: Slavery in the Ante-Bellum South*. New York: Alfred A. Knopf, 1956.

Starobin, Robert S. "The Economics of Industrial Slavery in the Old South." *Business History Review* 44:2 (1970): 131–74.

The State v. Wm Jackson F.P.C. Offence Aiding & Abetting Negro Stealing, Enticing a Slave to Run Away. Simons & Simons. SCHS.

Steinfeld, Robert J., and Stanley L. Engerman. "Labor—Free and Coerced? A Historical Reassessment of Differences and Similarities." In *Free and Unfree Labour. The Debate Continues*, edited by Tom Brass and Marcel van der Linden, 107–26. Bern: Peter Lang, 1997.

Stevenson, Brenda E. *Life in Black and White: Family and Community in the Slave South*. New York and London: Oxford University Press, 1996.

Stith, G. *Message of the Mayor to the Common Council*, October 11, 1859. In Richard C. Wade, *Slavery in the Cities: The South 1820–1860*, 219. London, Oxford, and New York: Oxford University Press, 1964.

Stuart, John Esq. "Three Years in North America." *Westminster Review* 18:36 (1833).

Sweeney, Shauna J. "Market Marronage: Fugitive Women and the Internal Marketing System in Jamaica, 1781–1834." *William and Mary Quarterly* 76:2 (2019): 197–222.

Tadman, Michael. *Speculators and Slaves: Masters, Traders, and Slaves in the Old South*. Madison: University of Wisconsin Press, 1996.

Takagi, Midori. *'Rearing Wolves to Our Own Destruction': Slavery in Richmond, Virginia, 1782–1865*. Charlottesville: University Press of Virginia, 1999.

Tansey, Richard. "Out-of-State Free Blacks in Late Antebellum New Orleans." *Louisiana History* 22 (1981): 369–86.

Taylor, Alan. *The Internal Enemy: Slavery and War in Virginia, 1772–1832*. New York: W. W. Norton, 2013.

Taylor, Michael. "Free People of Color in Louisiana. Revealing an Unknown Past." *LSU Libraries. A Collaborative Digital Collection*. https://www.lib.lsu.edu/sites/all/files/sc/fpoc/history.html#historyintro. November 29, 2018.

Testimony of Angelina Grimké Weld. April 6, 1839. In *American Slavery As It Is: Testimony of a Thousand Witnesses*, edited by Theodore Dwight Weld, 52–57. New York: American Anti-Slavery Society, 1839.

Thompson, John. *The Life of John Thompson, a Fugitive Slave: Containing His History of 25 Years in Bondage, and His Providential Escape*. Worcester: C. Hamilton, 1856.

Thompson, Michael D. *Working on the Dock of the Bay: Labor and Emancipation in an Antebellum Southern Port*. Columbia: University of South Carolina Press, 2015.

Tilly, Charles. "Cities and Migration." Center for Research on Social Organization (CSRO) Working Paper #147. Ann Arbor: University of Michigan, 1976.

———. "Migration in Early Modern European History." *Center for Research on Social Organization* (CSRO) Working Paper #145. Ann Arbor: University of Michigan, 1976.

Tomich, Dale W. "The Second Slavery and World Capitalism: A Perspective for Historical Inquiry." *International Review of Social History* 63:3 (2018): 477–501.

———. *Through the Prism of Slavery: Labor, Capital, and World Economy.* Lanham, MD: Rowman & Littlefield, 2004.

Tocqueville, Alexis de. *Democracy in America.* Translated by Henry Reeve, Esq. With an Original Preface and Notes by John C. Spencer. Fourth Edition Vol. II. New York: J. & H. G. Langley; Philadelphia: Thomas, Cowperthwaite, & Co.; and Boston: C. C. Little & J. Brown, 1841.

Towers, Frank. *The Urban South and the Coming of the Civil War.* Charlottesville and London: University of Virginia Press, 2004.

Transcriptions of Parish Records of Louisiana. Prepared by The Historical Records Survey Division of Professional and Service Projects. Works Project Administration. No. 26 Jefferson Parish (Gretna). Series I. Police Jury Minutes. Vol. I: 1834–1843. New Orleans: Police Jury, Parish of Jefferson, June 1939. HML.

Tyler-McGraw, Marie, and Gregg D. Kimball. Exhibit catalogue *In Bondage and Freedom: Antebellum Black Life in Richmond, Virginia.* Richmond: Valentine Museum, 1988.

United States Department of Labor and Bureau of Labor Statistics. "History of Wages in the United States from Colonial Times to 1928." *Bulletin of the United States Bureau of Labor Statistics* 604 (1934).

United States Manuscript Slave Census. Richmond. 1st Ward, 1860. 2nd Ward. In Loren Schweninger. "The Underside of Slavery: The Internal Economy, Self-Hire, and Quasi-Freedom in Virginia, 1780–1865." *Slavery & Abolition* 12:2 (1991): 1–22.

U.S. Bureau of the Census. *Aggregate Number of Persons within the United States in the Year 1810.* Washington, DC, 1811.

———. Population of the 100 Largest Cities and Other Urban Places in The United States: 1790 to 1990. https://www.census.gov/library/working-papers/1998/demo/POP-twps0027.html. January 8, 2019.

Veen, Marjolein van der. "Rethinking Commodification and Prostitution: An Effort at Peacemaking in the Battles over Prostitution." *Rethinking Marxism* 13:2 (2001): 30–51.

Virginia Department of Corrections. Brief History. https://vadoc.virginia.gov/about/history.shtm. March 21, 2019.

To the Virginia General Assembly. 1848. Petition by Ely Ball and Henry Satterwhite. Petition 11684607. Race and Slavery Petitions Project. University of North Carolina at Greensboro.

Vlach, John Michael. "'Without Recourse to Owners': The Architecture of Urban Slavery in the Antebellum South." *Perspectives in Vernacular Architecture* 6 (1997): 150–60.

Wade, Richard C. *Slavery in the Cities: The South 1820–1860.* London, Oxford, and New York: Oxford University Press, 1964.

Walker, Daniel E. *No More, No More: Slavery and Cultural Resistance in Havana and New Orleans.* Minneapolis: University of Minnesota Press, 2004.

Walker, David. *Walker's Appeal, in Four Articles; Together with a Preamble, to the Coloured Citizens of the World, but in Particular, and Very Expressly, to Those of the United States of America, Written in Boston, State of Massachusetts, September 28, 1829.* Boston: David Walker, 1830.

Walker, Juliet E. K. *The History of Black Business in America: Capitalism, Race, and Entrepreneurship.* New York: Macmillan Library Reference, 1998.

Weis, Tracey M. "Negotiating Freedom: Domestic Service and the Landscape of Labor and Household Relations in Richmond, Virginia, 1850–1880." PhD diss., Rutgers University, 1994.

Weld, Theodore Dwight, ed. *American Slavery As It Is: Testimony of a Thousand Witnesses.* New York: American Anti-Slavery Society, 1839.

Wells, Jonathan Daniel. *The Origins of the Southern Middle Class, 1800–1861.* Chapel Hill: University of North Carolina Press, 2004.

West, Emily. *Chains of Love: Slave Couples in Antebellum South Carolina.* Urbana: University of Illinois Press, 2004.

———. *Family or Freedom: Free People of Color in the Antebellum South.* Lexington: University of Kentucky Press, 2012.

"What was the Three-Fifth-Compromise?" *Laws.* https://constitution.laws.com/three-fifths-compromise. May 30, 2019.

"Where Free Blacks Lived." *SCIWAY* (2019). https://www.sciway.net/hist/chicora/freepersons-3.html. June 11, 2019.

White, Deborah. *Ar'n't I a Woman?: Female Slaves in the Plantation South.* New York: Norton, 1987.

White, Shane, and Graham White. "Slave Clothing and African-American Culture in the Eighteenth and Nineteenth Centuries." *Past & Present* 148:1 (1995): 149–86.

Whitman, T. Stephen. "Diverse Good Causes: Manumission and the Transformation of Urban Slavery." *Social Science History* 19:3 (1995): 333–70.

———. *The Price of Freedom: Slavery and Manumission in Baltimore and Early National Maryland.* Lexington: University Press of Kentucky, 1997.

William Ellison to Henry Ellison. March 26, 1857. Ellison Family Papers. SCLC.

William Prentis, William Moore, Robert Bolling, Jack Hammon, and Nathaniell Harris to the Honble The Genl. Assembly of Virginia. December 1805. Accession #11680507. Legislative Petitions. VSA. Race and Slavery Petitions Project. Series 1. Legislative Petitions. LOC.

William R. Cox to William Cobbs. January 27. 1830. William Cobbs Letters. LVA.

William Read to Jacob Read. February 14, 1800. Read Family Papers. SCHS.

William Walden, John Peyton, Churchill Berry, John R. Tanesly, and Charles E. Dodge to the General Assembly of Virginia. December 9, 1831. Culpeper County, Virginia. Legislative Petitions. VSA. Race and Slavery Petitions Project. Series 1. Legislative Petitions. LOC.

Wilson, Tamar Diana. "What Determines Where Transnational Labor Migrants Go?" *Human Organization* 53:3 (1994): 269–278.

Wolf, Eva Sheppard. *Race and Liberty in the New Nation: Emancipation in Virginia from the Revolution to Nat Turner's Rebellion.* Baton Rouge: Louisiana State University Press, 2006.

Woodson, Carter W., ed. *Free Negro Owners of Slaves in the United States in 1830. Together with Absentee Ownership of Slaves in the United States in 1830.* Washington, DC: Association for the Study of Negro Life and History, 1924.

Wright, George C. *Life Behind a Veil: Blacks in Louisville, Kentucky, 1865–1930.* Baton Rouge and London: Louisiana State University Press, 1985.

Wright, James M. *The Free Negro in Maryland 1634–1860.* New York: Longmans, Green & Co.; and London: P.S. King & Son, Ltd., 1921.

Wyatt-Brown, Bertram. *Southern Honor: Ethics and Behavior in the Old South.* Oxford: Oxford University Press, 2007.

X, Malcom. "Message to the Grass Roots." In *Malcolm X Speaks: Selected Speeches and Statements,* edited by George Breitman, 3–18. New York: Grove Press, 1965.

Zaborney, John J. *Slaves for Hire: Renting Enslaved Laborers in Antebellum Virginia.* Baton Rouge: Louisiana State University Press, 2012.

Zeuske, Michael. "Die Nicht-Geschichte von Versklavten als Archiv-Geschichte von 'Stimmen' und Körpern." In *Jahrbuch für Europäische Überseegeschichte* 16 (2016): 65–114.

General Index

Index of Names

Index of Occupations and Work

CPSIA information can be obtained
at www.ICGtesting.com
Printed in the USA
BVHW040831190922
647389BV00001B/19